Praise for *Modernity as Apocalypse*

"Thaddeus Kozinski wrestles in this book in a disarmingly honest way with the difficult question of how to be genuinely Catholic in the modern world, demonstrating brilliantly that even the retreat into the fortress is a capitulation. Each of the brief chapters makes some thought-provoking proposal that keeps the reader from slipping back unwittingly into the categories that seem to be the only ones modernity permits."—D.C. SCHINDLER, author of *Freedom from Reality*

"This demanding but exciting book is a first-rate guide to modernity as apocalypse, to the kind of religion that has been appearing in recent times, and to what we might expect of this form of modernity."—GLENN W. OLSEN, author of *The Turn to Transcendence*

"*Modernity as Apocalypse* is a penetrating exploration of our cultural crisis. Kozinski knows that neither the nature of this crisis nor a plausible response to it can evade coming to grips with the cultural and historical impact of the Christian revelation. Laudably, he has discovered in the legacy of René Girard both the anthropological insight and the deeply Catholic sensibility demanded by our present predicament."—GIL BAILIE, author of *God's Gamble*

"Thaddeus Kozinski has attempted an ambitious undertaking: a comprehensive understanding of the Great Desolation of modernity in terms equal to its depth and magnitude. The result is a book rich enough that everyone will find something to disagree with. Nevertheless, its premise that modernity is an event of apocalyptic proportions, and its conclusion that Christian mysticism is a nonoptional necessity for traversing this desert, are both unassailable."—MICHAEL HANBY, author of *No God, No Science*

"It has been said that a fish does not know it lives in water. To those of us doomed to live within modernity, it is at least helpful if *we* know our address. Thaddeus Kozinski's new book, *Modernity as*

Apocalypse, does a fine job of telling us where we ourselves dwell—even if the news will not be welcomed by everyone. Let this book help show you where you are, where we all are, and what it might mean."—THOMAS STORCK, author of *An Economics of Justice and Charity*

"Is modernity good? Bad? Illusory? What should Catholics do about it? And how can we know, when it's so much with us? *Modernity as Apocalypse* is a panoramic report on where such issues seem to stand today, written from the standpoint of a philosopher and teacher who loves Christ and his Church as well as Socrates and liberal education, and who is alarmed by the eclipse of reason and return of sanctifying violence in our time."—JAMES KALB, author of *Against Inclusiveness*

"Modernity's manifold path to domination of a natural world it boasts of exalting, and yet inevitably destroys, has been forged in ways both open and subtle, through the hands of master builders as well as unwitting day laborers unaware of exactly where this road to nowhere was actually leading them. Dr. Kozinski offers us a fresh, extremely creative, highly readable, and uniquely valuable guide to modernity's serpentine penetration into the heart of a once great civilization, the character of the sickness it has spread therein, the tragic existence of many victims who refuse to recognize their infection by this disease, and the spiritual cure which alone can arrest the march into the abyss."—JOHN RAO, author of *Removing the Blindfold*

"Kozinski's wide-ranging and penetrating work builds on, and in certain respects improves upon, the critique of secular modernity laid down by scholars such as Alasdair MacIntyre, Charles Taylor, and William Cavanaugh. In addition to exposing the hollowness and hypocrisy of the modern secular nation state, Kozinski also demonstrates the inadequacy of both the neo-conservative attempt to harness and redeploy its powerful tools and the 'Benedict Option' to simply drop out and live in the wilderness."—BRIAN M. MCCALL, author of *To Build the City of God*

Modernity as Apocalypse

Sacred Nihilism and the Counterfeits of Logos

Thaddeus J. Kozinski

Modernity as Apocalypse

Sacred Nihilism
and the
Counterfeits of Logos

✢ Angelico Press

Cover design: Michael Schrauzer

CONTENTS

To Tami, Anatolia, Sophia, and T. J.

The general public is being reduced to a state where people not only are unable to find the truth but also become unable to *search* for the truth because they are satisfied with deception and trickery that have determined their convictions, satisfied with a fictitious reality created by design through the abuse of language.

∿ Josef Pieper

Do not accept anything as the truth if it lacks love. And so do not accept anything as love which lacks truth! One without the other becomes a destructive lie.

∿ St Teresa Benedicta of the Cross

Nowadays the devil has made such a mess of everything in the system of life on earth that the world will presently become uninhabitable for anybody but Saints. The rest will drag their lives out in despair or fall below the level of man. The antinomies of human life are too exasperated, the burden of matter too oppressive; merely to exist, one has to expose oneself to many snares. Christian heroism will one day become the sole solution for the problems of life.

∿ Jacques Maritain

The Christian of the future will be a mystic, or he will not be at all.

∿ Karl Rahner

Introduction:
The End of Modernity

Modernity's Soteriology

Modernity is inadequately characterized as a mere chrono-logical time-period, on the one hand, or a timeless, abstract idea, on the other. Perhaps it is better described as a culturally and historically embodied consciousness or cast of mind, a "social imaginary."[1] Indeed, modernity functions in practice and in the souls of many as a full-fledged religious culture: it possesses a sacred origin (the Renaissance's rebirth of man and the Enlightenment's birth of Reason); a sacred event or set of events (the Reformation, the Treaty of Westphalia, the Glorious, American, and French Revolutions); sacred texts (Kant's *sapere aude*, the UN Declaration of the Rights of Man, the Declaration of Independence, the American Constitution); sacred dogmas (the separation of Church from state and religion from politics, the sanctity of individual rights, the political toleration of all beliefs, "the right to define one's concept of existence, of meaning, of the universe, and of the mystery of human life"[2]); a perpetual enemy and source of evil (dogmatism, religious war, intolerance, racism, sexism, hierarchy); and lastly, and most importantly, a soteriology. If we define soteriology as what makes lasting and ultimate peace between competing individuals,[3] modernity's soteriology is many-sided: the political hegemony of the nation-state with the exclusive right to employ coercive force, the privatization and liberty of religious

---

1. Charles Taylor, *A Secular Age* (Cambridge, MA: Belknap Press, 2007).
2. Planned Parenthood of Southeastern Pa. v. Casey, 505 U.S. 833, 851 (1992).
3. William T. Cavanaugh, *Theopolitical Imagination* (London: T&T Clark, 2002).

belief and practice, inexorable scientific advancement, and commercial prosperity. We late-moderns can add private self-creation, moralistic therapeutic deism, and a globalistic market and multicultural state eschewing objective moral and spiritual truth to ensure perpetual peace and stability.

To its devotees, modernity is just the way things really are: a nonideological, worldview-neutral account and practice of human flourishing bereft of the superstitious, irrational, freedom-suppressing and ruler-serving, ancient-medieval theoretical and practical apparatus of scholasticism, priestcraft, oppression, and feudalism. But to those more resistant to and skeptical of its soteriology, modernity is Christendom's rotting corpse, having been murdered sometime in the Enlightenment by the sword of de-hellenization, the poison of nominalization, and the stranglehold of secularization. And modernity has divided up the body, giving us Christ without the cross, in its liberal-democratic half, and the cross without Christ, in its totalitarian half. Modernity is nothing more than a counterfeit of and parasite on the Mystical Body of Christ.

There are, of course, other "just so" stories in this traditionalist vein, as well as many non-theological, secularist-friendly, progressivist narratives. Indeed, the narratives of modernity are seemingly endless and incommensurable, notoriously resistant to definitive adjudication and harmonious negotiation. What is needed is an adequate synthesis in which the partial truths of all the myriad stories and accounts can come together.

The "Immanent Frame" and the "Great Separation"

In *A Secular* Age, Charles Taylor tells us:

> We have undergone a change in our condition, involving both an alteration of the structures we live within, and our way of imaging these structures. This is something we all share, regardless of our differences in outlook. But this cannot be captured in terms of a decline and marginalization of religion. What we share is what I have been calling "the immanent frame"; the different structures we live in: scientific, social, technological, and so on, constitute

such a frame in that they are part of a "natural," or "this worldly" order which can be understood in its own terms, without reference to the "supernatural" or "transcendent."[4]

Mark Lilla, in *The Stillborn God*, describes this change in our condition as

> the liberation, isolation, and clarification of distinctively political questions, apart from speculations about the divine nexus.... Politics became, intellectually speaking, its own realm deserving independent investigation and serving the limited aim of providing the peace and plenty necessary for human dignity. That was the Great Separation.[5]

Understanding the genealogy of modernity is not of merely academic interest, for it is, as suggested above and demonstrated below in the chapters that follow, not just a chronological period or set of ideas—it is an ineluctable existential reality. And if, as Taylor claims, the world we live in now is literally God-less, what does that entail for the billions of religious believers?

In the remainder of this introduction and in several chapters in this volume, I wish to pursue the following questions: where did this "immanent frame" and "great separation" come from, and what caused it? When did our condition supposedly "definitely and irreversibly change," and is this truly the case? How would one know? Is this change unprecedented, and if so, why? And most importantly, should we be celebrating or repudiating our new situation, or should we be dispassionately neutral? Even with Charles Taylor's exhaustively detailed and magisterial book treating these questions, *A Secular Age*, the questions remain. Indeed, if anything, Taylor has rendered them more pressing and complex.

In his excellent revisionist intellectual history, *The Theological Origins of Modernity*, Michael Gillespie has made a persuasive case that the origins of modernity are primarily theological:

4. Taylor, *A Secular Age*, 594.
5. From Mark Lilla, *The Stillborn God*, quoted in Charles Taylor, "Why We Need a Radical Redefinition of Secularism," in Judith Butler, Jürgen Habermas, Charles Taylor, and Cornel West, *The Power of Religion in the Public Sphere* (New York: Columbia University Press, 2011), 51.

Modernity is better understood as an attempt to find a new meta-physical/theological answer to the question of the nature and relation of God, man, and the natural world that arose in the late medieval world as a result of a titanic struggle between contradictory elements within Christianity itself. Modernity, as we understand and experience it, came to be as a series of attempts to constitute a new and coherent metaphysics/theology.[6]

According to Gillespie, Erasmus, Petrarch, and Luther, on the one hand, and Hobbes, Locke, and Descartes, on the other, were working within a nominalist theology bequeathed to them from fourteenth-century Franciscans, a theology not always explicit and consciously understood or referred to by these thinkers, but working in and through their minds nevertheless. This theology cleaved nature from grace, God's will from His nature, faith from reason, particulars from universals, history from rationality. These Renaissance and early Enlightenment thinkers inherited and radicalized an already latently desacralized notion of the world and man, and they attempted to carve out an autonomous sphere for nature, will, knowledge, morality, and political life within a now (to use Max Weber's term) *disenchanted* cosmos, including the new conception of man as *imago voluntatis*, in the image and likeness of the new voluntaristically-conceived God with and against whom they were now engaged. This God was becoming more and more inscrutable and, indeed, arbitrary. For Luther, God was still bound by his "ordained will," discovered now *only* in Sacred Scripture, through the lens of his and all later Protestants' idiosyncratic, personal interpretation. According to Gillespie, we moderns have never transcended our nominalist, voluntarist, and desacralized origins.

Inescapable Modernity

The main point of Gillespie's compelling revisionist intellectual history is the ostensible inescapability of modernity. For Taylor, it is the inescapability of the immanent frame, the buffered self, and the

6. Michael Gillespie, *The Theological Origins of Modernity* (Chicago: University of Chicago Press, 2008), xii.

"spins" through which moderns interpret the world. For Gillespie, there is an intellectual impregnability to the inner structure of nominalist metaphysics, ethics, and theology, with even modernity's most radical critics caught up and complicit in what they attempt to escape and critique. One sees this especially in Nietzsche and Marx, both of whom rail against bourgeois moral consciousness and material worldliness but end up promoting a more radical version of them. Within the ambit of nominalist metaphysics, which nowadays all but a minority of radically orthodox and paleoconservatives accept as normative and inevitable, there seems to be no resolution of the crisis of modernity, a crisis brought to a head in the thoroughly unexpected and seemingly impossible contemporary resurgence of primitive, sacrificial violence.[7]

Voluntarism, nominalism, disenchantment, and desacralization: these were the background theological assumptions of the Enlightenment, but they are now, it seems, *foregrounded* social, cultural, and political dogmas. The Regensburg Address of Pope Benedict XVI, with his account of the three waves of dehellenization, is a key text for grasping this development. Dehellenized reason closed to intelligible, noetic being, a voluntarist God beyond good and evil, and a non-participatory cosmos mechanically construed—all undergirded by the replacement of analogy with univocity—are the metaphysical, epistemological, and theological roots of modernity. As the pope suggests, these roots have nourished a misshapen cultural tree, nay, a forest; and it cannot be simply cut down and replanted. It the forest we call home, and there seems nowhere else to go.

Nonetheless, all these conceptions and relationships and genealogies are being negotiated and renegotiated, challenged and reconfigured, in our post-secular, post-disenchanted, intellectual, spiritual, and cultural climate. Jürgen Habermas talking *to* Benedict XVI, and not *at* him, a conversation published as *The Dialectics of Secularization*,[8] is one of many examples of such non-polemical and fruitful

7. See chapters 18 and 19 below.

8. Jürgen Habermas and Joseph Ratzinger, *The Dialectics of Secularization: On Reason and Religion* (San Francisco: Ignatius Press, 2007).

negotiation. But where is this unstable yet pregnant dialectic going? Will it be transcended, replaced, or further developed, and in which direction? Will we see a return to traditional ideas and practices, but now more highly developed and nuanced, in a new synthesis of faith and reason, a new Christendom incomparably richer than the old one exemplified by St Thomas in theory and medieval Christendom in practice? Or, will we see only an exacerbation of the fissiparous and centrifugal tendencies of a nihilistic, nominalist modernity, a further rejection of tradition and the *philosophia perennis*, devolving into a truly apocalyptic, nightmarish, post-human world? Or will it be both of these scenarios at the same time?[9] As I see it, the question comes down to this: can men live together in peace and flourish under a purely human canopy in which the eschaton has been thoroughly immanentized? Thomas Molnar puts the question this way:

> Must the political order be derived from a cosmic model (or, at any rate, from an external, transcendent reference point), or are there valid and effective substitutes? Can unaided humanity, through the mobilization of its faculties, create a sacred, or at least a myth, powerful enough to convey a model? If the answer to these questions is no, we must ask: can a community exist without the sacred component by the mere power of "rational" decisions and "intellectual" discourse?[10]

The Dialectic of Modernity

So, how to respond to our peculiar situation, as tradition-minded theists? One cannot just discount the social, cultural, political, and religious fruits that have come through our humanist forebears. One can and must regret the evil of the breakup of Christendom

---

9. For an incomparable argument for this, see Glenn Olsen, *The Turn to Transcendence: The Role of Religion in the Twenty-First Century* (Catholic University of America Press, 2010); cf. Thaddeus Kozinski, "The Turn to Transcendence," *The Imaginative Conservative*, May 26, 2018, available at https://theimaginativeconservative.org/2018/05/turn-to-transcendence-glenn-w-olsen-thaddeus-kozinski.html.

10. Thomas Molnar, *Twin Powers: Politics and the Sacred* (Grand Rapids: Eerdmans, 1988), 137.

and the great evils the ensued in its wake,[11] but one must accept and appreciate the good that broke free, as it were, as well:[12] the immense progress of the sciences and medicine (though these have been thoroughly corrupted by money and politics), the aspiration to universal human rights (though incoherently and hypocritically applied), the concern for and vindication of victims (though not without further scapegoating), the historical consciousness of the evil of ritual scapegoating to maintain political order (though it happens now more than ever, under the surface),[13] the affirmation of the great good of ordinary, non-clerical life (though new and oppressive hierarchies have arisen), the emergence of a large, politically and economically active middle-class (though it is constantly besieged), the heightened consciousness of the dignity of the human person (though helpless babies and the dying are murdered), and, as José Casanova has presented it,[14] the structural differentiation of spheres of human activity rightly given relative autonomy from the ecclesial, religious, and sacred, such as politics, science, and economics (though the autonomy has become absolute).

It is plausible to maintain that these aspirations and values and institutions, though replete with incoherence and hypocrisy, did develop, and relatively quickly, within the modern period. Yet were these developments worth the price—the genocidal atheistic totalitarianism and fascism of the twentieth century, and the godless, scientistic dictatorship and psychopathic new world order of the twenty-first? I do think Taylor radically undervalues the blessings and merits of the Christendom model, both historically and ideally, for he underestimates the evil that partial goods and half-values, however universally and sincerely pursued and held, can wreak, and have wreaked, on a society not unified, grounded, and integrated in and through the moral and spiritual authority of the *philosophia*

---

11. The best recent book on this is Brad Gregory, *The Unintended Reformation* (Cambridge, MA: Harvard University Press, 2012).

12. On this, see Charles Taylor, *A Catholic Modernity?* (Oxford: Oxford University Press, 1999).

13. See Part V of this book.

14. See his *Public Religions in the Modern World* (Chicago: University of Chicago Press, 1994).

perennis and the Catholic Church. And Taylor is wrong, along with Jacques Maritain and John Courtney Murray and neoconservative Christianity, to renounce the project of creating a new Christendom based firmly upon Sacred Tradition, employing its metaphysics and political theology, and incarnating it in politics, economics, and culture.[15]

Nevertheless, one point here is well taken. In the words of Maritain, there has been a certain maturation of the political order, and it does look like the Gospel seed has come to a greater fruition now in certain temporal areas—though there is room for much more growth, and there have been many misshapen and misbegotten stalks, as well as abortive fruits. This maturation, and the awesome responsibility that it demands, is the true message of *Gaudium et Spes* when interpreted correctly according to the hermeneutic of continuity; not as a replacement of the *Syllabus of Errors* of Pius IX, but as its dialectical complement. After Vatican II, no Catholic can interpret the prior Leonine social teaching and theology as a wholesale rejection of modernity, but neither can he reject or dismiss the prior teaching as outdated or simply mistaken.

Yet we must not celebrate modernity unequivocally. Exclusive humanism, that is, the faith of atheism plus good works, certainly gets things right in terms of demanding the dignity of human freedom and personhood, and in being on the side of victims—things that paganism got really wrong. But these good affirmations of humanism have come at too steep a price. We celebrate freedom and the dignity of persons as never before, but we as a society do not really know what these things are, as witness the condoning of abortion, euthanasia, and gay marriage, legally enforced political correctness and hate crimes, the normalization of torture, eroticized and violent mass consumer culture, unmanned drone attacks on civilian "enemies," and the seeming inability of Western nations to cease scapegoating, genocide, and war. That is why Taylor, as well

---

15. I try to show that confessional politics, whatever the confession, is not just a historical feature of the pre-modern world, but of any world, in my book *The Political Problem of Religious Pluralism: And Why Philosophers Can't Solve It* (Lanham, MD: Lexington Books, 2010).

as Habermas, insists that for the genuine goods of modernity to endure—healthy secularity, non-exclusive humanism, just democracy, authentically human human rights, non-Jacobin equality—modernity must recognize its theological roots, or at least not be ungrateful or in denial of them, as were the leaders of the European Union in their refusal explicitly and officially to recognize Europe's Christian genealogy and historical character. Thomas Molnar has written:

> We are thus approaching societies without the sacred and without power. To use the words of Gauchet again, the political enterprise is no longer justified in calling itself the concretization of the heavenly law. Political power is subverted in its symbolic foundation and sacred identity. Its roots, hence its mediating legitimacy, have been removed by a quiet revolution. Liberal democracy has proved to be a passage from society founded on the sacred to society founded on nothing but itself.[16]

The jury is still out on whether or not theoretically and practically political power can be authorized and exercised in a purely immanent and secular mode, and whether or not the foundation for political authority has actually been transferred from the traditional sacred to the modern profane. As Remi Brague warns, "Such a contract, precisely because it has no external point of reference, cannot possibly decide whether the very existence on this earth of the species *homo sapiens* is a good thing or not."[17] Such ambivalence about human existence itself is intolerable, of course, but is it the price we must pay for desacralization? The vast majority of political theorists and actors for over four hundred years have been telling us that the Great Separation has occurred and is irreversible, with even many Christian thinkers in agreement. Yet it is not clear that Christians can make complete peace with a thoroughly desacralized political order, though the Catholic Church has come a long way toward *rapprochement* from the time of Gregory XVI's *Mirari Vos* and Pius IX's *Syllabus of Errors.*

16. Molnar, *Twin Powers*, 116.

17. Remi Brague, "Are Non-Theocratic Regimes Possible," *The Intercollegiate Review* (Spring 2006), 11.

Modernity as Apocalypse

The question remains as to the limits the retention of an integrally Catholic worldview places on full reconciliation with secular modernity and liberal democracy. According to St Thomas, men cannot adequately understand in theory, let alone fulfill in practice, the precepts of the natural law without the help of its author, God, and its divinely appointed interpreter, the Roman Catholic Church. With regard to a non-sacral foundation for political order, the Thomist Joseph May in the 1950s stated: "The only true doctrine is that civil society cannot prescind from the ultimate end both because the temporal welfare implies an ordering to the spiritual and supernatural, and because the individual citizens are directly and positively bound to tend to it."[18] And even *Dignitatis Humanae* insists that it "leaves untouched the traditional Catholic doctrine about the moral duty of men and societies toward the true religion and the one Church of Christ" (Sec. 1). As Pope St John Paul II often reiterated, the face of Jesus Christ is the only true mirror in which man can fully and accurately contemplate and comprehend his own nature and destiny; thus, only therein can he discern the moral values and goods most perfective of himself and the political order.

The two extremes to avoid, then, are a complete rejection of "the secular," on the one hand, and a belief in its complete self-sufficiency, on the other. Where to find the balance? Reading Catholic Social Teaching, from Leo XIII to Pope Francis and through the lens of the hermeneutic of continuity, can provide much light. In so doing, one can see how unchanging Catholic principles—such as the social reign of Christ the King, the rights of God in both the religious and temporal orders, the error of the divorce (though not the distinction) between Church and state, the inadequacy of the anti-Aristotelian, social contractarian, Lockean/Rousseauian foundation for political authority, and the moral obligation, objectively speaking, of every political community to recognize in some capacity the True Religion—are not at all rejected by later teachings. The right of the human person to religious freedom and the necessity of a healthy political secularity do not contradict the right of the Church

---

18. Joseph R. May, *The State and the Law of Christ* (Rome: Ponta Grossa, 1958), 51.

to certain social and political privileges, and the cooperation of Church and state for the good of both the political and ecclesial communities. Those who aver that the more recent teachings are obvious repudiations of a theocratic, paternalist, antimodern, and fanatical past are blinded by their spun-modernity, enslaved to the spirit of the age from which, as Chesterton insisted, the Church alone can save us. *All* the Church's teachings, even when they evince prima facie tension, are coordinated and resolved in a delicate synthesis by the Magisterium to preclude both the imbalanced, *tout court* rejection of modernity and the blind adulation of it.

But how to apply these teachings effectively, here and now? Can we aspire to something more than private practice? Should we not be engaging in Christian action directed toward the long-term goal of not merely a justly-managed pluralism wherein Christians can carve out a modest space for their own exercise of religious freedom, but a truly new Christendom where Christ reigns as King over all? Can we have a genuinely Christian, confessional political order that respects religious freedom and freedom of conscience within the centrally administered, gargantuan, liberal democratic nation-state without recourse to some level of cultural and even political secession of like-minded believers? Can we transform our ever-expanding Leviathan into a truly federated and decentralized polity, or is it simply, as the Pledge of Allegiance insists, indivisible? Are we caught in an inescapable tyranny of pluralism? Can such tyranny be peacefully subverted?

From Faith to Dialectic to *Aporia*

It would seem that the "marketplace of ideas" approach to obtain autonomy for tradition-constituted communities is being programmatically sabotaged from the top down by ideology and the ruling class's jealousy to preserve its hegemony. As Alasdair MacIntyre puts it: "Liberalism is often successful in preempting the debate . . . so that [objections to it] appear to have become debates within liberalism. . . . There is little place in such political systems for the criticism of the system itself, that is, for putting liberalism in question."[19] Thus, we would first need a nationwide ideological repudiation of centrally managed and controlled "pluralistic" secular liberalism as the inescapable political reality. But with the way political conversation is set up nowadays, culturally, legally, and juridically —that is, staged, controlled, policed, constrained, and shut down when necessary—any discourse whose outcome poses a threat to the status quo is doomed to failure, or made to fail.

Hence the vital need to secure political autonomy for those communities that already repudiate the status quo. But how does one obtain that? The real problem is psychological and spiritual. Too many Christians have been mentally colonized by the Lockean political paradigm, where "every Church is orthodox to itself," where religion is defined as private, divorced from politics. If MacIntyre is right, the precondition for getting out of the liberal cave, as it were, is robust and prolonged participation in tradition-constituted communities that are already out of it, so as to be inculcated in the habits of thought and practice of a truly supra-and-anti-liberal politics. For MacIntyre, we can achieve such communities right now, on a small scale, and many have already done so, but somehow this is to be enacted in and through communities without any legal and political teeth, or even any desire of obtaining them. This seems impossible, for such communities are just not genuine political communities, that is, not perfect societies in the Aristotelian sense, and hence too weak to do the job of virtue inculcation and orientation of souls to the transcendent. They must fall prey to the insidious individualism of modernity.

I have not yet encountered convincing and satisfying answers to these questions and their derivative and underlying questions posed throughout this book. MacIntyre, perhaps, comes closest in terms of a philosophical account, but his project is not powerful enough, and I think the reason it ultimately fails is its neglect to incorporate the power and authority of political theology and the reality of the spiritual—and political—authority of the Catholic Church. One needs more than philosophy to defeat the theological heresy and idola-

19. Alasdair MacIntyre, *Whose Justice? Which Rationality?* (Notre Dame: University of Notre Dame Press, 1988), 392.

trous church of secularist liberalism. William Cavanaugh recognizes this need, but his is a notion of political authority and state that borders on the anarchist.[20] Cavanaugh seems to repudiate the normative Leonine/Thomistic understanding of the state as possessing intrinsic moral authority and the obligation to offer God worship, that is, the infallibly taught political ideal of the Catholic confessional state. For Cavanaugh, the state appears to be a necessary evil at best, an intrinsic evil at worst, and it is not clear that he means only the post-Westphalian nation-state. All states, even the best of them, seem for him to be intrinsically evil to some extent. His model conceives of the state as inexorably beholden to the City of Man. However, the work of René Girard on scapegoating, treated below in chapter 19, makes Cavanaugh's dire conclusion seem inescapable, at least in terms of how the modern state has behaved and behaves.

So, after all this, what *is* Modernity? Apophaticism is probably the best we'll do. Modernity is *not* the progressive divinization of man and marginalization of God, socially, economically, politically, culturally, anthropologically, leading in postmodernity and beyond to the final rejection of His public reign on earth. But it may very well be that Enlightened humanism is to be succeeded by transhumanism, warned about by C. S. Lewis in his (hopefully non-prophetic) *That Hideous Strength*, in which an elite of the powerful few control and enslave the world's population via genetic engineering, mind control, and technological wizardry—to which we could add, based upon our experience since Lewis's time, a culture of super-eroticism and suicide, sex and death. Modernity, on the other hand, by God's grace, may be the site of a new synthesis, the transcending of stale and dichotomous categories of thought and practice in which a new Christendom can emerge, one in which the reign of God in His glory and love emerges side-by-side with the full dignity and flourishing of man in economic, political, moral, and spiritual freedom. It does seem that man has been given the freedom and power to determine the answers to these questions in practice as never before. Perhaps that freedom is the essence of our present age.

---

20. See especially his *Migrations of the Holy: God, State, and the Political Meaning of the Church* (Grand Rapids: Eerdmans, 2011).

Modernity as Apocalypse

In 1969, theologian Joseph Ratzinger wrote about the future. His sobering remarks leave room for hope, but only of the supernatural kind:

> The church will become small and will have to start afresh more or less from the beginning. She will no longer be able to inhabit many of the edifices she built in prosperity. As the number of her adherents diminishes . . . she will lose many of her social privileges. . . . As a small society, [the Church] will make much bigger demands on the initiative of her individual members. . . . It will be hard going for the Church, for the process of crystallization and clarification will cost her much valuable energy. It will make her poor and cause her to become the Church of the meek. . . . The process will be long and wearisome as was the road from the false progressivism on the eve of the French Revolution—when a bishop might be thought smart if he made fun of dogmas and even insinuated that the existence of God was by no means certain. . . .
>
> But when the trial of this sifting is past, a great power will flow from a more spiritualized and simplified Church. Men in a totally planned world will find themselves unspeakably lonely. If they have completely lost sight of God, they will feel the whole horror of their poverty. Then they will discover the little flock of believers as something wholly new. They will discover it as a hope that is meant for them, an answer for which they have always been searching in secret. . . . And so it seems certain to me that the Church is facing very hard times. The real crisis has scarcely begun. We will have to count on terrific upheavals. But I am equally certain about what will remain at the end: not the Church of the political cult, which is dead already, but the Church of faith. She may well no longer be the dominant social power to the extent that she was until recently; but she will enjoy a fresh blossoming and be seen as man's home, where he will find life and hope beyond death.[21]

This book is the outcome of my sundry attempts over the past decade to grapple with the question of modernity in the areas of

21. Joseph Ratzinger, *Faith and the Future* (San Francisco: Ignatius Press, 2009), 116–17.

philosophy, theology, spirituality, psychology, education, and politics. I hope they shed some light within this cave we live in, a cave into which God Himself descended and out of which He ascended, gifting all men with the power to ascend as well, but only if we allow ourselves to be united to Him. Karl Rahner's prophecy that "the devout Christian of the future will either be a 'mystic,' one who has experienced 'something,' or he will cease to be anything at all,"[22] and Romano Guardini's bracing depiction of the future, ring all the more true:

> Loneliness in faith will be terrible. Love will disappear from the face of the public world, but the more precious will be that love that flows from one lonely person to another, involving a courage of the heart born from the immediacy of the love of God as it was made known in Christ.... Perhaps love will achieve an intimacy and harmony never known to this day.[23]

The vanquishing of these unprecedented evils will come, I believe, from nothing other than the power of God, who is now flooding the world with graces unprecedented—witness St Faustina, Luisa Piccarreta,[24] and Elizabeth Kindelmann[25]—enabling a level of mystical union with God greater than ever before. Come, Divine Will! Holy Mary, Mother of God, flood humanity with the blessings of thy Flame of Love!

---

22. Karl Rahner, "Christian Living Formerly and Today," in *Theological Investigations VII*, trans. David Bourke (New York: Herder and Herder, 1971), 15, as quoted in Harvey D. Egan, *Soundings in the Christian Mystical Tradition* (Collegeville, MN: Liturgical Press, 2010), 338.

23. Romano Guardini, *The End of the Modern World* (Delaware: ISI Books, 1992), 10.

24. The best introduction to the writings of Luisa Piccarreta is Daniel O'Connor's *The Crown of Sanctity: On the Revelations of Jesus to Luisa Piccarreta* (self-published), 2019. Available at https://danieloconner.files.wordpress.com/2015/06/the-crown-and-completion-of-all-sanctity.pdf.

25. The "Flame of Love" is, according to Elizabeth Kindelmann, "the greatest Grace given to mankind since the Incarnation" (http://www.flameoflove.us/brief-history-overview-flame-love-movement-immaculate-heart-mary/).

I

Modernity

1

Modernity: Disease and Cure

In contemporary Western nations, individuals and groups live in distinct social networks, engage in myriad cultural practices, learn in diverse educational institutions, and communicate in idiosyncratic imaginative and conceptual idioms. Yet they are neighbors. Many of the people we see and interact with every day live within virtually airtight intellectual, moral, and spiritual universes radically divergent from ours, holding beliefs utterly incompatible and irreconcilable with our own. One unfortunate ideological upshot of this strange situation is an *a priori* public incredulousness regarding anyone "having the whole truth." It is no wonder that the Roman Catholic Church, whose Founder identified the whole truth with His very *Person*, is at best tolerated in Western society, and really only when lost in translation, as one denomination among others, juxtaposed with other equally "true" belief expressions in a multicultural, pluralistic boutique. Indeed, any dogmatic belief system in its raw, untranslated form is portrayed in the culture as a dangerous and inhuman cult, an intolerable opponent of the indisputable reign of freedom and pluralism.

The existence of a pluralism of incompatible "truths" is not a good thing, for Truth is one, and error about first principles and ultimate ends is the result of *sin*, not, as the late John Rawls put it, "the free exercise of reason." Radical religious pluralism, in short, must be seen as a grave defect of human existence, a spiritual, intellectual, moral, social, and political *dis*order. *Pace* the Enlightenment, perpetual and increasing religious pluralism is not the ideal for politics, nor the "best we can hope for this side of paradise," and "the most prudent accommodation to the *real world*." The Church's perennial political ideal of the reign of Christ the King simply does not permit such resignation to sin, error, and worldliness.

Yet because this tragic pluralism has been mysteriously permitted by God, I think it could be an occasion for what Peter Leithart has called "deep comedy."[1] Perhaps our pluralistic milieu can provide Catholics and other men of good will open to the transcendent with a unique opportunity for an unprecedented encounter with the living God beyond all systems, paradigms, and concepts—including religious ones. As John Paul II wrote in 1999, "If by modernity we mean a convergence of conditions that permit a human being to express better his or her own maturity, spiritual, moral, and cultural, then the Church saw itself as the 'soul' of modernity."[2] Indeed, pluralism itself can be, if interpreted and utilized correctly, a potent catalyst for the New Evangelization. Modernity, as I shall try to show, is both the cause and the cure of its own existential disease, one that can best be described as a descent into *partial thinking*. But it is also precisely the deep pluralism of modernity that enables man to overcome it, if only he desires to do so.

Feeling the Pull

To borrow from the thesis of Charles Taylor's masterpiece *A Secular Age*, along with the peculiar "consciousness shift" that constitutes the essence of modernity comes a heightened capacity intimately to *feel the pull* of other worldviews and belief systems, especially those we might otherwise deem unworthy of our interest. Modern secular pluralism, though essentially defective, provides an unprecedented opportunity for persons to experience the *other*, and *from the inside*, that is, not just as an abstract possibility of thought and practice, as was possible in all ages, but *intimately and existentially*, as a living,

---

1. Peter Leithart, *Deep Comedy: Trinity, Tragedy, and Hope in Western Culture* (Moscow, ID: Canon Press, 2006).

2. Cited in Tracey Rowland, *Ratzinger's Faith: The Theology of Pope Benedict XVI* (Oxford: Oxford University Press, 2008), 152.

breathing, concrete, coherent (or perhaps not so coherent, as in the case of the tradition of liberalism) historical *tradition.* Alasdair MacIntyre describes this immersion in other traditions as akin to learning a second conceptual and imaginative language, and he judges it indispensable for the authentic understanding and practice of one's own tradition. Moreover, without such exotic immersions, we can lose the capacity to recognize and correct the defects in our own tradition, rendering us ineffective as participants in its further development.

By encountering the partial truths in other traditions, we are more able to recognize partial truths *as partial*, both in other traditions and in our own, including the partial way in which we finite and flawed humans inevitably appropriate and understand those *non*-partial truths contained within our own tradition. The tradition of which we are a member may indeed be the true tradition, providing the most intimate access to and limpid mediation of the deepest realities, yet reality is perceived and grasped by *me* in a partial and incomplete manner at best, and in a tendentious and distorted way at worst. *I* am not Tradition. Encountering reality through the lens of other perennial traditions can serve to expose that false dichotomy in our minds that leads us to interpret other views as nothing more than full-fledged errors and our own personal lenses as nothing less than the whole truth. Our particular tradition of rationality—say, Thomism—may, in an objective sense, contain the most truth and best method of knowing, inquiring about, and recognizing truth, but as finite, fallible, sinful creatures, our subjective grasp of it is inevitably partial.

Our modern, secular, godless culture, of course, due to its narcissistic ethos,[3] can cause us to lose the capacity to feel the pull of just those parts of the truth we need to see and accept in order to attain wholeness. The modern tendency to *liquidate the other*, in Josef

3. See Christopher Lasch, *The Culture of Narcissism: American Life in an Age of Diminishing Expectations*, rev. ed. (New York: Norton, 1991) and *The Minimal Self: Psychic Survival in Troubled Times* (New York: Norton, 1984). Also, Neil Postman, *Amusing Ourselves to Death: Public Discourse in the Age of Show Business* (New York: Penguin, 1985).

Pieper's phrase, is far from being a sign of loyalty and devotion to one's truth. Rather, it indicates a totalitarian solipsism of the self, an intellectual enslavement through a self-inflicted, epistemological seclusion that automatically translates any genuine experience of the other into the same. When this occurs, any part of the truth recognized and possessed loses its healing property, becoming deadly to the soul. Instead of being seen as the wonderful part of truth that it is, in the poisoned soul it is rendered a full-fledged error, and we are blind to what could render us whole again. In other words, truth, when encountered partially but interpreted totalistically, becomes a lie.

However, if the diseased mind could learn to see the parts *as parts*, and not simply as hateful errors to condemn and fear and from which to escape at all costs, he could recognize the prison into which his mind has fallen. As Plato's cave suggests, liberation from our intellectual and spiritual prisons can only occur through the dawning upon our souls of the light of the whole, the Good, which is both that by which all true knowledge occurs and the knowable *par excellence*.[4] And for our non-angelic, discursive, and fallen intellects, this can occur only through a persistent and often excruciating dialectical comparison of whole and part, a dynamic exemplified by Plato in his dialogues and brought to near perfection by St Thomas in his *Summa Theologiae*. It is a kind of ongoing intellectual crucifixion. Might modernity, for all its tragic evils, serve as our conceptual Calvary, bringing about a deeply comedic intellectual and spiritual resurrection?

None of this is meant to suggest that there are not full-fledged, pernicious errors and evils in the modern world, as distinct from merely partial truths—indeed, there are more and worse ones than ever before. St Pius X deemed modernism the "synthesis of all heresies." Nor am I suggesting that Catholicism is not the whole truth of Revelation, objectively speaking. But, again, often what we perceive to be absolute error is only a partial truth distorted into error by its being removed from the whole; and often what we perceive to be the whole truth is only an exaggeration of a partial truth. We must

4. See chapter 4.

22

consider whether the partial truths we tend to reject as unworthy of our consideration might be precisely those we need to embrace for the completion and correction of our thinking. In short, strategic and prudent intellectual immersions in our pluralistic milieu, always preceded and followed, of course, by extensive and intensive periods of nursing at the bosom of Holy Mother Church in study and contemplation, is, I think, a necessary regimen: 1) to enable us to recognize the partialness of our own and others' appropriation of the truth; 2) to transcend whatever in modernity holds us back from self-knowledge, wisdom, and union with God; and 3) to help end the reign of relativistic pluralism and bring about a new Christendom.

But why risk plunging ourselves into pluralism? Why play around with alien traditions that we know to be fundamentally false? Again, it is the *Church alone* who sees and possesses the whole truth (at least implicitly and latently; the *expression* and *recognition* of the whole truth by the Magisterium is time-bound and discursive, being historically mediated and occasioned, as Cardinal Newman has taught us). But we, the Church's members, are always, subjectively speaking, *approaching* this whole truth, and if we forget this, we fall into idolatry. What we think to be the whole truth is often only our own partial appropriation of it, and, even worse, *a part pretending to be the whole*. This idolatry is the spiritual disease of modernity, and the practice of Catholicism, including above all daily silent contemplation, is the cure of all spiritual maladies. However, the occasion for the remedy to be applied is to be found, paradoxically, within—indeed, through—modernity itself.

Catholics in a pluralistic society are uniquely positioned to accomplish the "whole and part" dialectical exercise, for we possess both the whole by grace and through the Church, and the parts through the charity and humility that prompt us to vulnerable and humble dialectical encounters with our neighbors' and our own partial-truth fragments. Fragmentary, partial knowledge, unrecognized as fragmentary and partial and substituting for comprehensive holistic knowledge, is the intellectual condition of our fallen nature, and modernity serves to exacerbate it. But with the intrinsic help of grace, the extrinsic help of the Magisterium, and our cooperation through courageous intellectual analysis, imaginative immersions in the *other*, and generous dialogue coupled with imaginative, intellectual, and silent contemplation,[5] we can ascend, at least partially, to the whole that awaits us personally and fully in the Beatific Vision.

I would like now to offer three examples that illustrate the disease of partial thinking: the fall of Lucifer, the sin of Adam and Eve, and Saul the Pharisee's rejection of Christ. I shall try to show how a partial yet subjectively significant truth, when eclipsing a truth of momentous and fundamental import, becomes a full-fledged error, that is, how complementary partial truths, when pitted against each other as contradictions, become illusory, self-sufficient whole-truths. When this occurs, even the partial truths are lost, and a totalitarianism of the psyche ensues. The only cure for this is a radical, vulnerable openness to the *other*, through relentless Socratic questioning and existential wonder.[6]

Lucifer's "Truth"

Did "partial thinking" cause Lucifer to fall from heaven? An angel, that is, an intuitive, non-discursive intellectual being, can never grasp truth in the partial way humans do; yet perhaps there is something analogous to partial thinking even in the angelic intellect. What "thoughts" preceded the complete perversion of Lucifer's will? As St Thomas teaches in his treatise on the angels, an angel receives knowledge of the supernatural order through the mediation of angelic intellects higher than itself. Thus, an angel in the choir of powers could not receive knowledge of God's plan for the

---

5. On how to practice silent contemplation, I have found the writings and talks of Father John Main to be of incomparable clarity and profundity, as well as practicality. See, among many others, his *Word into Silence: A Manual for Christian Meditation* (Norwich: Canterbury Press, 2006), and the talks grouped at YouTube under the heading "Set your Mind on the Kingdom by John Main 1926–1982."

6. For a profound and exhaustive account of the problem with dualistic thinking by a thinker deeply learned in both Western and Eastern thought, see Raimon Panikkar, *The Rhythm of Being* (New York: Orbis, 2013).

salvation of man through the intellect of an angel in the choir of, say, the archangels, but only from principalities, cherubim, seraphim, etc. Lucifer knew that spirit is superior to matter, and God's plan, as it might be supposed, was to reveal and effect the salvation of men through the lowly intellect of a human being, uniting not only spirit and matter, but *divinity* and matter. "Now, since the purpose of creation is to give glory to the Supreme Being, and since *I* am second only to God," Lucifer might have considered, "then how could He be justified in his plan to unite divinity with anything less than *my* angelic nature? Could it be that a *human woman* could possibly mediate the divine? Moreover, am I absolutely certain that this being calling himself God actually is what he claims to be? After all, I did not actually witness my own creation."

For *humans* to engage in such critical analysis of and *a priori* skepticism towards supernatural matters is not necessarily malicious, for, as Pope Benedict XVI made clear in his Regensburg Address, it is incumbent on man to bring *all* truth claims to the bar of reason, even claims supposed to be from God Himself. Truth can never contradict truth. However, for an unfallen angel, things are not so simple. For Lucifer to have "reasoned" this way (whatever that would mean for a non-discursive intellect) would have been unspeakably malicious and perverse. And this is not because his logic may have been flawed, for angelic logic is always *valid*, if not always sound; but because to doubt God *in an unfallen angelic state*, no matter the pretext, is to have entered deliberately and irreversibly into an abyss of unreality. I suggest that Lucifer's very *hesitation* to submit, metaphorically speaking, was at the basis of his "creation" of evil and error, the origin of hell. Prudent deliberation and speculation about the proper course of action to take in any given situation is, for us fallen men, an indispensable means to virtue. However, for an unfallen angelic intellect, any hesitation or doubt regarding the will of God must constitute the gravest of sins, a violent ripping of one's being away from the loving bosom of reality, the rejection of the whole and one's part in the whole for the virtual nothingness of the isolated part.

It is true that once we humans begin to think about the mere possibility of not submitting to God's plans, the reasons justifying such a possibility can begin to look quite reasonable. Perhaps some such apparently reasonable justification is the "partial truth" that Lucifer embraced, so to speak, but the price paid for it was the loss of the overwhelmingly more fundamental truth of the perfect goodness and infinite love of God. The origin of such angelic questioning, however subtle, forceful, and coherent it may have seemed to Lucifer, is not mere intellectual error, but willful malice, the sin of *disbelief*, which, as Josef Pieper maintains, is the rejection of God's revelation with full knowledge of it as the revelation of God.[7] It was, for Lucifer, it seems, the rejection of the revelation of the identity of God as Love. Such disbelief, by the highest and thus most loving—at least potentially—of God's creatures, would be an unthinkable act if it were not revealed to us by the Church.

The Fall into Fragmentation

Adam and Eve had not yet obtained the fullness of human happiness or perfection in their short sojourn in paradise; for, like us, only in heaven would their lives be brought to complete fullness. Before the fall, all creatures, from the most humble to the most exalted, were to form Adam's and Eve's ladder to this eventual fullness, both through contemplation—the stars, the order of nature, each other—and by consumption—the bountiful and unimaginably delicious fruits and vegetables provided by the Lord God for their sustenance and delight. Yet, they were not permitted to consume or contemplate *every* creature (they were forbidden to contemplate disobedience); the only other rational being they knew, the one who called himself God, willed it so. It was the first "doctrine of conditional joy," which Chesterton discusses in his wonderful chapter from *Orthodoxy* called "The Ethics of Elfland."

However, they had now met another rational being who had suggested to them that by not consuming *every* fruit, they would be depriving themselves of the fullness of reality; if *some* creatures would bring them *some* fulfillment, then *all* creatures would bring

---

7. Josef Pieper, *Faith, Hope, and Love* (San Francisco: Ignatius Press, 1997), ch. 1.

them *all* fulfillment. And nothing could possibly justify their missing out on the very purpose for which they were created. God's proscription, then, must be interpreted as a prescription, else God becomes a miser. Moreover, precisely the fruit "forbidden" to them was necessary for their fulfillment, for it alone could complete their knowledge of reality, which included, by God's own description, good and evil. The fulfillment of souls made to be capax omnium requires complete, not partial, knowledge. Finally, they perceived this fruit both immediately and upon reflection as good, for every existing being is ontologically good, and, since error did not yet exist in their minds, it would be sinful not to bring this fruit to the perfection for which it was made by being consumed.

Admittedly, one can see in these arguments a justification for at least some hesitation on the part of Adam and Eve when confronted with the command not to eat the forbidden fruit. The essential problem with these arguments, however, is not the content or structure of the arguments themselves—some absurdity, incoherence, or implausibility to be found in them. It is, I think, their *partialness.* They are sound and valid arguments as far as they go, but only if taken completely out of the existential and ontological context to which they owe their very intelligibility. It is *God* who has given this command, after all, and Adam and Eve are His creatures, brought into being out of the slime. In *that* context, partial truths in their argument become lies. By the mere consideration of these partial truths ripped out of the whole truth, Adam and Eve had already lost God, the source of all truth. How otherwise could it possibly have seemed reasonable to them to disobey God in order to obey Him? To perfect themselves by severing themselves from the only possible source of perfection?

As the whole truth began to fragment before their eyes, disobeying God, which at first was only a hint of a possibility, now became a valid consideration, and finally, in their act of eating the fruit, a categorical imperative. Like Lucifer's disbelief in the identity of God and love, Adam and Eve, through an external temptation but still by an act of their own free will, lost their trust in Him. Immediately, their integral perception of the truth was shattered, and the whole in whose light the fragments of truth could be seen precisely as fragments and thus as unworthy of isolated consideration was lost to them. And through them it was lost to us, until the time of the descent of the Whole into His now fractured world.

Saul: the Pharisee vs. the *Logos*

The final and perhaps most illustrative example of how fundamental error can arise through the totalistic embrace of partial truth is the Pharisees' rejection of Christ, particularly, that Pharisee-turned-Apostle named Saul. In his remarkable *Jesus of Nazareth*, Benedict XVI has brought out the plausibility and power of the Pharisees' indictment against Christ.[8] In his discussion of Rabbi Jacob Neusner's book, *A Rabbi Talks to Jesus*, the Holy Father explains why, for a Pharisee, the threat Jesus posed to Judaism was far more dangerous than any that came before. Throughout the history of Judaism, there were always formidable foes to its survival and God-pleasingness: subversive teachers, heretics, fanatics, traitors, worldlings, indifferentists, blasphemers. But never before did one man embody the very antithesis of the Judaic belief in the utter transcendence and holiness of God. Jesus, by his claim to be the definitive and full embodiment of God, the chosen *Person*, threatened to destroy the Jews' claim to be the chosen *People*. And by his defiant abrogation of the most sacred of Jewish laws, he was poised to dismantle the cornerstone that underlay the entire edifice of Jewish culture, tradition, society, and life—the *Sabbath*.

Benedict pulls no punches in his explication of Neusner's argument—it *is* powerful, and Benedict depicts it as such, with the utmost respect and sympathy. Saul was only acting upon the force of the argument's truth when he persecuted the infant Church, for the Nazarene's power to destroy the chosen people of God through his followers' fanaticism required a violent and ruthless extermination, as violent and ruthless—and even more so—as, say, Joshua's, Gideon's, or David's extermination of the much lesser threats of the

---

8. Benedict XVI, *Jesus of Nazareth: From the Baptism in the Jordan to the Transfiguration*, trans. Adrian Walker (New York: Doubleday, 2007), 103–27.

Jerichoites, Midianites, and Philistines. However, just as the trenchant and seemingly ironclad arguments of Lucifer and Adam and
Eve splintered into fragments when applied to the infinite solidity
of God's holiness, so did the Pharisees'. As Benedict argues, from the
Pharisees' perspective the desire to destroy Jesus and persecute His
followers was the epitome of loyalty, piety, courage, and devotion to
God—*if* Jesus was only a human being. If He were the incarnate
God, however, then these virtues would become vices, indeed, the
epitome of sacrilege and blasphemy.

Saul was a self-condemned prisoner to partial thinking. Nothing
but an unforeseen, undesired, violent encounter with Him who, to
his diseased spirit, was *the Other*, a Jewish man claiming to be God,
would liberate him. If Saul had been allowed by Christ to remain in
the isolated, blinded world of the Jewishdom of his day—the way in
which some traditional Catholics would like to remain within the
isolating and alienating "Christendoms" of their fears and gnostic
certainties[9]—his blindness would never have been revealed to him,
and he would never have become St Paul, the Apostle to the Jewish
other, the Gentiles. Christ Himself had to break Saul out of his partial thinking, which was indicative not of authentic Mosaic Judaism,
but of Talmudic, anti-*Logos* fanaticism. Such violent divine inter-
vention (in the manner of a Flannery O'Connor story) had to
occur, for Saul's was a particularly virulent case of partial thinking.
We Christians, however, have the unique chance to invite Christ
freely into our minds and hearts by inviting into intimacy the
salvific "others" we would rather not meet. I would argue that such
encounters are providentially available as never before, if we would
only accept them, in our modern pluralistic world.

In a remarkable passage, Alasdair MacIntyre zeroes in on the
essence of modernity's peculiar disease:

> We have within our social order few if any social milieus within
> which reflective and critical enquiry concerning the central issues
> of human life can be sustained.... This tends to be a culture of
> answers, not of questions, and those answers, whether secular or

9. See my article "The Gnostic Traditionalist," *New Oxford Review* (June 2007).

religious, liberal or conservative, are generally delivered as though meant to put an end to questioning.[10]

What MacIntyre is saying, I think, is that the culture of modernity is a culture without wonder, and since without wonder there is no awe, as Plato taught us, modern culture tends to preclude the experience of that which is most awesome, God. What is the antidote to this? MacIntyre once said that we need a new St Benedict, but I wonder if we couldn't add Socrates to the list. Dietrich von Hildebrand describes the Socratic, questioning, wondering spirit as

> the inner willingness which is not closed against even the most unpleasant truth, which is really free from bias, ready to make friends with things, open to the proof of all objective existence, not looking at things through a colored lens that allows only such things to pass into the understanding as do not offend our pride and self-complacency.[11]

The existence of even one person with a genuine spirit of erotic, Socratic questioning, a soul with true metaphysical courage, is, I think, the most effective antidote to the suffocating, anti-questioning, partial-truth culture we live in, in both its traditionalist and modernist varieties. Those who believe themselves to have obtained answers without having first endured the existential agony of questioning the darkness, whether because they have judged that there are no answers, or because they believe themselves to be already quite securely possessed of dogmatic certitude, need to recognize in such an attitude neither a humble disposition of ignorance nor a pious submission to God's word, but a type of idolatry, the idolatry of partial thinking. Paul Evdokimov, an Eastern Orthodox theologian, writes:

10. Alasdair MacIntyre, "Philosophy Recalled to its Tasks," in *The Tasks of Philosophy: Selected Essays, Volume 1* (Cambridge: Cambridge University Press, 2006), 182.

11. Dietrich von Hildebrand, "Catholicism and Unprejudiced Knowledge," in *The New Tower of Babel: Modern Man's Flight from God* (Manchester, NH: Sophia Institute Press, 1994), 141.

The outdated religious person and the modern sophisticated irreligious individual meet back to back in an immanence imprisoned within itself.... The denial of God has thus permitted the affirmation of man. Once this affirmation is effected, there is no longer anything to be denied or subordinated.... On this level total man will not be able to ask any questions concerning his own reality, just as God does not put a question to himself.[12]

Perhaps what secular modernity provides to those who are open to it is a greater existential awareness of the primacy of *questioning*, as well as the heightened urgency of discovering and asking the right questions. If so, secular modernity is, in essence, a second—and perhaps final?—Axial Age. This time around, however, we are *all* called to be Socrates, with others, and more urgently, with ourselves.

What really is important in life is not so much to provide answers, as to discern true questions. When true questions are found, they themselves open the heart to the mystery. Origen used to say: "Every true question is like the lance which pierces the side of Christ causing blood and water to flow forth."[13]

---

12. Paul Evdokimov, *Ages of the Spiritual Life* (Crestwood, NY: St. Vladimir's Seminary Press, 2002), 17, 27.

13. Archbishop Bruno Forte, "Religion and Freedom: Searching for the Infinitely Loving Father-Mother," a lecture given at a meeting of the bishops of England and Wales, November 12, 2007, available at http://www.catholic.org/featured/headline.php?ID=5262.

2

Becoming Children of Modernity

As the benefits of Revelation disappear even more from the coming world, man will truly learn what it means to be cut off from Revelation.... The rapid advance of a non-Christian ethos, however, will be crucial for the Christian sensibility. As unbelievers deny Revelation more decisively, as they put their denial into more consistent practice, it will become more evident what it really means to be a Christian.

Romano Guardini[1]

No One Gets Out of Here Alive

Christian modernists and anti-modernists, and those falling somewhere in between, have offered innumerable definitions, characterizations, and genealogies of secular modernity, and none seems entirely adequate. There is something asymptotically elusive about modernity: the depth and comprehensiveness of our definitions increase with abstractness and distance; the accuracy, nuance, and precision of our characterizations increase with narrowness and obscurity. Modernity is nearly as immune to exhaustive intellectual comprehension and description, nearly as impossible to escape or transcend, as reality itself. Even what we take to be "anti-modern" theoretical and practical constructs, and our resistances and rejections of the pernicious constructs of others, are ineluctably erected from within and in virtue of the existential consciousness that is secular modernity itself. This is the main thesis of Charles Taylor's *magnum opus*, *A Secular Age*, and I think it is

---

1. *End of the Modern World*, 101.

a compelling one. Modernity is, in a very important sense, inescapable. As Taylor puts it—we are *in it*.

Even though we are talking about an artifact, a *cultural* and *historical* phenomenon, not a natural or supernatural phenomenon equivalent to a change in *being* itself (I am no Hegelian), cultural and historical being is nevertheless, at least for *us*, that is, for the culture-dependent rational animals that we are, the mediator of any "pure" being or nature that we may experience. As Alasdair MacIntyre has argued persuasively, *pace* the Enlightenment's "view from nowhere," we never encounter reality unmediated by *tradition*, that is, the cultural artifacts of human language, conceptual schemes, social practices, ritual and narrative, moral norms, symbols, etc. And although we are equipped with intellects and imaginations that can ultimately transcend tradition, history, and culture to attain timeless truth, goodness, and beauty, we do so only through the cultural resources and productions that we both create and are created by. Louis Dupré writes:

> Those who in a particular epoch impose a new pattern of meaning on the life and thought of their time do more than apply a different film of thought to an indifferent reality. They transform the nature of reality itself. If the preceding carries any metaphysical weight, it would be contained in the original thesis that Being must not be conceived as a substance moved by thought. Cultural changes leave a different reality in their wake.... Culture, then, consists not in what humans add to the real, so to speak. It is the active component of the real itself transforming the passive one.[2]

Be that as it may, it would seem obligatory for not only Christians but all men of good will to be against modernity—whatever its ontological status—in light of the notorious, anti-Christian and anti-human fruits that appear to have grown solely in the soil of secular modernity. And it seems quite plausible to a Christian that with enough prayer, education, and effort, by apprenticing oneself to the supreme culture-transcending teacher that is the Church, and

---

2. Louis Dupré, *Passage to Modernity* (New Haven: Yale University Press, 1995), 11.

by immersing oneself in her pristine formative hands, one could more or less escape at least its worst effects. Should Christians not try to create adequately anti-modern domestic, social, cultural, political, educational, and liturgical environments if the ones that secular modernity has given threaten their salvation? Christians are indeed obliged to resist and ultimately "escape" from secular modernity, but that is because we are called to transcend in spirit all finite times and places, especially when they become idols preventing the attainment of union with the timeless and placeless God.

The End of Naïveté

Of the many trenchant descriptions of modernity Taylor offers us, this one is especially helpful for our purposes:

> There has been a titanic change in our western civilization. We have changed not just from a condition where most people lived "naïvely" in a construal (part Christian, part related to "spirits" of pagan origin) as simple reality, to one in which almost no one is capable of this, but all see their option as one among many. We all learn to navigate between two standpoints: an "engaged" one in which we live as best we can the reality our standpoint opens us to; and a "disengaged" one in which we are able to see ourselves as occupying one standpoint among a range of possible ones, with which we have in various ways to coexist. . . . The shift to secularity in this sense consists, among other things, of a move from a society where belief in God is unchallenged and indeed unproblematic, to one in which it is understood to be one option among others. . . . A secular age is one in which the eclipse of all goals beyond human flourishing becomes conceivable; or better, it falls within the range of an imaginable life for masses of peoples.[3]

Note that Taylor's characterization of secular modernity (SM) is eminently non-ideological and non-condemnatory; it is neither the traditionalist's rigid denunciation nor the humanist's insouciant glorification. Rather, Taylor identifies SM as something more akin

---

3. Taylor, *A Secular Age*, 12, 19–20.

to a radically new paradigm or consciousness shift, in itself neither moral nor immoral, neither true nor false, neither good nor evil, neither pro-Christian nor anti-Christian. For, according to Taylor, SM has engendered diverse ideological interpretations and embodiments, structures of thought and practice that have been built upon and with secular modernity's peculiar consciousness and potentiality, what he calls the "immanent frame." What Taylor means by this phrase is not a rejection of all transcendence, but just that the default position is a world and self experienced in such a way that transcendence is merely an optional "spin" one is free to place as a filter on one's experience. But the "given" filter lacks any sense of transcendence.

"An age or society would then be secular or not, in virtue of the conditions of experience of and search for the spiritual."[4] Thus SM is the inescapable mode, background, and context for all thought and practice in the contemporary West, rather than any particular ideological or cultural expression of it. It is a deeper reality than culture, for it is *existential*. We encounter it deep within our lived experience of reality, *before* we have the chance to reflect on it. It is not so much the reflective description or account we give ourselves of a more fundamental, pre-philosophical and pre-reflective experience, but is itself this fundamental experience, embodied in the warp and woof of our lives in such a way that to attempt to disengage or extricate ourselves from it is equivalent to the attempt to escape reality itself. Because SM is so intimately bound up with our experience of reality, it serves as the *background* to and *structure* of the very form and content of our thinking, akin to grammar and rhetoric as the background to and structure of the matter and expression of our words. Although we can think about and thus gain some distance from the background and structure, we cannot entirely escape and transcend it.

This is a bracing claim. However, I think there is one short and powerful demonstration of its essential accuracy. Ask yourself this question: does any religious believer in the modern West *experience* his religion in a *naïve* manner, that is, in the way a small child raised

4. Ibid., 3.

within a sheltered, integrally and robustly religious home might experience it? Is it simply the way things are, that is, immune to all experiences of the "other"? Can one completely avoid being disengaged from one's naïve experience of what is and must be, losing all awareness of what is not and might not be? Is it even possible for a religious child to retain this sort of naïveté nowadays? What I am describing is not the perennial and age-indifferent capacity of human reason to abstract from one's lived experience and entertain other possible philosophical and theological accounts of reality through and in one's imagination and intellect. If that were the case, there would be nothing new in secular modernity in this respect, for even the most sheltered and parochial medieval peasant could thereby escape from the Christianity he imbibed with his mother's milk. What does seem radically unique to secular modernity is an entirely new *in*capacity to *experience* the reality of a particular worldview in a *naïve* way, that is, without the consciousness of there being other viable options.

For the Christian, then, the end of naïve religious consciousness would entail an experience of reality as perpetually open to the possibility or at least the awareness of a non-Christian interpretation and experience of the world, of the possible *absence* of God. Might such a characterization of our epoch explain the experiences of St Teresa of Calcutta and St Thérèse of Lisieux, who, as we know from their personal writings, experienced this sense of the absence of God with an intensity we cannot imagine—even while possessing a fervent supernatural faith? Perhaps what St Teresa experienced in an extraordinary manner was the ordinary communal consciousness of secular man. These and other saints in our day are representative of what seems to be a peculiarly modern form of spiritually, what Fr Aidan Nichols has called *existential* prayer: "accepting in a generous spirit our deprivation of many of the conventional props and assurances of a culturally transmitted religion ... [we] may be ushered with peculiar immediacy into the presence of the living God."[5] Obviously, these saints did escape secular modernity to some extent; however, it occurred precisely through a peculiarly

5. Aidan Nichols, *Christendom Awake* (Edinburgh: T&T Clark Ltd, 1999), 213.

intense experience of the existential absence of God, written into the very fabric of modern secular consciousness. It would seem that these saints *escaped* it by going *through* it.

Assuming that this characterization of secular modernity is more or less accurate, what would happen if one were to deny secular modernity, attempting to escape it by going against or around it? To answer this question we must first answer the more fundamental question of why one would desire to escape SM in the first place. One reason, perhaps, would be the conviction that SM is evil, for aversion is, as St Thomas teaches, the passion of the soul naturally evoked by the presence of evil. However, if we are correct in our assessment of SM as being something preceding or situating morality, being virtually ontological, at least, subjectively and experientially, then this conviction and its ensuing passion would be gravely mistaken and disordered. What *is* evil, of course, are the predominant ideological interpretations of SM, which Taylor identifies as certain "spins" on the culture of secular modernity that are often mistakenly taken to be the reality itself: "But this order of itself leaves the issue open whether, for purposes of ultimate explanation, or spiritual transformation, or final sense-making, we might have to invoke something transcendent. It is only when the order is 'spun' in a certain way that it seems to dictate a 'closed' interpretation."[6] This "closed spin" Taylor calls "exclusive humanism." We can see it today in both its "right" and "left" versions, with its twofold Janus-like embodiment in "conservative," nation-worshipping, secular-messianic militarism, on the one hand, and relativistic, Protagorean, managerial totalitarianism, on the other—relativism and fundamentalism being equally narcissistic, practically atheistic, and nihilistic.

If we take these "closed spins" to be secular modernity itself, we would rightly respond by either attacking them or attempting to escape them, or both. However, if Taylor is correct, though we must renounce and avoid all errors and evils, we should not renounce and avoid the larger background conditions or consciousness-form— the "immanent frame"—that has both enabled their existence and

6. Taylor, *A Secular Age*, 594.

our capacity to choose radically different theoretical and practical alternatives to them. In short, by choosing an alternative *content* built upon and within the background of secular modernity, we do not thereby escape the background itself—nor should we wish to. The lack of awareness of the *twice-removed nature* of secular modernity is, perhaps, a main reason for the disordered interpretations and embodiments of it, for fundamentalism (Islamic, Zionist, or Americanist) and relativism (liberal or conservative) are motivated by a mistaken aversion to what they consider evil, namely, this or that particular aspect of secular modernity itself.

Whatever modernity is, one thing we can say for certain is that it, and it alone, has been the mid-wife for the birth of the *choice-making individual*. As MacIntyre has pointed out, the "individual" is not a natural type of human being, but a kind of scripted role created in modernity according to its own peculiar dramatic exigencies. Whatever we eventually become—whether postmodern, isolated, fragmented, secularist, therapeutic urban connoisseurs of private self-creation, or anti-modern, communitarian, traditionalist, paleo-conservative, "back to the land" aspirants of a neo-medieval Christendom—we do so by *choice* as *individuals*, before we do and are anything or anybody else. For all the alternatives that modernity offers, modernity does not permit us to escape this fundamental precondition for the shaping of our identities. The non-chosen and communally provided identity of the choice-making individual is, like secular modernity itself, neither good nor evil in itself, but becomes good or evil depending upon the "spin" we put on it. As Taylor argues in his essay "A Catholic Modernity?," the greatest mistake secular moderns have made regarding their new identity is to construe the radical responsibility and high dignity that attends it for radical autonomy and spiritual independence.[7] This, and not secular modernity *per se*, is arguably the main cause of the culture of death.

What, then, is the alternative to such a construal? Josef Pieper provides a clue:

7. See Taylor, *A Catholic Modernity?*

I refer of course to the life of our fellowmen under the conditions of tyranny. As we all know, under such conditions no one dares trust anyone else. Candid communication dries up; and there arises that special kind of unhealthy wordlessness which is not silence so much as muteness. Under conditions of freedom, however, human beings speak uninhibitedly to one another. How illuminating this contrast is! For in the face of it, we suddenly become aware of the degree of human closeness, mutual affirmation, communion, that resides in the simple fact that people listen to each other and are disposed from the start to trust and "believe" each other.[8]

Our enlightened, free-thinking age is, ironically, a culture of suffocating dogmatism, and so it becomes vitally important for us to take the great gift we have been given in these times, a heightened capacity for god-like freedom, and use it for *others*. But to give to others the gift of ourselves, we must first have an intimate experience of what is *not* ourselves, for, as St Teresa Benedicta of the Cross (Edith Stein) taught, we can know ourselves adequately only through the eyes of others. All of this requires a willingness to expose ourselves to the other in the most vulnerable way, to ask, to seek, to venture out existentially in humble questioning of ourselves and all that is around us—even when we know the answers given to us by the gift of Faith. Do we *experience* these true answers as answers *to questions*, to *our* questions? Those who do not, who believe themselves to have obtained all the answers without having first endured the existential agony of searching in the darkness, whether because one has judged that there are no answers, or because one believes them to be already securely "possessed," should recognize in such an attitude neither a humble plea of ignorance nor a simple and pious submission to God's word, but a type of idolatry.

8. Pieper, *Faith, Hope, and Love*, 41.

II

Logos

3

What's Good?
Wherefrom Ought?

Wat is it that makes any human action obligatory? We have all had the experience of *ought*, of something that, at least in a subjective sense, renders my imminent action morally relevant, so that what I am about to do or not do is more than a mere question of what will be pleasing to me, socially frictionless, psychologically comfortable, or useful for some self-serving plan of action. How to understand the character of this moral experience? Wherefrom *ought*?

Innumerable accounts have been given of this universal experience, ranging from cavalier dismissal, as a psychological vestige of our ancestors' primitive taboo cultures that the Enlightenment began to expunge from our communal consciousness without having quite completed its task, to its robust embrace as the voice of a righteous God in the depths of the soul demanding us to act according to that righteousness in obedience to divine commandments. Somewhere in the middle of these is the Aristotelian, eudaimonistic interpretation of the moral *ought* as an emotional and intellectual impetus pointing us toward happiness, not so much to *do* right but to *be* good, which is to say, to follow the natural, rational path to self-fulfillment, perfection, flourishing, or well-being. Depending upon one's philosophical or cultural tastes, this could be psychological adjustment, à la stoicism or Sigmund Freud, or virtuous activity, à la Aristotle or Benjamin Franklin. And then there is always the Kantian third way, combining the ethos of both a divine command and the ethics of well-being, but without the need of a revealed set of divine commandments or a feeling of well-being. In other words, "Follow reason, God's internal command in the soul, and you will be rendered worthy for happiness ... later." Jack Bauer from the television series *24* exemplifies this mentality, the contemporary hyper-Kantian doing his duty without quite knowing why it's his duty, why he should do his duty, and if he'll ever be happy doing it.

Which theoretical and practical interpretation of the indisputable, universal human experience of *ought* makes the most sense? It seems to me that there are two fundamental features of the experience that must be affirmed and explained. On the one hand, there is the sense of *duty* to the *other*, of what is *right*: something or someone outside or above me requires me to act in a certain way, regardless of my individual likes or dislikes, notwithstanding my understanding of how or whether the imminent act will contribute to my personal well-being, satisfaction of desire, happiness, or aspirations. On the other hand, there is the sense of *desire* for *self-fulfillment*, of the *good*: the attraction, regardless of any sense of duty I might also have or not have, to things in the world that I experience as desirable, simply because they are good for *me*, as somehow related to my own happiness, which I pursue for its own sake.

Any explanation of the subjective experience of ought should encompass and synthesize both these features. And herein lies the problem, for these features appear to be mutually exclusive, or at least in very great tension with each other. If I am obliged to do or not do something, whether this obligation comes from knee-jerk taboo, social contract convention, categorical reason, or God, I cannot at the same time do this action for the sole purpose of my well-being, perfection, or subjective satisfaction. But if I feel obliged as well as attracted, then I cannot be doing what I ought to do merely because I am attracted to it personally. For then my happiness has become my duty. Conversely, if I find that I am personally attracted to what I also consider my duty, then I am not doing it *because* it is my duty, for my duty has now become for me a desirable good and thus a means to my personal happiness. Happiness and fulfillment of duty seem to be opposite motivations.

I think this phenomenological dialectic of *right* and *good* would be resolved if we could understand what is at the heart of human moral experience; but to understand this heart we require more than what unaided, human moral experience and purely philosophical speculation on this experience can provide. My argument for this conclusion is this: what the duty aspect of moral experience suggests is the reality of *justice*, which is inherently relational or communal, and thus irreducible to any interpretation of morality as mere personal fulfillment. What the happiness aspect of moral experience suggests is the reality of our *desire for the good*, which is inherently personal and thus irreducible to an interpretation of morality as social or divine obligation. So, any explanation of the moral ought must include both other-related justice and self-related desire, and this is precisely what is provided by a theological ethics of *creation* and *gift*: if we are creatures, then we are inherently relational, with our actions related above all to our creator; and if creation is a gift, then we are obligated to enjoy creation as a good.

If God created us and the world for a purpose, then we are obliged, by definition and through our very nature, to act according to this purpose. Even if we have been given free-will to decide whether to correspond with our natural *telos*, we are not really capable of re-creating or re-designing ourselves to become something other than purpose-fulfilling creatures. And if God created the world as a gift, then our main purpose as the only creatures that can receive and recognize a gift *qua* gift—not simply as something desirable—is to receive this gift as any gift is meant to be received, in love and gratitude for both the gift and the giver. In short, we are *obliged* to be happy because we have a duty to love the gift of a divinely bestowed, happy-making existence, and we are encouraged to *desire* happiness for its own sake because that is precisely the way we justly show our gratitude for the good gift we have been given. The gift we have been given, after all, is eternal happiness, begun here and perfected in the next life.

So, am I saying that only an ethics rooted in the divinely revealed truth of creation-as-gift and creator-as-love can coherently and adequately make sense of the universal experience of ought? Indeed I am. I think that purely philosophical explanations are helpful, for creation is replete with secondary causality, and grace and revelation can complete nature and reason only if nature and reason have a relative integrity and intelligibility. Thus, I am open to purely philosophical accounts that do justice to our experience. But I have not yet come across any that adequately accounts for the infinite desires and absolute obligations I experience.

We need a balanced synthesis of Platonic and Aristotelean metaphysics and ethics, for then we would have the most attractive and obligatory pre-Christian account of ethical experience, combining both a divine-order (Plato's *Good*) and happiness (Aristotle's *phronemon*)[1] ethics. Synthesize this with Christian revelation, as in St Augustine's Platonic-Christian and St Thomas's Augustinian-Aristotelian ethics—but these themselves need to be synthesized and held in balance! And integrate with all this the legitimate speculative and practical advances of modernity, such as the immense dignity of *every* human person, the extraordinariness of ordinary human life, and the integrity and relative autonomy of the temporal social and political order. Now add to these the insights of postmodernism, such as the tradition-and-history-constituted character of rational enquiry, the bankruptcy of the Enlightenment "view from nowhere," and the myth of "the secular." Charles Taylor and Alasdair MacIntyre have done incomparable work in this regard. Now all we need is a new St Benedict to show us how to put all this theory into practice.

1. *Phronemon* is the term used by Aristotle to indicate a practically wise person.

4

Plato:
Being in Exile

All education is conversion.[1]
Pierre Hadot

We know as Catholics, from the divine revelation that has come down to us from the Apostles, that we are exiles in this world. We also know that, nevertheless, this world is neither illusory nor evil, but real, good, and beloved by God. But we also know from Revelation that it is a fallen world, and that this fall is due to human sin: the willful rejection of God by our first parents, and the mysterious participation in this rejection by every human being born into this world. We also know that the exile we suffer is tragic, but temporary, and ultimately comedic, for there is a way out. God Himself entered into our exilic state by becoming a human being, and through His life, death, and resurrection overcame our exile and put an end to it. By uniting ourselves in faith, hope, and love to the God-Man who now reigns in heaven but remains intimate with us even in this fallen world, we are enabled to do what He did, through the power of His grace, and conquer death. "After this our exile," we, if we obey Him, are promised a life in our true home with our Father forever.

Every human being is born into exile, and the experience of and various responses to it constitute what we call religion, which, etymologically, is *re-ligio*, a binding or tying back. There is a universal

1. "Conversion," *Encyclopaedia Universalis* (Paris: Encyclopaedia Universalis France), 4:979–81.

recognition in the major religions of the world, including non-the-istic religions such as Buddhism and Hinduism, of a radical separa-tion of human existence from its true ground; an alienation from something more real than what we normally experience; an estrangement from a transcendent source; a blindness to a unifying, resolving, perfecting, guiding, guarding, nurturing, and loving presence; a deafness to a voice that answers infallibly to "why?" In short, we are homeless and cannot find our way home by ourselves.

Though the major religions of the world indicate our exilic status and give hints to a way home, Christianity—and as a Catholic, I would say Catholic Christianity—alone provides the accurate rea-son for our exile, the correct map, indefectible navigational tools, and an unsinkable vessel to carry us to our homeland. If this is the case, and if we have been permitted this exile only to learn how to overcome it, it would seem prudent to keep to the map with the limited time we have in our pilgrimage: to keep our hearts focused on the Sacred Scriptures and Catholic theology, to practice the sci-ence of the saints, and to seek only the wisdom of the Cross.

This is all a preface to the question: why read Plato? Indeed, why study philosophy at all, the *search* after wisdom, if Wisdom, in the person of Jesus Christ, has already been found? Why perpetuate unnecessarily the asking of questions about the nature of the good, the purpose of existence, the immortality of the soul, etc., since these questions have already been answered by Revelation, and thus can only distract us from the one thing necessary—knowing and loving Jesus Christ? And why study the philosophy of a pagan who lived before the Incarnation, and thus whose grasp of and solution to the problem of exile is bound to be incomplete at best and erro-neous at worst? As St Paul wrote, speaking to the pagan philoso-phers on Mars Hill, Jesus Christ is a stumbling block for the Jews, who preferred an earthly savior with a military program, and fool-ishness to the Greeks, who didn't really want answers, but rather only to keep up their fruitless and decadent questioning.

Why Plato and Greek philosophy? Consider this: the Gospel of St John was written in Attic Greek, which, due to its precision and unique capacity for abstract articulation, was the language of ancient philosophy; the word that the beloved disciple chose for the very identity of the Second Person of the Holy Trinity was *Logos*, a word with profound philosophical resonances and connotations; the bishops and theologians of the early Ecumenical Councils that gave us definitive declarations of the nature of the Trinity and Jesus Christ were able to do so only because they were steeped in Platonic metaphysics, and thus their doctrinal formulations, such as the hypostatic union and the distinction of nature and person, were indebted to distinctions made in Greek philosophy; the greatest Church Father, St Augustine, would most probably not have been a Church Father, and perhaps not even a Christian or saint, if it were not for his initial conversion to spiritual reality through reading Plotinus, the great pagan theologian of Platonism.

But these are essentially arguments for the good of Greek philosophy in general, and for Plato in particular, on account of *something else*—in this case, for understanding the history and the development of Christian theology. With all the wonderful Catholic theology there is to read in a lifetime, theology that we know with certainty to be true and salvific, should we not just read the great Christian Platonists, St Augustine and St Bonaventure, and leave Plato, and philosophy—solid scaffolding, yes, but better to be discarded with the completion of the building—to the scholars and academics? Does Plato deserve our attention in himself?

Yes. But why? One must simply read Plato. Read the "Allegory of the Cave" from *The Republic*, or the "Ladder of Love" from the *Symposium*, and if you have an open mind and inquiring heart, you will recognize something wonderful in Plato's writings, a profound resonance with the most essential of Christian teachings. The Cave is a masterful metaphor for the soul trapped in sin, and the Ladder is a striking description of the ascent of the soul from creation to Creator. But again, though there is certainly an amazing foreshadowing of Catholic theology in Plato—e.g., his suggestive trinity of the One "beyond being," the Intellect comprising the perfect forms of created things, and the World-Soul as their agent in this word—Plato is essential reading on his own terms. This is especially the case when we consider the theme of exile.

Before grace can divinize the soul, the soul must yearn for divinization. What makes us so yearn? A sense of the inadequacy and shadow-like nature of this world, an intense feeling of alienation and homesickness, a profound intuition that there is much more to reality than what ordinarily appears to us. Plato's dialogues evoke these senses, feelings, and intuitions. Eric Voegelin, the great twentieth-century German Platonist, wrote: "There is no answer to the Question other than the Mystery as it becomes luminous in the acts of questioning."[2] Paradoxically, the answer to spiritual questions is found in the questions themselves, or better, in the very act of questioning, the art of which was brought to perfection in practice by Plato's teacher Socrates, and in writing by Plato himself. In his capacity to prompt recognition of our alienation from true reality, evoke yearning for it, and enable us, through the dialectical method of inquiry he invented, to achieve participation in it, Plato is simply indispensable, both as a precursor to Faith, and a guide along the way home.

Philosophy as Spiritual Exercise

We touched on the Christian understanding of spiritual exile from God as originating in our banishment from the Garden of Eden through original sin, and culminating in, not tragic loss, but a comedic recovery of everything—and more. The ancient pagan world also possessed a deep sense of exile, of having fallen from an original perfection and harmony, but tragedy was its inexorable upshot, with any comedy only the soothing salve for an inevitable, irretrievable pain and loss. As Peter Leithart has written in his profound book, *Deep Comedy*:

> For Greeks and many other ancient peoples, history was essentially tragic. Things had begun well in a world of plenty and joy, but the world was bound to degenerate and decline until it sputtered and whimpered to a halt. For some, history was seen as a turning wheel, so that the pathetic end was a prelude to a new

2. Eric Voegelin, *Order and History, Volume 4: The Ecumenic Age*, in *The Collected Works of Eric Voegelin*, vol. 17, ed. Michael Franz (Columbia, MO: University of Missouri Press, 2000), 404.

beginning. Cyclical views of history such as these look more optimistic, but that is only apparent. If it is cyclical, history merely repeats the story of decline again and again, unto ages of ages, the tragedy becoming more banal with each repetition.[3]

There was only one pagan author who held a real hope for a return to the bliss of the golden age, and it was not Plato, but Virgil, who, in his *Fourth Eclogue* written only forty years before the birth of Christ, prophesied the birth of a child who would inaugurate a new age in which all wars would eventually cease, and earth and man would obtain a harmony such that commerce and agriculture would no longer be necessary—a return to Eden.

But if Virgil, and (we must add) the mysterious figure of Job—who, neither a pagan nor a Jew, and exiled on his dung heap 1,500 years before Virgil, cried, "I know that my redeemer lives" (Job 19:25)—are the closest that non-Christians ever got to hope in a redemption from exile, Plato got the closest to grasping what this post-exilic reality might be like. For he hoped for something more than this life and the shadow world of Hades in his unshakable conviction, modeled by Socrates through his courageous indifference to his death (read *Phaedo*!), of the immortality of man's soul and of eternal reward for the proper care of it. Through his dialogues, Plato invites all men to grasp the transcendent world of perfection for which the soul yearns. "The nature of man is openness to transcendence."[4] Eric Voegelin learned this from Plato, and, while it is a truth expressed to some extent in all the ancient religions of the world, Plato was the first to treat it scientifically, so to speak, by providing intellectual justification for its truth not only through myth,

3. Leithart, *Deep Comedy*, 3.
4. "In the aftermath of the Montreal lecture that gave rise to 'In Search of the Ground,' one of Voegelin's auditors asked this question: 'Is it possible that a synthesis of all the current theories on the structure and operation of the human psyche could produce a new concept of the nature of man? And would this not produce a new ideology?' Voegelin responded: 'The nature of man is in principle known. You can't produce by new insights a new nature of man. The nature of man is openness to transcendence.'" See Thomas F. Bertonneau, "Liberalism and the Search for the Ground: Another Visit with Eric Voegelin," *The Brussels Journal*, February 2, 2010, available at https://www.brusselsjournal.com/node/4308.

which he employed generously in his dialogues, but also through rational discourse and logical argument.

Alfred North Whitehead, the great twentieth-century British mathematician and philosopher, once quipped, "The safest general characterization of the European philosophical tradition is that it consists of a series of footnotes to Plato." That's the truth, for Plato was the inventor of philosophy—whose living embodiment and exemplar was Socrates—at least as a form of written discourse, and his dialogues cover every possible philosophical issue. It is important to understand that philosophy for Plato and for the ancient Greeks in general, whether stoic, cynic, epicurean, or skeptic, was not a mere academic exercise or quest for abstract knowledge. It was, as Pierre Hadot has shown in his many pioneering works on ancient philosophy, a *way of life*, and the practice of philosophy for the ancient Greek, whether alone with his thoughts, in his study with a tablet, or in dialogue with others on the portico or in the agora, was more a personal spiritual exercise than an abstract academic pursuit. As Voegelin put it, "Philosophy in the classic sense is not a body of 'ideas' or 'opinions' about the divine ground dispensed by a person who calls himself a 'philosopher,' but a man's responsive pursuit of his questioning unrest to the divine ground that has aroused it."[5] The life of philosophy for the ancient was more akin to the life of prayer for the Christian, with contemplation, reception of the sacraments, and attendance at the liturgy constituting the "responsive pursuit of our questioning unrest to the divine ground that has aroused it."

The great difference, of course, is that Christian spiritual exercises are, when most authentic, practiced by the Holy Spirit in us through our receptive consent. And while our souls remain in "questioning unrest" in this life, aside from those rare mystical moments where we find ourselves immersed in God's ineffable peace, we do have, through our participation in His very life, "the answer" in Christ, along with the peace that surpasses understanding. Nevertheless, reading Plato's dialogues more as sacred texts

---

5. *Anamnesis*, in *The Collected Works of Eric Voegelin*, vol. 6 (Columbia, MO: University of Missouri Press, 2002), 96.

than as academic works is surely a spiritual exercise. On every page of Plato, from the most tedious logical argumentation to the most fantastic myths and sublime allegories, are hints, suggestions, and sometimes what feels like revelations of that mysterious and transcendent reality he had first experienced in the person of Socrates and then in his own soul as he pursued, with more passion, intelligence, and determination than perhaps any pagan before and neopagan since, the divine ground that aroused his wonder.

Dialogue, Dialectic, and the Good City

So, what was Plato trying to teach the fourth-century B.C. Athenians of his day, and what can he teach us, particularly about exile? Two things must be said before we delve into Plato's main teachings. The first is that Plato was not only critical of poetry and literature due to their being twice removed from reality, a copy of a copy, but also of writing itself, including philosophical writing. Truth for Plato was primarily found not in books or lectures, but in the soul, and all the more when it is actively engaged in inquiry and contemplation. A written account of a philosophical insight or argument is only the lifeless and shadow-like vestige of the original ecstatic experience, one that cannot ask or answer questions, and just keeps saying the same thing to the reader over and over again. An oral lecture is better, for it exists interactively in present time, but it is also second-rate, as it is primarily rhetorical, the attempt to persuade another to right opinion or action, and not dialectical, the attempt to justify an opinion or action in truth or the good. Even if the belief or action is a true or good one, the listener is not enabled through lecture alone to recognize this truth as true and this action as good for and in himself; the back and forth of dialogic and dialectical inquiry is required for this.

Of course, Plato recorded his thoughts in writing, but not in the form of oral or written treatises; rather, it was through that unique literary form he invented: philosophical dialogues. For Plato, writing at its best should aim to imitate the drama of the face-to-face conversation in which the soul's movements occur at *this* place and in *this* time and with *this* person. Like the Apostles, whose lives were transformed not by reading Old Testament texts but by meeting in person the living embodiment of those texts, Plato experienced a radical *periagoge*, a turning or reorientation of the soul, and a *metanoia*, a change of mind, by listening to and speaking with Socrates in the Agora and at the homes of wealthy aristocrats. Like the writers of the Gospels, Plato wanted to convey something of his experience to those not privileged to meet the master, so that they, too, could be transformed. To do this, Plato invented the philosophical dialogue, and he wrote over thirty of them, some the length of a book. As Plato reflected on the master's words in the privacy of his study, he eventually became a master himself, and his dialogues contain both Socrates' teaching and his own, sometimes quite hard to distinguish.

About the Platonic dialogue, Voegelin wrote: "The dialogue is the symbolic form of the order of wisdom, in opposition to the oration as the symbolic form of the disordered society. It restores the common order of the spirit that has been destroyed through the privatization of rhetoric."[6] Voegelin was primarily a political philosopher, but then, so was his master. Plato wrote his dialogues not just for the purpose of personal *periagoge*, the conversion of individual Athenians, but for the conversion of the entire Athenian *polis*, which was radically in need of it, having suffered a tremendous defeat at the hands of Sparta in the Peloponnesian War, ending in 404, after twenty-eight years of fighting and five years before the execution of Socrates by that same defeated Athenian so-called democracy. The public political culture of the Athens of his day was dominated by a cynical desire for power among the young aristocracy, of whom Plato was a member, and by a ruling class of politicians and educators, or sophists. These, for a large fee, would deign to teach the aspiring politician the secret of political success, namely, the manipulation of the populace through clever, self-serving rhetoric. It was a situation not unlike our own, with expensive education ordered to career success and power instead of the good

---

6. *Order and History, Volume 3: Plato and Aristotle*, in *The Collected Works of Eric Voegelin*, vol. 16, ed. Dante Germino (Columbia, MO: University of Missouri Press, 1999), 66.

of the soul and wisdom, and with politics a game of struggle for dominance ordered to the preservation and extension of private freedom or empire, instead of the common good and virtue. This is what Plato had to say about his beloved *polis* in his *Seventh Letter*:

> Finally, it became clear to me, with regard to all existing communities, that they were one and all misgoverned. For their laws have got into a state that is almost incurable, except by some extraordinary reform with good luck to support it. And I was forced to say, when praising true philosophy, that it is by this that men are enabled to see what justice in public and private life really is. Therefore, I said, there will be no cessation of evils for the sons of men, till either those who are pursuing a right and true philosophy receive sovereign power in the States, or those in power in the States by some dispensation of providence become true philosophers.

In other words, unless philosophers rule, politics fails, and it was for the purpose of making philosophy and the good, not sophistry and might, the ruling religion of the state that Plato set out to write his dialogues. Plato sought to replace the reigning educational curriculum of Athens—an incoherent and unstable synthesis of the older, informal education of music, stories, and gymnastics, with the newer, formal education of sophistical rhetoric and a dialectic of cleverness—with his own curriculum, combining the best of the old and the new, but arranged in proper order in the light of the highest wisdom. Socrates had discovered this wisdom, and Plato systematized and developed it. Education, or *paideia*, was to be ordered to the good of the soul, which is nourished solely on the Good, the True, and the Beautiful. Plato was not alone in desiring educational reform, being part of the fourth-century movement towards a more systematic and rigorous formation of the Greek citizen by the state. But he was far ahead of his time in the moral, intellectual, and spiritual depth he sought in this formation. Richard Tarnas puts it this way:

> This ideal of man was the pattern and model toward which all Greek educators and poets, artists and philosophers always looked. It was this universal ideal, this model of humanity which

all individuals were to imitate. As this ideal was to be embodied in the community, the goal of education was to make each person in the image of the community. Plato's primary directive for philosophy focused on the strenuous development of the intellect, the will, and the body, motivated by a ceaseless desire to regain the lost union with the eternal, for the recollection of the ideals is both the means and the goal of true knowledge. Education, therefore, for Plato is in the service of the soul and the divine. Under Plato, the classical paideia assumed a deeper and metaphysical dimension in his Academy, holding forth the ideal of inner perfection realized through disciplined education.[7]

For Plato, what began as a meeting with an unkempt bricklayer walking around the marketplace bothering people with his incessant questions was to end, through the establishment of his Academy and hopefully schools modeled on it throughout Athens, in a vast educational system producing rulers for Athens who, being brought into intimate soul-contact with the Real, would, like an artist gazing upon beauty in his mind and incarnating it on canvas, incarnate the just political order by gazing on the eternal and immutable Forms and effecting a constitution mirroring eternal wisdom in this time-bound and mutable world.

Intimations of Christ:
The Cave and the Ladder of Love

Although Plato's teachings are spread out among the over thirty dialogues he wrote, I think we need look no further than his description of the Ladder of Love in the *Symposium* (210a–212c) and the Allegory of the Cave in the *Republic* (VII, 514a2–517a7) to encounter the core of Plato's teachings. "Man is born free, and everywhere he is in chains." So goes the opening line of *The Social Contract* by Jean-Jacques Rousseau, intellectual architect of the French Revolution. For Rousseau, the chains were political ones, to

---

7. Richard Tarnas, *The Passion of the Western Mind: Understanding the Ideas that Have Shaped Our World View* (New York: Ballantine Books, 1991), 42–43.

be broken only by the revolutionary institution of his social contract. For Plato, however, and this is the essential meaning of the cave allegory, they are chains binding the soul, only to be broken by an intimate encounter with the Real, culminating in a vision of the Good. The Real is bright and undeniable as the Sun, but we the unenlightened seemed doomed to mistake the shadows it casts for the Real itself. The teaching of Plato that we discover in the cave allegory is that our true exile is from ourselves, who, though divine and destined for immortality, have somehow forgotten our true identity. And the way to recover our true selves, and thus the true world that is our home, is through the moral, intellectual, and spiritual exercise of philosophy. But such contemplation must be translated into action—though many contemplators would have it otherwise!—and by being formed in an educational system and state ordered by and to the Good, we the exiled in mortal bodies can best prepare ourselves for the liberation of the soul unto the life that never ends.

The cave, then, is not an actual place but a state of mind or consciousness, one in which the soul, our true self, is eclipsed by the false self and the illusory world it mistakes for reality. It is akin to the Christian tradition's identification of the three main sources of evil as "the Flesh, the World, and the Devil." The flesh for St John the Evangelist meant a life intent on the goods of the body at the expense of the goods of the soul; the world connoted the desire for prestige above truth; the Devil was, well, the Devil. For Plato, the true evil we face is deception, in whatever form and through whatever agency, through the abuse of language, an evil against which the philosopher must fight incessantly with the sword of dialectic and passionate philosophical inquiry. In short, the material world we live in is not the cave—the cave is our unenlightened perspective of this material world. If we look with the eyes of the soul, which requires great discipline and ordered desire, we would see not a dark, suffocating cave full of flickering shadows cast by lying manipulators upon the eyes of slaves, but an infinite and eternal heaven of truth, goodness, and beauty overseen and pervaded by a mysterious, transcendent source whose essence is pure giving and who is mysteriously present in what He gives. If this sounds like

Christian theology, then the reader is beginning to understand something of the miraculous wisdom of Plato. But how do we look with the eyes of our soul? Who can show us how to do this? Who can break the chains of us prisoners? And how did the mysterious person described in the allegory who descends into the cave to liberate the prisoners break his own chains? Does Plato give us answers, or even hints? Read Plato and find out, especially his vivid description in Book II of the *Republic* of the perfectly just man deemed unjust by all and crucified. That Plato had an intimation of the Just Man is indubitable.

Finally, let us consider Plato's "Ladder of Love" from the *Symposium*. What this passage articulates is Plato's teaching on *participation*. The particular, changeable, and multiple realities that appear to us *are* precisely because they, to a certain extent, *are not*. For Plato, things of this material world are real, but in, by, and for themselves only as real as shadows—real to the extent that they borrow reality from something else that possesses reality in itself, as a reflection, imitation, image, and copy are parasitical, so to speak, on their original hosts. Nevertheless, there are not *two* realities: the individual material things in this world, on the one hand; the universal forms of which they are the reflections, on the other. There is only One, which appears *to us* as particular things and distinct ideas due to our unenlightened state. The material things we see are just the Forms, though perceived on a lower level of consciousness; and the forms are, when properly perceived, just the One. To use the *Symposium* example, it is Beauty itself that appears to us in beautiful things.

We are exiles from Being only because we do not see what is right in front of us. But how are we to escape this myopic exile, and is such escape even possible? These are questions that Plato the pagan, however noble and enlightened, was not able to answer adequately, for only divine revelation can tell us these things. What he did teach the world is that the examined life is alone worth living, and that such questions are the very life of the soul—and he taught us how to ask them.

5

The Good, the Right, and Theology

Divine revelation has been a curious non-interlocutor in public debates among conservative theists regarding how best to defend the objectivity, intelligibility, and communicability of moral truths, along with their application to contemporary legal issues, such as racial discrimination, human rights, and abortion. One such debate occurred in the pages of *First Things*.[1] The main issue of the debate is not the content of basic moral principles, but their epistemological, ontological, and rhetorical aspects: the fundamental structure of moral thinking and judgment, its relation to what precisely is being thought about and judged, and the most reasonable and effective mode of public ethical and legal discourse. The two interlocutors agree "that the source of morality is human nature, that human nature is essentially a rational nature, and that moral truths are discoverable through reason apart from revelation," and they both condemn the moral evil of racial discrimination. What they are at odds about is exactly why this or any evil act is evil, and what makes an act good and a moral principle true. The question comes down to the precise ontic and epistemic character of "ought."

For Hadley Arkes, racial discrimination is a big "ought not" because—and only because—it is *unreasonable*; it is an act that violates a known principle of reason, that humans have moral status

---

1. For a summary of and commentary on the debate, see Micah Watson, "A Tale of Two Philosophers," *First Things* Web Exclusives (February 18, 2002), available at https://www.firstthings.com/web-exclusives/2011/02/a-tale-of-two-philosophers.

and dignity by virtue of what makes them human, namely rationality and freedom. Thus, treating a human being as less than human
based upon what does not define him essentially as human, such as
skin color, is unreasonable and therefore wrong. And since reason is
ultimately anchored in the law of non-contradiction, racial discrimination, as well as any other moral evil, is evil because it violates this
most fundamental and self-evident law of human reason. If a
human being is properly defined as possessing an essential equality
with all other humans, then it is self-contradictory to commit racial
discrimination, since it treats a human being as not having this
equality. Thus, legal proscriptions against this evil practice, for
Arkes, should be explicitly grounded in and justified by this sort of
explanation. Matthew O'Brien, on the other hand, identifies Arkes's
characterization of the location, derivation, and justification of
moral knowledge as essentially Kantian and therefore problematic:
"To have substance, morality needs to go beyond mere rational con-
sistency and find its grounds in the form of 'rational animality,' as
Aristotle and Aquinas saw, but which Kant mistakenly rejected as
'heteronomous.'" For O'Brien, moral evil is evil not primarily
because it is self-evidently unreasonable in light of some sort of *a
priori*, abstract conception of the rational being as such, but because
it is *vicious*, in light of concrete, personal, historical, tradition-constituted, community-informed *experience*—in terms of a conception of human flourishing and happiness that answers not so much
the question why one ought to do this or that, but what we, qua-
members-of-this-community-and-tradition, need in order to live
well.

As it seems to me, this debate is a scuffle in an ongoing human
feud, begun in the wranglings between ancient Stoics and Epicure-
ans. It is a war between "two rival versions of moral enquiry," to use
MacIntyre's expression, between eudaimonism and deontologism:
an ethics of happiness, flourishing, virtues, *eros*, and the *good* versus
an ethics of self-sacrifice, duty, law, *agape*, and the *right*. This feud is
not going to end any time soon, at least not without some mediation by a third, peacemaking interlocutor. As I said at the outset,
theology, unlike in the ancient debates, has not been an interlocutor
in this or virtually any academic and public discussion of ethics and

politics. Sure, the theologian is allowed to have his say, but he is barred from ever having an *authoritative* say, from being one of those insiders whose deliberations and speculations are to become an integral part of "public reason." The theologians have a compelling story, the philosophers and public policy folks admit, but we need a story more appropriate and more compelling for our pluralistic, secular, political culture.

However, when dealing with the foundations of ethics, the Christian theologian's story is not just one story among others; it is one that must be read by everyone, as it is meant for everyone. It is ultimately everyone's story. Moreover, as the Radical Orthodoxy school has shown, the ostensibly a-theological, secular stories that automatically pass the muster of public reason are nothing if not theologically implicated. Now, although the Christian story is everyone's story, only a very select audience has heard it in its entirety, believed it fully, and made it a model for their own life's stories. Yet, even for the unbeliever, the theologian's story has clear and arguable logical, ethical, philosophical, legal, and political ramifications and components, just as the "non-theological" stories have implicit theological moorings. Let those who have ears, that is, those who have taken out their old and decrepit, modernist, Enlightenment earplugs, hear: "we are all theologians now."

The inseparability of faith and reason in both theory and practice is one of the main points of Benedict XVI's teaching. We can debate the political and philosophical ramifications of the affirmation that we are made in the image of God, that God loves us, and that He *commands* us to "be perfect as our Father in heaven is perfect"; however, in the end, we either affirm these truths or we do not, based upon whether we have or have not encountered the living Christ, *caritas in veritate*, or perhaps just encountered those Christians who have. So, if human acts are a matter of experience, choice, and grace, not just logic, evidence, and demonstration (whether Aristotelian-eudaimonistic or Kantian-deontological in mode), then any debate about the metaphysical, epistemic, and rhetorical aspects of ethics must invite theology as an interlocutor. And this neglect of theology is the reason that the debate between Arkes and O'Brien is, as it stands, irresolvable.

The problem is that they are both right. O'Brien is correct that arguments about and declarations of principled moral prescriptions and proscriptions, even rigorous and true ones, cannot ensure a public commitment to and embodiment of Christian or even humanistic values in our post-Enlightenment, neo-pagan, pluralistic political culture. Moral principles are experiential, cultural, and historical in their genealogy and in the subjective apparatus of human recognition. But Arkes is also right that we can and must transcend these contingencies to see and act on principles in an absolute and universal mode. In other words, although reason is tradition-dependent (*pace* Kant), it is also tradition-transcendent (*cum* Kant). Somehow we must hold these together, and my argument here is that we cannot do so outside of a theological narrative and discourse.

Western nation-states lack a shared intellectual tradition to provide grounding for the abstract meaning of universal human rights and moral values. They also lack a communally-shared ethos, which is required for the effective, authentic, and integral political and legal embodiment of rights and values. However, as O'Brien's argument suggests, the discourse-of-moral-principle-alone, in prescinding from experiential genealogy and a moderate historicist sensibility, is ultimately sterile. On the other hand, public reason in today's secular culture eschews any theological dogmas that might shed authoritative light on the ultimate meaning, derivation, and fulfillment of human life and experience. And, as Arkes maintains, a discourse-of-moral-experience-alone, absent the universal, history-and-experience-transcending *logos*, is ultimately indeterminate, for it is deficiently rational. The right and the good must live together or die alone.

Critiquing Maritain's "democratic charter," where natural law norms without religious or philosophical particularity are to ground the political consensus, MacIntyre sums up what he considers the essential problem with a natural law morality and argumentation that tries to transcend contingency and experience:

> What Maritain wished to affirm was a modern version of Aquinas' thesis that every human being has within him or herself a natural

knowledge of divine law and hence of what every human being owes to every other human being. The plain pre-philosophical person is always a person of sufficient moral capacities. But what Maritain failed to reckon with adequately was the fact that in many cultures and notably in that of modernity plain persons are misled into giving moral expression to those capacities through assent to false philosophical theories. So it has been since the eighteenth century with assent to a conception of rights alien to and absent from Aquinas' thought.[2]

According to this view, Arkes's model would be analogous to Maritain's, and so not sufficiently aware of the fact that while men may argue and think about moral truth, and value and pursue moral goods without conscious deference to a particular philosophical theory or religious belief, they nevertheless possess implicit and unconscious philosophical commitments that influence and condition the character and interpretation of that evaluation and pursuit. These commitments determine to some extent the character of behavior that is the conclusion of the practical reasoning that begins with the evaluation and pursuit of particular goods. Since rationality itself is a practice, it inevitably takes on the shape of the particular lived tradition of which it is a part. In practice, then, there is no rationality as such, but only particular rationalities informed by particular religious, philosophical, anthropological, and epistemological commitments that condition the manner in which that rationality is understood and applied to practical questions. Therefore, with citizens divided in their ultimate concerns, one should not expect rational agreement on practical matters of a moral nature, especially not on the foundational moral values of the political order. As MacIntyre argues in *Whose Justice? Which Rationality?*:

> There is no way to engage with or to evaluate rationally the theses advanced in contemporary form by some particular tradition except in terms which are framed with an eye to the specific character and history of that tradition on the one hand and the specific

2. Alasdair MacIntyre, *Three Rival Versions of Moral Enquiry: Encyclopaedia, Genealogy, and Tradition* (Notre Dame: University of Notre Dame Press, 1990), 76.

character and history of the particular individual or individuals on the other.[3]

For MacIntyre, a strictly principled, obligation-laden, logic-derived articulation of moral goods and rights cannot serve as the political foundation of a tradition-pluralistic regime. For we are "tradition-constituted, culturally dependent rational animals" who cannot effectively separate our metaphysical beliefs from our values and the actions derived from them. Though the citizens in a pluralistic polity may share a common lexicon of "human rights" and "democratic values," it is a house built on sand with a sinking foundation of entirely disparate understandings of that lexicon and radically disparate traditions of practical rationality: Thomist, Humean, Kantian, Rousseauian, Nietzschean, Deweyan, et al. For MacIntyre, shared moral evaluation and understanding is extremely limited, if not impossible altogether, in the absence of a shared tradition of practical rationality, including a common reservoir of theological, philosophical, ethical, and anthropological concepts, and common virtues and goods attained and obtained in and through various practices, especially the architectonic practice of politics, that constitute a shared tradition. And this is why we have so much moral disagreement in our public discourse. Tracey Rowland summarizes MacIntyre's position: "MacIntyre's analysis raises the question of whether there can be any such things as 'universal values,' understood not in a natural law sense, but rather . . . the idea that there is a set of values which are of general appeal across a range of traditions, including the Nietzschean, Thomist, and Liberal traditions."[4] MacIntyre again:

> Abstract the particular theses to be debated and evaluated from their contexts within traditions of enquiry and then attempt to debate and evaluate them in terms of their rational justifiability to any rational person, to individuals conceived as abstracted from their particularities of character, history, and circumstance, and you will thereby make the kind of rational dialogue which could

3. MacIntyre, *Whose Justice?*, 398.
4. Tracey Rowland, *Culture and the Thomist Tradition after Vatican II* (London: Routledge, 2003), 141.

move through argumentative evaluation to the rational acceptance or rejection of a tradition of enquiry effectively impossible.
Yet it is just such abstraction in respect of both the theses to be
debated and the persons to be engaged in the debate which is
enforced in the public forms of enquiry and debate in modern liberal culture, thus for the most part effectively precluding the
voices of tradition outside liberalism from being heard.[5]

Let us suppose it is true that citizens belonging to the same narrative tradition would form a more unified, robust, stable, and
strong political order, so that exceptionless and self-evident rights
and laws deriving ultimately from the law of non-contradiction and
man's end-in-himself dignity would serve as the most effective public discourse. Unfortunately, the demographic and sociological exigencies of the modern, pluralistic nation-state preclude such
narrative unity. We cannot have forced conversions to our narrative
of choice, and so we must accept the limitations of our "concrete
historical ideal," as Maritain would say. The "fact of religious pluralism" requires us to attempt, even if it seems impossible, the separation of the public, legal, political sphere from the particularity of
our tradition. But can such be done? Is this kind of acquired schizophrenia necessary to be a good pluralist citizen?

Conservative theists endorse wholeheartedly the infusion of integrally religious practices and discourse into the naked public
square; yet they also tend to limit the participation in and scope of
these practices and discourses to the in-house crowd, as it were. For
those outside their tradition, and for the secular public sphere in
general, it is to be a program of *translation*—a translation of
dogma, ritual, charitable acts, and especially the natural law. It is
urged to speak only the language of principled, universal "public
reason" to strangers, thereby secularizing, moralizing, and politiciz-
ing what is distinctly theological and spiritual in our tradition, both
in doctrine and in practice, to render it intelligible to non-theists
and practically effective for secular society.

However, this strategy presupposes two fundamental claims that
are highly dubitable. The first is that there is such a thing as the

5. MacIntyre, *Whose Justice?*, 399.

"secular," that is, an ideologically neutral, universal, public world accessible to and based upon a universal public reason, independent of the practical and speculative particularities of tradition. For, as the argument goes, if there is no objective, public reason accessible to all, then we are left with the postmodernist hermeneutics of suspicion and the will to power, where any affirmation of true or good is unmasked as either mere idiosyncrasy or the will to dominate. The second dubitable idea is the separability of *theoria* and *praxis*, such that one can effectively strain out from the concrete practices and particularist discourse of one's tradition a secular, universally accessible remainder that is intelligible to all regardless of traditional allegiance.

Regarding the existence of a secular reason or public space neutral to any particular tradition, MacIntyre writes:

> *Either* reason is thus impersonal, universal, and disinterested *or* it is the unwitting representative of particular interests, masking their drive to power by its false pretensions to neutrality and disinterestedness. What this alternative conceals from view is a third possibility, the possibility that reason can only move towards being genuinely universal and impersonal insofar as it is neither neutral nor disinterested, that membership in a particular type of moral community, one from which fundamental dissent has to be excluded, is a condition for genuinely rational enquiry and more especially for moral and theological enquiry.[6]

For MacIntyre, it is only through active participation in particular authentic traditions that men are rendered capable of discovering and achieving their ultimate good. For it is always *through* a particular tradition that we ascend to universal truth. Indeed, without tradition we are unable to make any sense of reality at all. As body and soul composites, our encounters with reality are mediated and influenced by bodies, which are themselves mediated and influenced by history and culture. Even the words and concepts we use to interpret and make sense of the brute facts of reality originate and develop in what MacIntyre calls "traditions of rationality." All men

---

6. MacIntyre, *Three Rival Versions*, 59.

are necessarily habituated into a particular tradition, even if it is an incoherent and considerably defective one like the tradition of liberalism. Outside of tradition, coherent knowledge and discovery of the good is practically impossible. We are, in MacIntyre's improvement on Aristotle's classic definition, "tradition-dependent rational animals." As Paul Griffiths puts it: "To be confessional is simply to be open about one's historical and religious locatedness, one's specificity, an openness that is essential for serious theological work and indeed for any serious intellectual work that is not in thrall to the myth of the disembodied and unlocated scholarly intellect."[7]

Regarding the capacity to translate particular religious truth into non-religious public reason, MacIntyre articulates the traditionalist dilemma:

> The theologian begins from orthodoxy, but the orthodoxy which has been learnt from Kierkegaard and Barth becomes too easily a closed circle, in which believer speaks only to believer, in which all human content is concealed. Turning aside from this arid in-group theology, the most perceptive theologians wish to translate what they have to say to an atheistic world. But they are doomed to one of two failures. Either [a] they succeed in their translation: in which case what they find themselves saying has been turned into the atheism of their hearers. Or [b] they fail in their translation: in which case no one hears what they have to say but themselves.[8]

Is there a solution? Is there a resolution between Arkes and O'Brien, between eudaimonism and deontologism? If there is, the indispensable condition for its realization is the recognition of the illusory nature of secularist liberal pluralism. Indeed, there is really no such thing as "liberalism," if this means a sphere of reason or action or culture that escapes the particularism and exclusivity of tradition. For there is also no such thing as "the secular," since traditions of

---

7. Paul J. Griffiths, "The Uniqueness of Christian Doctrine Defended" in *Christian Uniqueness Reconsidered: The Myth of a Pluralistic Theology of Religions*, ed. Gavin D'Costa (Maryknoll, NY: Orbis Books, 1996), 200.

8. Alasdair MacIntyre, *Against the Self-Images of the Age* (New York: Schocken Books, 1971), 19–20.

rationality are distinguished by the particular way they grapple with matters of ultimate concern—all traditions are ultimately *religious*. This has immense political implications. David Schindler writes: "A nonconfessional state is not logically possible, in the one real order of history. The state cannot finally avoid affirming, in the matter of religion, a priority of either 'freedom from' or 'freedom for'—both of these priorities implying a theology."[9]

If believing theists of diverse traditions do not think, speak, and act distinctively as Catholics, Protestants, Jews, and Muslims, bringing their intellectual, moral, and liturgical traditions wherever they go in imitation of Socrates, whom Catherine Pickstock once described as a "walking liturgy,"[10] then our "ecumenical jihad" stands no chance at converting the liberal traditionalists of the culture of death, who have no qualms about communicating to themselves and others exclusively in their religious parlance of tolerance and diversity, and inviting all into their liturgical practices of aggressive war, false-flag terror, scapegoating, abortion, same-sex marriage, and euthanasia. Indeed, they see *themselves* as the "true believers," the only ones truly defending "life," with us as the heretics, obsessed only with death and control.

How can these deluded devotees have any hope of ever renouncing their enslaving tradition unless they are made aware of its enslaving character? And how can they become aware unless they have some palpable *experience* of an alternative? The tradition they inhabit deprives them of the existential conditions required to see moral truths, let alone religious ones, as Tristram Engelhardt has pointed out: "In the grip of Enlightenment dispositions regarding religion, few are inclined to recognize that the moral life once disengaged from a culture of worship loses its grasp on the moral premises that rightly direct our lives and foreclose the culture of death."[11] D. Stephen Long puts the point powerfully:

9. David Schindler, *Heart of the World, Center of the Church* (Grand Rapids: Eerdmans, 1996), 83.

10. Catherine Pickstock, *After Writing: On the Liturgical Consummation of Philosophy* (Oxford: Blackwell, 1998), 40.

Beginning with the flesh of Jesus and its presence in the church, theology alone can give due order to other social formations—family, market, and state. The goodness of God is discovered not in abstract speculation, but in a life oriented toward God that creates particular practices that require the privileging of certain social institutions above others. The goodness of God can be discovered only when the church is the social institution rendering intelligible our lives. . . . For a Christian account of this good, the church is the social formation that orders all others. If the church is not the church, the state, the family, and the market will not know their own true nature.[12]

Moral judgments are certainly principled judgments, and we should search for and declare these principles, even enforce them in law when prudent and possible. Yet all principles of reason, whether moral or logical, are first and foremost expressions of the divine *Logos*, who can be encountered *in* and *through* his manifold, principled, universal expressions. But in the absence of a personal, experiential encounter with Him through Faith, in the very particular place and time where His Flesh becomes available to touch, eat, and experience, principles are just principles—fleshless, bloodless, and dead.

11. H. Tristram Engelhardt, Jr., "Life & Death after Christendom: The Moralization of Religion & the Culture of Death," *Touchstone* (June 2001), available at http://www.touchstonemag.com/archives/article.php?id=14-05-018-f.

12. D. Stephen Long, *The Goodness of God: Theology, the Church, and Social Order* (Grand Rapids: Brazos Press, 2001), 26, 28.

6

Where Top and Bottom Meet: Public Discourse Rightly Understood

> Without bad will, political philosophy cannot refuse to consider revelation's insight into political things when politics does not solve its own problems in its own terms about its own subject matter.
>
> James V. Schall[1]

Purely philosophical, natural, rational explanations of moral experience exist and are necessary, but they are not adequate without a complementary theological account. This is not to say that theology is the *starting* point for our understanding of the phenomena of obligation and of our orientation towards goods and the Good, but rather that it is and must be the *ending* point. This is not to say that reason can provide *no* grounding for or direction to our moral experience and thinking, nor to advocate a mode of public discourse that *begins* with revelation. Instead, I would like to consider a public discourse where "top and bottom meet," as it were, with the central nexus being an *ethics of gift*. This certainly does not exclude a bottom-up approach; indeed, it presupposes it. Beginning with the natural law is often the standard operating procedure for theists and conservatives in out pluralistic culture, as it should be, but this does not mean we should always *end* with the natural law,

---

1. James V. Schall, *Roman Catholic Political Philosophy* (Lanham, MD: Lexington Books, 2004), 157.

or that we cannot offer a supra-rational foundation for the existence, universality, force, and intelligibility of the natural law. Of course, a human person without the light of faith can *recognize* genuine goods that evoke authentic obligatory sentiments and reasons, and he can *act* upon those sentiments and reasons through a rational decision that can achieve a real, particular good; but reason cannot—as reason itself concludes, when it is honest and humble—*adequately* account for and motivate those sentiments and decisions without some help from above. Reason, as James Schall has argued persuasively,[2] is bound to close in on itself when it is not internally open to the transcendent, becoming a distorted, hidden theology.

Though I am not entirely sure a gift anthropology and theology is something that reason can *discover* on its own, I do think that reason can *recognize* its truth, as well as its beauty and goodness, and that a person can act morally with this recognition as the main—but not necessarily exclusive—emotional, existential, and intellectual ground and motivator. And wouldn't actions based on such a recognition be morally superior to those that are not, all other things being equal? If so, an ethics of gift should be argued for *publicly* as that way of approaching and dealing with reality that best explains and perfects what reason can know to be true about the good, human nature, and God, without fully knowing how, what, and why it knows.

To make the case for a discourse neither exclusively top-down nor bottom-up, but one where top and bottom meet, where faith and reason unite, I would like first to discuss Jacques Maritain's arguments for the impossibility of a purely rational ethics, and then conclude with an examination of Pope Benedict XIV's last encyclical.

2. James V. Schall, *At the Limits of Political Philosophy* (Washington, DC: Catholic University of America Press, 1996).

Philosophy Rightly Understood

For Jacques Maritain, a Thomist who was vigorously engaged in the public discourse of the mid-twentieth century, any science of human action that excludes the realm of the supernatural from its purview is deficient, and radically so. There is no such thing as "pure ethics" if that means a discourse or methodology that excludes consideration of what God has revealed about the destiny of man. Maritain does distinguish between moral philosophy and moral theology, with the former *relatively* autonomous in its methodology and conclusions, resolving its judgments in the light of human reason alone; yet the philosopher of Christian Faith, when engaged in public discourse with non-Christians and even non-theists, cannot consider his philosophizing to be theologically neutral, since his faith presents to him at least two incontrovertible and ethically relevant supernatural truths about man's existence in this world: man is fallen and redeemed, and his happiness is not to be found in this world. But even the non-Catholic or non-theistic ethical philosopher cannot adopt a purely agnostic stance towards the existence of an ethically and politically relevant supernatural reality, because his understanding of and particular prescriptions for the fundamental structure of the social and political order necessarily imply either an affirmation or denial of the supernatural end of man, and so of any other fundamental fact about human existence. The denial of this end is at the heart of secular modernity in general, and of John Rawls's project in particular. It fundamentally explains the failure of his attempt to articulate a "purely political" conception of justice able to serve as a generic module fitting into any comprehensive doctrine whatsoever—as long as it is "reasonable." Maritain writes:

> Man is not in a state of pure nature, he is fallen and redeemed. Consequently, ethics, in the widest sense of the word, that is, in so far as it bears on all practical matters of human action, politics and economics, practical psychology, collective psychology, sociology, as well as individual morality—ethics in so far as it takes man in his concrete state, in his existential being, is not a purely philosophic discipline. Of itself it has to do with theology, either to

become integrated with or at least subalternated to theology.... Here is a philosophy which must of necessity be a superelevated philosophy, a philosophy subalternated to theology, if it is not to misrepresent and scientifically distort its object.[3]

Ethical enquiry is incomplete and bound to err if it is not "subalternated" to theology. What Maritain means by this term is philosophically complex, but at the risk of oversimplification, we can characterize Maritain's conception of moral philosophy as neither completely autonomous from theology nor essentially identical to it; it is distinct from yet dependent upon moral theology. It is dependent upon theology because it is incomplete without it; it is distinct from theology in that it resolves its judgments in the natural light of practical reason and experience, not in the light of divine revelation.[4] "Theology looks on the supernatural ultimate end first and foremost as a sharing of the intimate life of God, and ... moral philosophy adequately considered looks on this same ultimate end above all insofar as it brings completion to human nature."[5] Maritain explains that because in a practical science ends serve as principles, any practical science that does not know the ends of its subject matter does not possess its own principles. Since man's ultimate end is unknowable by the light of human reason alone, and since man's end is the first principle of both moral theology and moral philosophy, then moral philosophy without the light of divine revelation does not possess its first principle; therefore, moral philosophy must be subalternated to theology. In this subalternation, moral philosophy makes the data offered to it by moral theology its own, shines the light of human reason on this data, and thus arrives at first principles and conclusions of a philosophical character. In this way, moral philosophy is "superelevated" and perfected so that it can become "adequate to its object," namely, man's end.

It is not that Maritain denies that natural truths about moral reality are accessible to human reason, for he affirms the validity of

---

3. Jacques Maritain, *An Essay on Christian Philosophy*, trans. Edward H. Flannery (New York: Philosophical Library, 1955), 39–40.

4. Ibid., 72.

5. Ibid., 81.

the distinction between and the autonomy of both moral philosophy and moral theology. But for Maritain, man is not in a state of pure nature, since God created a world both natural and graced; consequently, a purely natural ethics can be neither adequate nor entirely accurate.

Caritas in Veritate

To be rhetorically effective, a writer must construct his argument carefully with an eye to the presuppositions, beliefs, attitudes, sentiments—the *mindset* of his audience. Thus, the discourse of choice for a professor at, say, a Christian college speaking to like-minded but not confessionally identical conservatives, or, for that matter, a pope speaking to a post-Christian West about love and truth, would, one might think, be one that avoids the particular, tradition-exclusive truths of Catholic theology, proposing instead the universal, tradition-inclusive principles of the natural law; for, "men of good will," although sinners, are by definition cognizant of it. As St Augustine says in *The Confessions*, "Thy law is written in the hearts of men, which iniquity itself effaces not." In his dialogue with the atheist philosopher Jürgen Habermas, Pope Benedict wrote: "The natural law has remained (especially in the Catholic Church) the key issue in dialogue with the secular society and with other communities of faith in order to appeal to the reason we share in common and to seek the basis for a consensus about the ethical principles of law in a secular, pluralistic society."[6]

However, the most remarkable characteristic of Benedict XVI's encyclical *Caritas in Veritate* is its theologically rich mode of discourse. Although it employs language and encourages values intelligible and attractive to men of good will, especially in its more practical analyses of and prescriptions for remediating the universally recognized, worldwide economic crisis, it is nevertheless pervaded with substantive argument that is unapologetically Trinitarian and Christological in nature, based in a strong theological

6. Joseph Ratzinger and Jürgen Habermas, *Dialectics of Secularization: On Reason and Religion* (San Francisco: Ignatius, 2007), 69.

anthropology of person and society as *gift*, and delivered in a peculiarly Platonic and Augustinian rhetorical mode. This stands in great tension with, and counts as a departure from, the strategic project of recent magisterial documents that use only the language of "secular reason," while quietly informing it with theologically particular philosophical and anthropological content.

In his dialogue with Habermas, then Cardinal Ratzinger went on to say:

> Unfortunately, this instrument [the natural law] has become blunt. Accordingly, I do not intend to appeal to it for support in this conversation. The idea of the natural law presupposed a concept of nature in which nature and reason overlap, since nature itself is rational. With the victory of the theory of evolution, this view of nature has capsized.

Going further than the pope, I would say that we are contending not merely with formidable anti-nature and anti-reason *ideas*, but with a systematic and consistent body of such ideas, united by a historical narrative, and embodied in well-entrenched and concrete habits, attitudes, customs, rituals, institutions, and practices—a full-fledged *tradition*. I wonder, then, how effective a purely natural law discourse is, even as a starting point, in this milieu of nihilistic, anti-*logos* traditionalism. As Benedict XVI warned on the day before his election to the pontificate, "we are building a dictatorship of relativism that does not recognize anything as definitive and whose ultimate goal consists solely of one's own ego and desires."[7] It is as if the culture that Western man inhabits today embodies an alternative, *un*natural law with radically different notions of nature and law, as well as being, the good, the human person, and the relation of all these to each other. Charles Taylor writes: "It is not that we have sloughed off a whole lot of unjustified beliefs, leaving an implicit self-understanding that had always been there, to operate at last untrammeled. Rather, one constellation of implicit understandings of our relation to God, the cosmos, other humans, and time

---

7. Homily for the Mass *Pro Eligendo Romano Pontifice*, April 18, 2005.

was replaced by another in a multifaceted mutation."[8] But if there is no longer a consensus in Western culture on natural law truths and values, and if revelation is even more incomprehensible to it, how can those who still believe in God help save the world?

Benedict suggests a more complex yet satisfying and credible solution in *Caritas in Veritate*. In both proclaiming to believers and unbelievers alike the postmodern insight (though the Church had it first) of the inescapable intertwining of *theoria* and *praxis*, of reason and faith, in all personal and social human activity, and revealing the ultimate explanation and foundation of this intertwining in the person of Christ, the very embodiment and integration of truth and love, the pope has written the first truly postsecular encyclical, one that strategically and spiritually capitalizes on the contemporary, post-Enlightenment weariness with secular reason, and its new openness to religiously-informed narrative and practice. From Ratzinger's "Subiaco Address":

> The attempt, carried to the extreme, to manage human affairs disdaining God completely leads us increasingly to the edge of the abyss, to man's ever greater isolation from reality. We must reverse the axiom of the Enlightenment and say: even one who does not succeed in finding the way of accepting God, should, nevertheless, seek to live and to direct his life *veluti si Deus daretur*, as if God existed. This is the advice Pascal gave to his friends who did not believe. In this way, no one is limited in his freedom, but all our affairs find the support and criterion of which they are in urgent need.[9]

The pope does not expect his Trinitarian, Christological, Catholic-tradition-constituted encyclical, calling for an economics and politics of gratuitous, self-giving love informed by the truth of the Gospel, to be immediately embraced by a non-believing audience. What he is attempting instead is to meet his audience in its interior state of emergency—where bottom meets top, as it were—as well as

8. Charles Taylor, "Two Theories of Modernity," *Hastings Center Report* (March–April 1995), 24, 27.

9. An address given at the convent of Saint Scholastica in Subiaco, Italy, April 1, 2005.

to help bring about a state in which the choice for God becomes desperately urgent and overwhelmingly attractive in the face of the only alternative—a culture of death, force, fraud, meaninglessness, and despair.

MacIntyre has written:

> There is no way to engage with or to evaluate rationally the theses advanced in contemporary form by some particular tradition except in terms which are framed with an eye to the specific character and history of that tradition on the one hand and the specific character and history of the particular individual or individuals on the other.[10]

Western culture in both theory and practice has moved, in the words of Archbishop Javier Martínez of Granada, "beyond secular reason."[11] The era of enlightened, modernist, foundationalist, universalist, and tradition-prescinding *rationalism* has been displaced by post-Enlightenment, postmodernist, anti-foundationalist, particularist, and tradition-constituted *narrative*. And for all of postmodernism's nihilism and its disdain for any normative understanding of nature and truth, it is radically skeptical of the knee-jerk, anti-religious, reason-idolizing, autonomy-seeking discourse and practices of the Enlightenment; it is intrinsically open to a new "story" (though not necessarily inclined to the *true* one), to radically new hermeneutics and explanations, to radically "other" ontologies and epistemologies, indeed, to alien theologies and spiritualities. The "new atheism" of Hitchens, Harris, and Dawkins is not new at all, but the outdated, pathetic, "last gasp" of modernity, to use the phrase of James K. A. Smith. In short, Enlightenment secularism is dead. As Jürgen Habermas has stated, Western culture is now "post-secular."

The Enlightenment's reductionist explanation of truth and love as secular pragmatic reason and individual self-interest is no longer publicly authoritative in culture; it is now just one narrative among

---

10. MacIntyre, *Whose Justice?*, 398.
11. Javier Martínez, "Beyond Secular Reason: Some Contemporary Challenges for the Life and Thought of the Church," *Communio* 31.4 (2004): 557–86, available at https://archive.secondspring.co.uk/.

others. Can we now count on the power of straight Truth—truth both natural and supernatural, untranslated, unmediated, unfiltered—to help convert to the *good* and the *right* those who, precisely because they are now disillusioned by the Enlightenment's false promises of "reason alone," are newly open to both reason and revelation?

> Charity in truth, to which Jesus Christ bore witness by his earthly life and especially by his death and resurrection, is the principal driving force behind the authentic development of every person and of all humanity. Love—*caritas*—is an extraordinary force which leads people to opt for courageous and generous engagement in the field of justice and peace. It is a force that has its origin in God, Eternal Love and Absolute Truth.

For the unbeliever, such declarations are not immediately believable, self-evidently persuasive, or even fully intelligible. What *is* universally acceptable and, more importantly, evocative of love, is the human experience of love of others, desire for truth, the obligation of conscience, and the goodness of gifts, and so the pope chose to write an encyclical to be read by both theists and non-theists that provides the best explanation—one grounded in the Most Blessed Trinity—for these phenomena. This, to me, is public discourse at its best—and most reasonable.

III

Metanoia

7

An Apology for Uselessness

It is necessary for the perfection of human society that there should be men who devote their lives to contemplation.

St Thomas Aquinas[1]

Pragmatism is a matter of human needs; and one of the first of human needs is to be something more than a pragmatist.

G. K. Chesterton[2]

I would like to put liberal education in its place, by celebrating its essential uselessness to students and to society at large. And I would like to apologize for all the time wasted by my students and all liberal arts professors in trying to make liberal education useful. However, the place where I would like to put the liberal arts is at the forefront and foundation of education, as the *raison d'être* of every college and university in this country and the world. And my apology is to those who have suffered under any educational program not ultimately founded on and integrally oriented towards the study of the liberal arts, that is, to what is ultimately useless. Solely useful education is inherently dysfunctional; non-liberal education doesn't work.

There is, of course, an essential role for useful, non-liberal, vocational, career, and professional *training* in the typical university and college curriculum. I am not arguing for the *exclusivity* of liberal education, that every college and university should be wholly devoted to liberal arts education and nothing else. What I'd like to

---

1. Cited in Josef Pieper, *Leisure the Basis of Culture* (San Francisco, Ignatius Press, 2009), 41.
2. G. K. Chesterton, *Orthodoxy* (London: John Lane Company, 1909), 40.

propose instead is that the success, which is to say, the *usefulness*, of non-liberal education for individuals and society is inextricably bound up with and necessarily dependent upon 1) the uselessness of liberal education; 2) a widespread awareness of the preeminent value of this uselessness; 3) liberal education being at the very core of every college and university curriculum. Robert Hutchins, founder of St. John's College's integrated Great Books curriculum, sums all this up nicely:

> The liberal arts are not merely indispensable; they are unavoidable. Nobody can decide for himself whether he is going to be a human being. The only question open to him is whether he will be an ignorant, undeveloped one, or one who has sought to reach the highest point he is capable of attaining. The question, in short, is whether he will be a poor liberal artist or a good one.[3]

The tension between useful and useless knowledge has been around for millennia. Consider Plato's *Protagoras*. Here Socrates asks the sophist Protagoras what he teaches young men: "I teach them good planning, both in their own affairs, such as how one should best manage his own household, and in public affairs, how one can best speak and act in the city-state."[4] Contrast Protagoras's pragmatist notion of education to these notions:

> Of possessions . . . those rather are useful, which bear fruit; those liberal, which tend to enjoyment. By fruitful, I mean, which yield revenue; by enjoyable, where nothing accrues of consequence beyond the using. (Aristotle, *Rhetoric* I.5)

> In music, numbers, sounds, and measures; in geometry, lines, figures, spaces, magnitudes; in astronomy, the revolution of the heavens, the rising, setting, and other motions of the stars; in grammar, the peculiar tone of pronunciation, and, finally, in this very art of oratory, invention, arrangement, memory, delivery. (Cicero, *On the Character of the Orator*, 42)

---

3. From "The Great Conversation" in *Great Books of the Western World*, Book 1 (Encyclopaedia Britannica, 1952), 5.

4. *Protagoras*, 318a.

Such studies are the way to the highest things, the way of reason which chooses for itself ordered steps lest it fall from the height. The steps are the various liberal arts. (Augustine, *De Ordine* I.8.24)

The principle of real dignity in Knowledge, its worth, its desirableness, considered irrespectively of its results, is this germ within it of a scientific or a philosophical process. This is how it comes to be an end in itself; this is why it admits of being called Liberal. Not to know the relative disposition of things is the state of slaves or children; to have mapped out the Universe is the boast, or at least the ambition, of Philosophy. (Newman, *Idea of a University*, "Knowledge Its Own End")

What all these educational thinkers have in common is an idea of education as its own end. In other words, the end, goal, or use of liberal education is not found in anything outside of the study itself. So, is the mere studying of the liberal arts the purpose of the liberal arts? That does seem self-referential and circular. The liberal arts, as all arts, are tools, in a sense, but they are tools for making humans. They perfect the intellect, the highest part of man, and thus enable man to know the world, oneself, and God as these really are. Is this useful?

Consider an analogy. What do all humans desire for its own sake and never for something else? Nothing else but happiness. And in what activity or activities do we find our happiness? This is a difficult question, of course, for although we must agree that happiness is our ultimate goal, we disagree quite a bit as to the best means to get there, or else we say that the way to happiness is personal and not able to be judged objectively and universally. However that might be, we can all agree where happiness does *not* lie—in that which is only instrumental, a means, good for another thing. For whatever happiness is, we find it in those objects, persons, and activities that we consider good in themselves. Thus, happiness is the most useless thing, since it is never a means, but always an end. No one wants happiness in order to be healthy or to be rich or even to have pleasure, for one wants all these in order to be happy.

Again, unlike money or political order or freedom, liberal knowledge is a good in itself, for it is perfective of the human *qua* human, and not simply human *qua* worker or pleasure-enjoyer or freedom-employer. Just as happiness is the point and purpose of all our desires, the formation and perfection of ourselves as humans is the point of all our knowledge. Part of this formation and perfection is in the realm of the practical, since we are not intellects trapped in a body but integrated body-soul composites. In other words, we are meant to live in what Josef Pieper calls the work-a-day world, the world of instrumental goods, means-to-end knowledge, economic production, and materiality. But to confine knowledge only to this sphere, to say that all education must be ordered to use in the work-a-day world, is to imply that there is nothing that transcends it, that we are trapped in the realm of the temporal, material, and instrumental. And this is to make human happiness not an end but a means, bound to whatever we can *use* from this world: bodily pleasure, emotional satisfaction, wealth, honor, power, and the like. These are legitimate goods, and education can help us obtain these goods. But unless there is a transcendent reason for pursuing these goods, unless this work-a-day world is seen for what it is—a means and never an end—we end up making a means out of an end, and an end out of a means, and we thus make human happiness, and concomitantly true education, impossible.

In any means-end relationship, the existence of the means only makes sense if there is also something to which this means is ordered. If everything is a means, nothing is a means. The reason we study engineering or marketing is because it provides us with something else that we desire. Engineering provides a skill that we can employ to make, say, airplanes, but the making of airplanes is not the end, for that is to permit travel, which is a means to the societal good of mobility, which is a means towards the common good of political order and ultimately friendship. No one reads an engineering book to appreciate the aesthetic beauty of engineering, although this may be part of its attraction. Again, one goes for a walk. Why is one walking? It might be for the purpose of diet and health. It might also be because walking itself is enjoyable, but even in this case, it is the enjoyment that one is after, the *happiness* ensuing upon the activity of walking. No one would want to be happy so that he may walk! Similarly, if we see utility as all there is—if all we do and know are merely useful activities, with nothing serving as what these are useful *for*—then the whole notion of use collapses in on itself. If there is the useful, there must be the useless. What happens if we accept only the useful and deny the useless? What if the world-of-work encompasses us, so that any notion of leisure, philosophical speculation, contemplation of the whole, festivity, and enjoyment of God is construed as a means to an end, as merely useful? We rest and we philosophize and we celebrate—so that we can be more productive workers and successful consumers?

What underlies the argument so far is a claim that cannot be proven, but that there is no good reason to deny: *there is more to life than the work-a-day world.* The declining role of the liberal arts; the constant refrain of "what are you going to *do* with a liberal education"; the transfer of university funding away from the liberal arts to science, engineering, research, technology, and the practical professions; and the perversion of liberal education into purely subjective, emotional, and private concerns, on the one hand, and into the politicized categories of gender, class, race, and sex, on the other—all of this indicates that we, as a culture, believe, at least implicitly, that there is nothing other than the work-a-day world, the world of instrumental reason and goods, and that we think human happiness is to be obtained within this world alone.

But—and this is the claim of Josef Pieper in his book *Leisure the Basis of Culture*—the whole work-a-day world is itself only intelligible and livable as a *means.* To what? To the world of what he calls *leisure*, the world of goods that are good for their own sake, the world of knowledge that is worth having for itself, and the human encounter and celebration of this world. Education, then, is for leisure, to make leisure possible, and this means that all knowledge is preparatory for the contemplation of truth, goodness, beauty, and being—in short, the "philosophical act" by which man transcends the world of work and enters into the world of true freedom. The liberal arts are precursors and constituent parts of that one discipline that is the implicit goal of every other study: philosophy, in the broad sense of *theoria*, the contemplation of truth for its own sake. Philosophy as *wisdom* is the culminating discipline of the liberal arts and thus of all education whatsoever. The liberal arts are the arts of freedom, for they are pursued for their own sake, and thus are perverted when they become slaves to another master.

But this freedom means that philosophical knowing does not acquire its legitimacy from its utilitarian applications, not from its social function, not from its relationship with the "common utility." Freedom in exactly this sense is the freedom of the "liberal arts," as opposed to the "servile arts," which, according to Thomas, "are ordered to a use, to be attained through activity" [*Commentary on the Metaphysics* I, 3]. And philosophy has long been understood as the most free among the free arts (the medieval "Arts Faculty" is the forerunner of the "Philosophical Faculty" of today's university).[5]

What does it mean to transcend the world? Is this a "peak experience" only obtainable by a small elite of privileged and wealthy liberal artists? Not remotely! As Pieper writes, anyone who loves and truly yearns for true happiness has already experienced this transcendence:

> The lover, too, stands outside the tight chain of efficiency of this working world, and whoever else approaches the margin of existence through some deep, existential disturbance (which always brings a "shattering" of one's environment as well), or through, say, the proximity of death. In such a disturbance (for the philosophical act, genuine poetry, musical experience in general, and prayer as well—all these depend on some kind of disturbance) man senses the non-ultimate nature of this daily, worrisome world: he transcends it; he takes a step outside it.[6]

If we want to live in a world where there are only means to other means with no end in sight, where only the kitsch consumerist monuments of selfish human will and desire exist, where all knowledge is ordered to use, then we must say goodbye to liberal education. And to a large extent, this is precisely what we have done. But have we really eliminated the transcendent, true leisure, the philosophical act, and the liberal arts, or have we just transformed them into mere tools to contemplate the idols of our own making—the idols of consumerism, pleasure, power, and self-worship? If we no longer have a place for the truly useless, for the good-in-itself, for

---

5. Josef Pieper, "The Philosophical Act," in *Leisure*, 93.
6. "The Philosophical Act," 87.

speculation on the meaning of reality, then we ultimately have no place for the useful either. Those goods and truths that are so above our worldly needs as to remain transcendently useless are violently brought down into the work-a-day world, with the most useful goods and truths shoved into a transcendental world where they do not belong and must die. The end result is human degradation and unhappiness.

I conclude with the words of Simone Weil, one of the philosophers of our time most dedicated to the useless. She takes our argument to the next step:

> All study, whether inherently useful or useless, must ultimately be prayer. Our purpose in life is to imitate that Being whose very nature is useless, for out of the contemplation of His own uselessness comes the entire universe of useful things, useful, according to His plan, as steps on a ladder to Him, the only reality that can truly be said to exist for its own sake. Students must therefore work without any wish to gain good marks, to pass examinations, to win school successes; without any reference to their natural abilities and tastes; applying themselves equally to all their tasks, with the idea that each one will help to form in them the habit of that attention which is the substance of prayer. When we set out to do a piece of work, it is necessary to wish to do it correctly, because such a wish is indispensable in any true effort. Underlying this immediate objective, however, our deep purpose should aim solely at increasing the power of attention with a view to prayer; as, when we write, we draw the shape of the letter on paper, not with a view to the shape, but with a view to the idea we want to express. To make this the sole and exclusive purpose of our studies is the first condition to be observed if we are to put them to the right use.[7]

7. Simone Weil, "On the Right Use of School Studies with a View to the Love of God," in *Waiting for God* (New York: Harper Collins, 2009), 59.

8

Why the Philosopher
and the Catholic University
Need Each Other

As Alasdair MacIntyre has shown, human knowledge is "tradition-constituted" and "tradition-dependent," as well as,
paradoxically, "tradition-transcendent." And as he suggests
in *God, Philosophy, Universities: A Selective History of the Catholic
Philosophical Tradition*, that institution most indispensable for the
preservation, sustenance, and development of human knowledge,
or, in MacIntyrean terms, an intellectual tradition, is the university.
For, as MacIntyre writes:

> Philosophy is not just a matter of propositions affirmed or denied
> and of arguments advanced and critically evaluated, but of philos-
> ophers in particular social and cultural situations interacting with
> each other in their affirmations and denials, in their argumenta-
> tive wrangling, so that the social forms and institutionalizations of
> their interactions are important and none more so than those uni-
> versity settings that have shaped philosophical conversation, both
> to its benefit and to its detriment.[1]

The philosopher is created, nourished, and perfected in and by
the university (or college), for it can most effectively preserve, sus-
tain, develop, revise, and transform a philosophical tradition; the

---

1. Alasdair MacIntyre, *God, Philosophy, Universities: A Selective History of the
Catholic Philosophical Tradition* (Lanham, MD: Rowman & Littlefield Publishers,
2011), 1.

university is its institutional embodiment and the primary locus of philosophical practice, with the individual philosopher serving as the tradition's personal embodiment, as well as apprentice, interlocutor, and custodian. In short, Catholic universities have since the Middle Ages served as the philosophical *guilds* in which the Catholic philosophical tradition has been passed on from masters to apprentices, for it is through, in, and by universities that apprentices become masters. It is no different today, except for the fact that the typical modern university has become a guild for careerism and sophistry. Nevertheless, today's Catholic philosopher requires good Catholic universities not only for his philosophical flourishing, but also for his very existence *qua* philosopher; and, conversely, the Catholic university requires good Catholic philosophers, for no institution can survive, let alone flourish, without the personal influence, participation, and oversight of philosophy's personal practitioners.

Openness to the Other

As Cardinal Newman taught, the fullest embodiment, the culminating fruit of the liberal arts university, is the philosopher—not necessarily the academic or professional philosopher, but that humble lover of wisdom with a properly "enlarged" intellectual vista and distinctly "philosophical cast of mind." The philosopher should also be, as MacIntyre insists, first and foremost a servant of the "plain man," translating the non-philosophers' commonsensical and informal—though still vital and profound—questions into formal and rigorously examined philosophical questions, giving these questions philosophically rigorous answers, and then translating these philosophically purified questions and answers back into that commonsensical and informal, vital and profound, and existentially satisfying and intellectually intelligible discourse appropriate for the vast majority of non-philosophers in the world.

So, exactly how does one become this sort of philosopher? Indispensable, of course, is an apprenticeship to a master philosopher, as Plato was apprenticed to Socrates, St Augustine to Plato, St Thomas

The Philosopher and Catholic University Need Each Other

Aquinas to St Augustine and Aristotle, the whole Church to St Thomas Aquinas, Etienne Gilson, Jacques Maritain, and Alasdair MacIntyre to St Thomas Aquinas, and we to them. But, as important as are the erudition, skill, modeling, and experience only personal guidance can impart to the philosopher, it is to no avail apart from a certain indispensable existential attitude or condition: what might be called metaphysical courage or existential openness. The good philosopher must possess a radical existential openness to the incompleteness, myopia, and errors in his present philosophical understanding, and a metaphysically courageous orientation of the soul towards all aspects of being, one that evokes and sustains a perpetual desire for further inquiry, revision, and even conversion. He must cultivate a deliberate, relentless, and lifelong vulnerability to refutation, and an unquenchable passion for dialectical exchange with and enrichment by the *other*. As David Walsh puts it: "Socratic wisdom is indeed the deepest available to us, only now grasped as an existential condition rather than simply an attitude toward existence. It is because we now recognize that reason cannot contain itself that it possesses an openness toward being."[2] Again: "Speculation is not a separate avenue toward what is, but rather the result of a prior existential awareness."[3] Philosophy is, above all, a way of life.

The identity of this "other" for the aspiring good Catholic philosopher is not necessarily someone outside the Catholic philosophical tradition, but precisely that person, idea, argument, or tradition of argument most resistant to becoming merely a confirmatory mirror image of one's present philosophical understanding, that which is eminently immune to being narcissistically assimilated and sophistically manipulated by the philosopher. Now, while this openness is bound up with a perpetual readiness to be corrected, it in no way excludes a robust confidence in the truth of one's present understanding—as long as truth is secured and justified by rigorous and humble philosophical inquiry.

---

2. David Walsh, *The Modern Philosophical Revolution: The Luminosity of Existence* (Cambridge: Cambridge University Press, 2008), 16.

3. Ibid., 93.

The Good Philosopher—Institutionalized

It is philosophers who most of all need to be institutionalized, at least to protect the emotional well-being of everyone else. In any event, the qualities of the good Catholic university are analogous to the qualities of the good Catholic philosopher. Just as the good philosopher needs to be a master of his philosophical tradition and adept at the dialectical, analytical, synthetic, and imaginative skills with which his trade is plied, the good Catholic university requires a rigorous and sophisticated curriculum and pedagogy firmly rooted in the Catholic philosophical tradition. Taught without sufficient rigor, the liberal arts become jejune exercises in sentimentalism or self-expression, philosophy becomes sophistry, and theology becomes soft blasphemy. But just as one's commitment to Catholicism, philosophical erudition, and dialectical skill, without the proper philosophical attitude of metaphysical courage and existential openness, cannot render a philosopher a good one, so a Catholic university cannot be good without the right institutional ethos and *telos*. The perfection of the intellect is the proper *telos* for which university disciplines are taught, around which they are hierarchically integrated, and in the light of which their pedagogy is ordered. And such perfection requires a robust Catholic sacramental and virtuous culture in which the emotions, soul, and spirit can be effectively purified and perfected. Taught without the right *telos*, philosophical disciplines become sophistical and rhetorical linguistic skills to gain power for oneself and over others. If the university is Catholic and orthodox, but if its *telos* has an exclusively spiritual or moral orientation and focuses on moral formation at the expense of a robust intellectual life, then one ends up with a suffocating Catholic moralism, a world-contemptuous and suspicious Jansenism, or an anti-philosophical fundamentalism. If the university is secularist in foundation, this same misguided *telos* results in something like secular fundamentalism or political fanaticism. St Thomas Aquinas forbade a religiously fundamentalist notion of education, as MacIntyre points out: "Intellectual enquiry, like all other secular pursuits, is [by some] taken to have no worth whatsoever in itself, but to be worthwhile *only* as a means to salvation.

Contrast Aquinas, for whom many secular pursuits and, notably, intellectual enquiry are worthwhile in themselves and as such to be offered to God as part of that offering that is the path to our salvation."[4]

The ability to think clearly, accurately, deeply, and comprehensively about reality so as to come to a knowledge of the essential truths about the universe in their unity and diversity is the point and purpose of a Catholic university. The proper antidote to the tendency of today's Catholic universities to destroy the morals and faith of their students is not to turn the university into a retreat center or a training ground for piety and morals, even though moral and spiritual formation are higher goals than intellectual formation. For, when the primarily intellectual end of the Catholic university is eclipsed, ignored, or denied, through religious enthusiasm or power-pragmatism, the liberal arts lose their character as true arts, philosophy becomes ideology, and theology becomes something unholy.

A philosophically good attitude with respect to curriculum is also essential to the good Catholic university. The liberal arts are ends in themselves, surely, and should be taught as such, with literature taught in a primarily poetic, not philosophical, mode; but not all liberal arts are equal, and this should also manifest itself pedagogically: grammar must be ordered to logic, grammar and logic to rhetoric, the trivium to the quadrivium, all seven liberal arts to philosophy, and philosophy ordered to and practiced in the light of revealed theology. In turn, theology must be fecundated, enlivened, purified, and penetrated by philosophy and dialectics—indeed by all the liberal arts—to prevent the queen of the sciences from becoming rigid, graceless, fundamentalist, anti-liberal, and enslaving. That which is lower than theology should not be glossed over and given short shrift due to immoderate religious zeal or an orthodoxy-at-all-costs mentality, for this suggests a fanatical and eminently unphilosophical mindset. If either Socrates or Christ is banished from the curriculum and pedagogy of the Catholic university or the soul of the philosopher, the result is theological totali-

---

4. MacIntyre, *God, Philosophy, Universities*, 127.

tarianism or a dictatorship of relativism, in the one, and fanaticism or dilettantism, in the other.

Both extremes display an anti-dialectical, reactionary, "answers without questions" ethos, whether the answers are the true ones of divine revelation or the false ones of secular ideology. Such a university, if Catholic in affiliation and confession, offers true answers to its students, but perhaps at the expense of the necessary dialectical questioning and Socratic ethos that is indispensable to yielding answers to real questions in students' hearts. Similarly, on the personal level, such a philosophical "answer-man" might possess true answers, but they would be poisonous to his soul, a bulwark for his spiritual pride and gnostic, "inner circle" certainty. Neil Postman suggests the right balance:

> Knowledge is produced in response to questions; and new knowledge results from the asking of new questions; quite often new questions about old questions. Here is the point: once you have learned how to ask questions—relevant and appropriate and substantial questions—you have learned how to learn and no one can keep you from learning whatever you want or need to know.[5]

Just as philosophy and theology must be held in the right balance, the curriculum must also hold in fruitful tension the poetic and the philosophical. The liberal arts must not become mere poetic fodder for the "real" intellectual food of, for example, Aristotelian philosophy or Thomistic theology, nor poetic knowledge become hegemonic and all-encompassing, with philosophy dismissed as so much useless and pride-inducing abstract speculation, only good for the poetic meat one can glean from its scanty bones. To secure the right balance of the poetic and the philosophical is a complex matter, as Plato's ironic yet unassumingly sophisticated and nuanced treatment of it in the *Republic* reveals, but, as Peter Redpath has suggested, without the right balance, philosophy becomes neo-Protagorean, mytho-poetic sophistry under the aegis of political ideology, and poetry fails in its charge to keep both systematic

---

5. Neil Postman and Charles Weingartner, *Teaching as a Subversive Activity* (New York: Dell, 1969), 23.

philosophy and theology in touch with the earthly realities of man's senses, from which all human knowledge has its origin, and in the absence of which the human intellect becomes unmoored, delusional, and dangerous.

Lastly, the *pedagogy* of the university must be properly ordered and balanced, with pride of place given to Socratic tutorial over lecture and seminar. The lecture and seminar modes of teaching, though appropriate and necessary on certain occasions and with certain subjects, must never be the primary mode of teaching for the liberal arts and philosophy. When lecture predominates, the class becomes one of teacher-derived-and-promulgated questions, answers, and arguments, with the students serving as mere passive receptacles of catechetical knowledge, so that the vital student-derived-and-initiated questions and *aporias* that must precede and evoke any definitive answer or resolution are bypassed and repressed. Excessive and impertinent seminar teaching can result in an educational ethos of "questions without answers," resulting in misology and skepticism, and a false sense of intellectual sophistication and self-sufficiency.

In conclusion, what our anti-philosophical culture of death needs most is conversion and spiritual healing. An effective means to this is the reappropriation, rejuvenation, and rearticulation of the Catholic philosophical tradition, which both presupposes and requires a refounding of our Catholic universities firmly and integrally upon this tradition. Our Catholic philosophical tradition cannot flourish without integrally Catholic and Thomistic, that is, *good*, universities. But such universities, in turn, require an already flourishing Catholic philosophical tradition to inform them and render them good. It's a paradox, yes, but one that should not leave us without hope, as long as there are a few good Catholic philosophers in the world.

9

Catholic Education and the Cult of Theistic Evolution

Authentically Catholic liberal arts colleges and universities accept the harmony of faith and reason. The overall intellectual bent of Catholic schools should thus be, at least to some extent, and hopefully to a great extent, Thomistic. The teaching of Thomism and the *philosophia perennis* with regard to the philosophy of nature and science is, in contrast to nominalist, scientist, materialist, and fideist rationalities, that secondary causes are truly causal, and that God tends to do things in the world through them, even giving them genuine co-creative power. In other words, nature is distinct from God yet never separate from Him (for, through created *esse*, He is closer to all beings than they are to themselves), and nature possesses a relative autonomy and causal power that does not require God's perpetual interventions, though He can and does intervene. Nature is so powerful that it would appear to have *full* autonomy, and this is the misguided pretext and source of the prima facie credibility of materialism and atheistic scientism. Furthermore, nature's causal structures can be known through man's unaided reason, and the effects of these causes, including biological phenomena, can be explained without the use of Revelation, though, of course, not explained exhaustively, as all things, especially man, possess a certain unfathomableness due to their having been created and sustained in existence and activity by an ultimately unfathomable, transcendent, and mysterious God.

All this is to say that science should be taken seriously at any Catholic college or university, and where modern science has discovered truth about the material world, this truth should be embraced. "Fundamentalism" denies this, in a misguided attempt to vindicate Sacred Scripture. Scriptural interpretation must take such truths into consideration, and sometimes traditionally held views, such as six *literal* days of Creation and a 10,000-year-old universe, must be looked at anew in the light of the latest and *true* scientific evidence. But one has to be careful to discriminate between *genuine* scientific discoveries and counterfeit claims by the so-called "consensus of scientists." Regardless of what the "scientific community" now holds to be indubitable, I have yet to come across any scientific evidence that conclusively proves evolution or an old earth, and even today a serious case can be made for a motionless earth at the center of the universe.[1]

Science has the capacity and duty to take care of its own, as it were, without any undue interference from other disciplines, even the higher ones of philosophy, metaphysics, and theology—unless it oversteps its humble charge of cataloging, describing, predicting, interpreting, and making laws about matter in motion. But due to its deliberately narrow and superficial purview, it is obliged to offer up its material data to the higher sciences for ultimate, and more certain, interpretation and adjudication. If modern, empiriometric science attempts to teach on things that it knows nothing about, such as the metaphysical truths of the *philosophia perennis*, the purpose and meaning and origin of things, the mystery of man, the supernatural, and God, and dares to trespass against the natural and supernatural hierarchy of wisdom, then Aristotelian natural philosophy, Thomistic metaphysics, and orthodox theology are within their rights to step in and put science in its place.

Have there been some oversteppings and trespasses in the modern era up to the present? Catholics of a traditional cast know all about the Enlightenment, modernism, rationalism, etc., and the incessant and insufferably ignorant machinations of today's "four horsemen" of atheism. But the transgressions of the atheistic Darwinians are not the focus of this chapter. I wish to speak rather of

---

1. See the four-hour documentary of Robert Sungenis for a thorough review of the astronomical evidence: https://gwwdvd.com/.

the behavior of many Catholic theistic evolutionists. They overstep *science's* bounds when they claim that debatable theories, such as the theory of evolution, are "facts," a maneuver Pius XII condemned in *Humani Generis*. They overstep science's bounds again when they attempt to render certain unverified non-facts, such as common descent from monocellular organisms, as verified, indisputable facts by recourse to, not actual indisputable evidence, but the social force of the so-called "scientific consensus"—that same force that fires and character-assassinates people who publish peer-reviewed scientific articles that conclude to (for example) the intelligent design of certain cellular processes, and that excludes anyone but committed evolutionists to the Pontifical Academy of Sciences. They overstep *philosophy's* bounds when they teach debatable and idiosyncratic philosophical theories about causality in the natural world and its relation to God, claiming, for example, that God's providence over the world is compatible with genuine chance in nature—not just the *appearance* of chance, but chance!—as if this were the only rational and Thomistic way to explain things; as if serious philosophical challenges to it, such as found in the work of Robert Koons,[2] are *a priori* otiose and tending towards fundamentalism. They overstep *theology's* bounds when they dismiss the serious challenges not only to evolutionary theory, but to the very fact of evolution, found in the Catholic Magisterium and the Fathers of the Church—not to mention the latest scientific evidence, which has, it must be said, proved neither common descent of humans from primitive organisms, nor the generation of all life, in all of its glorious complexity and design, from mindless natural selection conserving random genetic variation and mutation.

There is surely scientific evidence for *micro*-evolution, namely, that living beings change and adapt, and that living species have genetic similarities. But, as there is no indisputable scientific evidence that all species have descended from a primitive ancestor, that species *macro*-evolve, and that evolution of species has taken place at all, we are dealing here with a dialectical topic, not a demonstra-

---

2. See especially Robert Koons and Logan Gage, "St Thomas Aquinas on Intelligent Design," *Proceedings of the ACPA* 85 (2012): 79–97.

tive one. In fact, the many missing transition fossils in the fossil record, the Cambrian species explosion, and the irreducible complexity of many biological phenomena, along with a host of other evidence that has been censored, belittled, or ignored by academia and the mainstream scientific community, seem to disprove Darwin's original theory as well as the neo-Darwinism of the theistic evolutionists, or at least make these highly debatable.

Intelligent design, and I would also include some of the findings of good creation scientists, is as scientific and confirmed by evidence as neo-Darwinian theistic evolution, and perhaps even more scientific and reasonable, but one would never know that intelligent design and non-evolutionary biological theories were even debatable, let alone possibly true, due to the irresponsible deference among so many in academia and media, including the vast majority of Catholics, to the idols of the tribe, the sacred cows of Darwin and the so-called "scientific consensus." Such deference bespeaks not loyalty to reason and science, but kneeling to the world.

What is the educational upshot of this? It is beyond obvious that a good case can be made for intelligent design—the debate has occupied the pages of *First Things* for years. For the sake of the students' intellectual good and the integrity of the school, Catholic colleges and universities should give as much deference to the possible truth of intelligent design as they do to neo-Darwinian theistic evolution, regardless of the private beliefs of any professor, which he is, of course, free to express to students. Students taking science in a Catholic liberal arts college should be led to investigate all the issues with an open mind, conducting dialectical inquiry into all the positions that are not "beyond the pale" of Catholic orthodoxy, philosophical possibility, and *real*, not just *claimed*, scientific evidence. The point of such courses is not to indoctrinate students into a certain debatable scientific or philosophical or theological viewpoint, but to teach them how to think scientifically, how to think philosophically and theologically about science, and how critically to assess scientific and philosophical theories so as to be able to arrive at truth. Of course, the teaching of the relevant scientific facts and *actually* confirmed theories is essential to such courses, but the status of "fact" and "theory" is not always something finalized in science, as any liberally educated, non-scientistic, scientific theorist knows, and this should also be made clear to students. The idolatry of science is ensconced in culture, as John West argued in *First Things*,[3] and Catholics must go against the grain to combat it. The proper suspicion of claims of science is not fundamentalism or conspiracism, but reasonableness and prudence.

There is simply no view-from-nowhere on the issue of evolution—no knockdown theological, philosophical, historical, or scientific argument that resolves the evolution issue to one side over the other. One's presuppositions and starting points, usually implicit and unconscious, tend to determine what kind of data is taken to be legitimate evidence, what data can be ignored, what kinds of arguments may be deemed "scientific," and which conclusions appear plausible. The claim to have "overwhelming evidence," made incessantly by pro-Darwinists like Laurence Krauss and theistic evolutionists, does not render a debatable issue a non-debatable one. Evolution, in both its factual and its theoretical claims, is, most certainly, debatable. It is, after all, being debated, at least among open-minded truth seekers, perhaps only a small minority these days. But even if it were no longer a topic of debate among mainstream scientists and intellectuals, this alone would not prove its having been definitively resolved and concluded.

The purpose of a Catholic college course on this debatable issue, as well as all the other ones at the nexus of science and religion, such as the historical existence of Adam and Eve, the age of the earth and the universe, and the geography of the cosmos, is to introduce students to the debates, and to present the best case for each side, even if the professor leans to one of them—and he is surely permitted, even encouraged, to share his leanings and the reason for them with the students. The purpose of both liberal and specialized education is not to teach only one side of a debatable issue as the only possible truth of the matter, whatever the so-called "consensus of scientists" says. Much evidence against both the fact and the theory of evolution is censored, belittled, or ignored by the scientific establishment, a sad fact so obvious that it can no longer be relegated to

3. John West, "The Church of Darwin," *First Things* (June–July, 2005).

"conspiracy theory." Just consider the work of Pierre-Paul Grassé (1895–1985), the renowned French zoologist and die-hard evolutionist, who himself admitted: "Through use and abuse of hidden postulates, of bold, often ill-founded extrapolations, a pseudoscience has been created. It is taking root in the very heart of biology and is leading astray many biochemists and biologists."[4] By the way, have you heard of the soft blood tissue found in dinosaur bones? Thought not.

The Church has surely given us strict guidelines on the legitimate interpretations of Genesis and other relevant sacred texts, but she has also approved of openness to the possibility of the truth of certain modern scientific theories, such as evolution. We do know that scientific, philosophical, and theological theories cannot be true if they trespass against known natural and metaphysical principles and revealed truths. Something cannot come from nothing, potency cannot actualize itself, unformed matter cannot alone cause form; Adam and Eve existed, Eve was created from Adam (she did not evolve from an ape!), they actually and literally committed the first sin from which Original Sin derives, God created the universe from nothing, and He specially creates every human soul from nothing. Positions that fall within the limits of *genuine* reason (not consensus-obsessed, secularist, scientistic, materialist or fideistic "reason") and Catholic orthodoxy (and this requires us not facilely to dismiss challenging statements of popes and Church Fathers as outdated or irrelevant) are genuinely debatable, and students need to learn to see them as such. Of course, the most difficult part of the dialectic is to determine definitively these limits and which positions fall within them, but this is the teacher's task.

If a professor thinks a particular debatable issue has been resolved in one way or the other, he is within his rights to say so to students and to present his case and the case of others. He would not be within his rights, however, to induce the students to think that his view of the matter is somehow indisputable and "the obvious truth of things," especially if this is done by presenting competing theories

4. Pierre-Paul Grassé, *Evolution of Living Organisms: Evidence for a New Theory of Transformation* (New York: Academic Press, 1977), 6.

as strawmen, with that exquisite condescension and sarcasm and selective use of evidence that is legion these days among Catholics. On controversial and debatable issues, it is a grave disservice to students for Catholic theistic evolutionists to use canards and conversation stoppers such as "science tells us," "we now know," "evolution is a fact." Of course, science does tell us some indisputable things, such as the fact of micro-evolution (since we have actually observed this taking place), and we do "now know" certain things we didn't know in the past, such as the existence of genetic similarities between different species. And, of course, there *are* indisputable facts (*pace* postmodernism) that modern science, and modern science alone, has enabled us to see, such as the unfathomable size of the universe. Macroevolution is simply not one of these facts, and thus it should be taught as precisely what it is, a debatable theory.

On a practical note, the policy upshot of my position relates to academic freedom. Professors who teach a course on evolution or other debatable scientific issues have the freedom to select the texts they think are most appropriate and excellent—some might choose Ken Miller's *Finding Darwin's God*, others Stephen Meyer's *Darwin's Doubt*, still others Gerald Keane's *Creation Rediscovered*—and, although the course should be taught dialectically, the professor is within his rights to teach one of the positions as the superior account, as long as he refrains from using his mere authority as a professor or as a degreed scientist to make unsubstantiated claims, and avoids the use of inappropriately dogmatic language (unless it's a matter of a self-evident philosophical principle, manifestly true established fact, or magisterial teaching) and facile arguments to influence the students to think that such-and-such *must* be true, that no other positions have any merit or plausibility, and that only "those people" would talk that talk way about the origin of species.

Am I saying one cannot support evolution as a Catholic? No, but I wonder about being an *adamantly* pro-evolution Catholic, which is the position of the Catholic theistic evolutionists. Nowadays, even to have an open mind about the possible wrongheadedness of the theory of evolution, let alone the fact, is to be cast into the outer darkness, to join Ken Ham and, as they would say, the biblical-literalist morons. However, the "evolution as fact" attitude goes directly against Pius XII's teaching in *Humani Generis*, which, if anything, is more germane now than ever. As Stephen Meyer has shown, and many biologists (Stephen J. Gould, for one) have now admitted, the evidence for Darwinian macro-evolution has become *less* compelling since 1950, so it makes Pius XII's condemnation of "rash transgression" even more pertinent:

> Some, however, rashly transgress this liberty of discussion, when they act as if the origin of the human body from pre-existing and living matter were already completely certain and proved by the facts which have been discovered up to now and by reasoning on those facts, and as if there were nothing in the sources of divine revelation which demands the greatest moderation and caution in this question.[5]

My main concern is that such moderation and caution is not being exercised by Catholic evolutionists and other Christians, especially in today's Catholic and Christian colleges and universities, and in Christian and Catholic intellectual circles in general. It seems to me that many academics and professors are afraid to question evolution for fear of being ridiculed or at least being put on the outskirts as "one of *those* people"—*a fortiori* the Catholic scientists who question the Sacred Cow, as all the smart Catholic science people *know* that evolution is the indisputable truth and the *only* position for the educated Catholic to hold. It seems to me that an evolution cult has developed among conservative Catholics. Father John McCarthy describes it well:

> The movement to accommodate traditional Catholic doctrine, as well as the traditional interpretation of the accounts in Sacred Scripture, to the supposed "fact" of the evolution of man from primitive matter by a relentless process of spontaneous transformations of species over an enormous period of time has become so widespread in Catholic intellectual circles that it has now assumed the appearance of a "mainstream" point of view. The assumed "fact" of biological evolution, as pictured in contemporary biological theories, has moved in our time from a far-out to a

---

5. Pius XII, Encyclical Letter *Humani Generis* (August 12, 1950).

central theological position and is now threatening to become a supposition of the updated "teaching of the Church," with all the inevitable consequences of such a development, not only as regards the two-thousand-year-old teaching of the Church on such issues as Original Sin, but also as regards the very credibility of Church teaching as such. At this moment in the historic assault of modern secular humanism upon Catholic belief, we are witnessing to our dismay more and more heretofore "solid" defenders of Catholic tradition ceding to Darwinism and its progeny ground without which they cannot survive for long as orthodox thinkers.[6]

It is my hope that a continuing conversation about this—most debatable—issue will help to expose and thus dispel an ideological approach and the "rash transgression of the liberty of discussion" that is its hallmark.

6. John F. McCarthy, "The Evolution of Original Sin," *Living Tradition* (Sept. 1991), 37, available at http://www.rtforum.org/lt/lt37.html.

10

Why Modern, Liberal, Pluralistic, Secularist Democracies Cannot Educate Themselves

In his masterpiece, *Paideia: The Ideals of Greek Culture*, Werner Jaeger writes:

> Education is the process by which a community preserves and transmits its physical and intellectual character. . . . The formative influence of the community on its members is most constantly active in its deliberate endeavor to educate each new generation of individuals so as to make them in its own image.[1]

For Jaeger, what education requires is a well-defined community capable of and willing to engage in deliberate, collective action. And for this action to effect a definite, effective, and lasting educational result, the community must possess a distinct, coherent, and intelligible image of itself, and be willing systematically and integrally to impose it upon its members. Do the communities we call modern, liberal, pluralist, secularist democracies meet these indisputable requirements for authentic and effective education of the soul? Can they educate themselves?

Of course, in a certain sense the answer must be yes, since millions of citizens in today's Western liberal democracies are, indeed, educated. Yet, if one asks precisely how such a high level and broad extension of education has occurred, the answer, as we shall see, is manifestly *not* through the deliberate, communal, image-making,

---

1. Werner Jaeger, *Paideia: The Ideals of Greek Culture*, 2nd ed., trans. Gilbert Highet (New York: Oxford University Press, 1945), vol. 1, xiii.

educational agency of the modern, liberal, secular, democratic *state*. At best, this state has provided some free yet ideologically tainted space for the true educational agents to do their work. The state is an educational agent by its very nature—but in order to function as such, it must first of all *be* a state, that is, a genuine political community embodying an intelligible and obtainable common good, and not a mere public interest organization or military alliance. Insofar as it is not an authentic political agent, it cannot be an authentic educational agent.

Not only does modern, liberal, pluralist, secularist democracy lack a distinct, coherent, and intelligible image of itself, but the image it does purport to have is an illusory spectre of an ideological ghost, an incoherent and insubstantial parody of *paideia* overseeing the *deliberate refusal* communally to impose any image whatsoever on its members. As Alasdair MacIntyre puts it:

> Every individual is to be equally free to propose and to live by whatever conception of the good he or she pleases, derived from whatever theory or tradition he or she may adhere to, unless that conception of the good involves reshaping the life of the rest of the community in accordance with it.[2]

If Jaeger's understanding of education is correct, such a "community" of private goods and private good seekers could not possibly educate its members. Yet as MacIntyre points out in the same passage, the collective refusal to impose an educational image irresistibly becomes itself a collective, imposed image! It's an anti-image imposed in a project of anti-education:

> And this qualification of course entails not only that liberal individualism does indeed have its own broad conception of the good, which it is engaged in imposing politically, legally, socially, and culturally wherever it has the power to do so, but also that in so doing its toleration of rival conceptions of the good in the public arena is severely limited.[3]

---

2. MacIntyre, *Whose Justice?*, 336.
3. Ibid.

If a community is defined both by its possession of an authentic self-image involving a definitive conception of the good and by a willingness to impose this image upon its members, then we can say that liberal democracy is a community only in spite of itself, a community trying its best not to be a community, with all the atrocious educational distortions that attend such social schizophrenia. Secular pluralism embodied in its pure ideological form—that is, without the authentic communal influences and embodiments that spring up in spite of its hegemony—is an anti-community devoted to the anti-education of its members. MacIntyre suggests just this in a powerful passage:

> Liberalism in the name of freedom imposes a certain kind of unacknowledged domination, and one which in the long run tends to dissolve traditional human ties and to impoverish social and cultural relationships. Liberalism, while imposing through state power regimes that declare everyone free to pursue whatever they take to be their own good, deprives most people of the possibility of understanding their lives as a quest for the discovery and achievement of the good, especially by the way in which it attempts to discredit those traditional forms of human community within which this project has to be embodied.[4]

By applying MacIntyre's community-defining terms—tradition, practice, *telos*, the good, reason, and revelation—we can see why the liberal secular state is incapable of *paideia*. Democratic pluralism fails as a community and therefore as an educational agent due to the lack of any substantive, intelligible realities that correspond to these terms in the community, and a radical confusion at best, ideological mendacity at worst, regarding such realities as may indeed be present in the community, but which serve an anti-communal and anti-educational agenda.

Communities are essentially embodied theories, and since education can be effected only in, by, and through communities, we can best understand the character and evaluate the effectiveness of any

---

4. Alasdair MacIntyre, "An Interview with Giovanna Borradori," *The MacIntyre Reader*, ed. Kelvin Knight (Notre Dame: University of Notre Dame Press, 1998), 258.

educational practice by examining the theoretical architecture its overseeing community embodies. Real education is concerned not primarily with job training, social, political, cultural, psychological, or spiritual indoctrination, or even the acquisition of knowledge, however sublime; education is primarily the development of intellectual and moral virtue, which renders us capable both of knowing and of achieving our good, the *telos* of all human activities. And virtues, whether moral or intellectual, are not acquired on our own through our own isolated powers, but in community with the help of the mentoring and cooperation of others, through participation in what MacIntyre calls practices:

> By a practice I am going to mean any coherent and complex form of socially established co-operative human activity through which goods internal to that form of activity are realised in the course of trying to achieve those standards of excellence which are appropriate to, and partially definitive of, that form of activity, with the result that human powers to achieve excellence, and human conceptions of the ends and goods involved, are systematically extended.[5]

Education, then, is a practice, involving and embodying internal goods, human excellences, and ends, the active and intelligent participation in and understanding of which enable us to make these goods and excellences our own and to render ends theoretically intelligible and practically appropriable. Just as virtues, because they are human powers that can develop only in and through communion with others, have their home, as it were, in communal practices that situate their performance and learning and thus enable their acquisition, so practices, because they embody and make intelligible to us goods, excellences, and ends, must be situated within an overarching *tradition*, giving to them both theoretical and practical point and purpose. For MacIntyre, all rational enquiry is inherently tradition-guided and tradition-bound, and

---

5. *After Virtue*, second edition (Notre Dame: University of Notre Dame Press, 1984), 187.

education is essentially a practice of rational enquiry—more specifically, a sharing of and participation in the fruits of rational enquiry. The social and cultural setting in which the practice of rational enquiry takes place is all-important, for it is the nutrient-rich soil without which no fruits can grow. For MacIntyre, rigorous philosophical conversation in the setting of the well-ordered university is the primary fertilizer.

Just as an individual life becomes intelligible only in the context of an historical life narrative, so a communal life, as well as the communal practices that constitute it, is made intelligible only through a historical, communal narrative. Tradition just *is* this communal narrative:

> A living tradition, then, is a historically extended, socially embodied argument, precisely in part about the goods which constitute that tradition.... Once again the narrative phenomenon of embedding is crucial: the history of a practice in our time is generally and characteristically embedded in and made intelligible in terms of the larger and longer history of that tradition through which the practice in its present form was conveyed to us; the history of each of our own lives generally and characteristically is embedded in and made intelligible in terms of the larger and longer histories of a number of traditions.[6]

Tradition, for MacIntyre, is the concrete, contingent, particular, and historically embodied realities of our daily lives, unified in a coherent system of thought and practice. It is any set of practices, customs, rituals, texts, arguments, authorities, institutions, artifacts (and any other type of historically extended and socially embodied phenomena) unified by a distinct narrative serving to interpret and order these phenomena, and affording the participant particular habits of knowing, judging, and feeling, and thus, intellectual access to an overarching comprehension of the world, the good, and his proper place in these. MacIntyre insists that it is only through active participation in particular authentic traditions that men are rendered capable of discovering and achieving their ultimate good; for

---

6. MacIntyre, *After Virtue*, 223.

it is only through a particular tradition that we can properly apprehend universal truth.

About the *telos* of education, MacIntyre writes:

> What education has to aim at for each and every child, if it is not to be a mockery, is both the development of those powers that enable children to become reflective and independent members of their families and political communities and the inculcation of those virtues that are needed to direct us towards the achievement of our common and individual goods.[7]

The powers and virtues that are developed in authentic education are ordered to the full flourishing of the human being, and thus to the human *good*—a good that must be known with a high level of certainty by the educational agent if it is to lead students to know it and achieve it. The good to be known and achieved is both individual and common: learned about, exercised, obtained, and finally perfected via, in, and for oneself *qua* member of community, whether family, educational, or political. Education enables us human beings to become the actual "dependent rational animals" we already are *in potentia*, fully actualized with the help of others more actualized than we, which is to say, by the mentoring of the teachings of *tradition*, the truth-and-good-embodying practices that transmit it, and the masters who personify it. Being animals, we find that such practices embody and enable the obtainment of bodily and emotional goods, as well as the truth of their essential yet subordinate role in human perfection. Being rational, we find that these practices include the good of reason—that is, natural and supernatural truth, offering an apprenticeship into the contemplative life we all must live to some extent. Being dependent, we find that they include the goods and virtues that cause, are made possible by, and are inherent in community—love, service, sacrifice, compassion, solidarity, and friendship—and the truth that no man is an island.

---

7. Alasdair MacIntyre and Joseph Dunne, "Alasdair MacIntyre on Education: In Dialogue with Joseph Dunne," *Journal of Philosophy of Education* 36.1 (2002): 3.

Ultimately, education is about developing the ability of human beings to *reason*, to become, as MacIntyre says, "independent practical reasoners." But the ability to reason is valuable only if used as a means to knowing and achieving the *good* of human beings, an essential aspect of which is the good of reasoning itself. What is this good? It is, as Aristotle made clear in the *Nicomachean Ethics*, happiness; but Aristotle did not know clearly and fully what, or rather, *whom* happiness ultimately is. For all of Aristotle's pagan wisdom regarding the nature of community, virtue, education, and the soul, any Aristotelian project of education must be incomplete, however well founded and rightly structured it is, without the God-revealed knowledge about man's ultimate good. Natural reason, and the tradition-guided and embodied practices that aim at its full development in its practitioner-apprentices, is itself not a fully competent educational agent. Reason itself requires a "master-craftsman" to guide and develop it, as MacIntyre suggests here:

> Part of the gift of Christian faith is to enable us to identify accurately where the line between faith and reason is to be drawn, something that cannot be done from the standpoint of reason, but only from that of faith. Reason therefore needs Christian faith, if it is to do its own work well. Reason without Christian faith is always reason informed by some other faith, characteristically an unacknowledged faith, one that renders its adherents liable to error.[8]

Modern, liberal, pluralist, secularist democracy not only rejects the master-craftsman, faith, but also its forever-budding, natural apprentice, reason. Secular liberal pluralism relegates Christian faith to the purely idiosyncratic, subjective, non-rational, apolitical realm of the "private," and reason to the reductively objective, inhumanly universal, instrumentally rational, and pragmatically utilitarian realm of the "scientific," which amounts to a reduction of reason to the purely pragmatic role of managing the private, irrational desires of individuals. The sole, unimpeachable, authoritative educational agents in modern liberal democracy, as MacIntyre makes clear, are the "managers," "bureaucrats," and "therapists," a self-

---

8. Alasdair MacIntyre, *God, Philosophy, Universities*, 152.

appointed elite who together execute, in the name of human liberation, equality, and well-being, a quite imposing *paideia* on the rest
of us.

Secular pluralism, because it has rejected both supernatural faith
and metaphysical reason as politically relevant *desiderata* and
authoritative communal guides, and because it has subjectivized
and privatized the good and the true, cannot possibly educate itself.
But because it still pretends to be—and, in a highly attenuated and
perverted fashion, actually *is*—a political community, it unfortunately does act as a powerful educational agent. It makes a mockery
of both education and community, seducing—when it is not
demanding—citizens' participation in defective practices embodying counterfeit goods and transmitting an anti-tradition of, ultimately, self-and-nothing worship. Secular liberalism's communal
telos is the aggrandizement of an elite class of sophist-educators
who teach their students to abandon the quest for their own good
and the common good for the pursuit of idiosyncratic ephemera,
and to seek, not the truth about God, the world, and man, along
with the political and cultural instantiation of these truths, but
purely practical "knowledge" ordered to nothing but the equal satisfaction of individual desires. Such a program serves only to require
and extend the hegemonic power of the state authoritatively to
manage and define this equality by preventing the existence and
flourishing of genuine common good organizations ordered by and
to the transcendent—in other words, by persecuting and neutraliz-
ing true educational agents.

The upshot of this pluralistic, inclusive, tolerant, and rational
"community" is, as MacIntyre puts it, "interminable moral argument with no prospect of resolution," "civil war by other means," a
controlled anarchy where power, profit, and fraud are the true educational agents, and where the citizen-student is taught—rather,
brainwashed—that such a state of affairs is good, and, what's more,
the only real possibility for free men. MacIntyre continues:

> What each standpoint supplies is a set of premises from which its
> proponents argue to conclusions about what ought or ought not
> to be done, conclusions which are often in conflict with those of

other groups. The only *rational* way in which these disagreements could be resolved would be by means of a philosophical enquiry aimed at deciding which out of the conflicting sets of premises, if any, is true. But a liberal order, as we have already seen, is one in which each standpoint may make its claims but can do no more within the framework of the public order, since no overall theory of the human good is to be regarded as justified.[9]

If "no overall theory of the human good is to be regarded as justified," then education in the proper sense of the term, *paideia*, is rendered impossible. Yet insofar as secular democracy retains the fundamental structure and function of community, an image of itself is indeed imposed on its unwitting members, even when this image is denied by the very imposers (imposters). What sort of an image is it?

> And now, I said, let me show in a figure how far our nature is enlightened or unenlightened. Behold! Human beings living in an underground den, which has a mouth open towards the light and reaching all along the den; here they have been from their childhood, and have their legs and necks chained so that they cannot move, and can only see before them, being prevented by the chains from turning round their heads. Above and behind them a fire is blazing at a distance, and between the fire and the prisoners there is a raised way; and you will see, if you look, a low wall built along the way, like the screen which marionette players have in front of them, over which they show the puppets.... To them, I said, the truth would be literally nothing but the shadows of the images.[10]

Of course, there are still many communities of education not yet wholly modeled on and obscured by modern liberalism's seductive shadow-images, and many of these exist as educational institutions chartered and overseen by secular democracy itself, such as the hundreds of public high schools, colleges, and universities, which, though tainted by the political correctness peddled by the cane puppeteers and unwittingly fostering anti-educational practices that promote the goods of effectiveness over the goods of excellence,

9. Alasdair MacIntyre, *Whose Justice?*, 343.
10. Plato, *Republic*, 514a-515a.

are still permitting good educational work to be done, through the efforts of those few educational craftsmen who have managed to acquire an "old school" education, and who are courageous and cunning enough to pass this "secret" wisdom on to new initiates and keep the true liberal arts guilds alive. Let us be vigilant to preserve and increase the autonomy and integrity of institutions that have not been entirely corrupted, and to build new ones to be as incorruptible as possible.

IV

Keep Yourself from Idols

11

Sacred Ambivalence

We are thus approaching societies without the sacred and without power. The political enterprise is no longer justified in calling itself the concretization of the heavenly law. Political power is subverted in its symbolic foundation and sacred identity. Its roots, hence its mediating legitimacy, have been removed by a quiet revolution. Liberal democracy has proved to be a passage from society founded on the sacred to society founded on nothing but itself.[1]

"Western democracy—at least as we have known it—turns out, itself, to be a kind of theocracy too."[2] Remi Brague's words suggest the inescapability of theocracy, for even the so-called secular regimes of modernity entail hidden, theocratic foundations. Though "the idea of divine law has been swept out of sight," it still works in the background, as it were, as the hidden, sacral underpinning of, say, the "dignity of moral conscience." In other words, it is not that modern liberal democracy has successfully desacralized politics, but rather it has changed the locus of sacralization from cosmic order, divine law, and the Church, to the human person, and the sacred freedom of individuals to choose their own sacred allegiances. Brague is skeptical of the attempt to radically desacralize politics, such that "the idea of the contract is even meant to put out of court whatever might claim an extra-human origin." Can we citizens of apparently secularized, desacralized, religiously pluralistic, liberal democracies be firmly committed to the funda-

1. Molnar, *Twin Powers*, 116.
2. Brague, "Non-Theocratic Regimes," 3.

121

mental principles and ethos of secular liberal democracy—freedom of conscience, consent, democracy, human rights, etc.—while remaining ambivalent about the sacrality of political order? Must we take a stand one way or the other?

But if religious truth is to have any influence in the public sphere, perhaps the primary task of its contemporary devotees is to bear prophetic witness to the possibility that the sacred is still as foundational to politics as it ever was, and, perhaps, always will be. Romano Guardini describes a very different conception of the power of religion in the public sphere:

> The law of the state is more than a set of rules governing human behavior; behind it exists something untouchable, and when a law is broken it makes its impact on the conscience of man. Social order is more than a warrant against friction, than a guarantee for the free exercise of communal life; behind it stands something which makes an injury against society a crime. The religious dimension of law suffuses the entire moral order. It gives to ethical action, that is, action necessary for the very existence of man, its own proper norms, which it executes from without and without pressure. Only the religious element of law guarantees the unity and cooperation of the whole order of human behavior.[3]

In any society, Christian or not, should not citizens attempt to create a political order whose public culture permits not only the free practice of one's religion, whatever that may be, but also, in a religiously pluralistic culture such as ours, a political and cultural ethos most conducive to discovering and practicing the *true* religion, or, if one is non-religious, the secular values most conducive to human flourishing? It is hard to see how the pluralistic, desacralized state could facilitate this sort of ethos better than the religiously unified, sacral state; thus, there is a good argument that the real "power of religion in the public sphere" must be a sacred power.

What is this good argument? It is one predicated upon Alasdair MacIntyre's concept of "tradition-constituted rationality," which, when applied politically, must be a tradition-constituted *theological*

---

3. Guardini, *End of the Modern World*, 112.

rationality. James Kalb characterizes liberalism as not only a tradition, but a *religious* tradition:

> The fundamental question of political legitimacy is the nature and purpose of authority, and thus the nature of man, the world, moral obligation, and the human good—in other words, which religion is correct. Liberalism cannot get by without answering that question, but it answers it indirectly, by claiming moral ignorance. We do not know what the good is, it tells us, so we should treat all desires the same. The satisfaction of all desires thus becomes the unquestionable good. Man becomes the measure, human genius the principle of creation, and individual will the source of value. The limitations on moral knowledge on which the liberal outlook is based lead to a definite result, and so become constituent principles rather than limitations. In short, they constitute a religion, a fact concealed by the moral doubt that is liberalism's first principle. This new religion, based on the denial of the knowability of truth, consists in nothing less than the deification of man. To refuse to talk about the transcendent, and view it as wholly out of our reach, seems very cautious and humble. In practice, however, it puts our own thoughts and desires at the center of things, and so puts man in the place of God. If you say we cannot know anything about God, but only our own experience, you will soon say that there is no God, at least for practical purposes, and that we are the ones who give order and meaning to the world. In short, you will say that we are God.[4]

Now, the liberal state never explicitly affirms "we are God," for in its official agnosticism, it does not explicitly deny or affirm even the possible or actual existence of a transcendent being. Moreover, it insists that it leaves open the possibility of some such being's revealing or having revealed himself and his will to man. Secular liberalism, in the form of the purportedly non-theocratic state, simply does not deem it necessary to recognize any such being and revelation for the purposes of either political philosophy or political practice. It claims public ignorance about, but does not deny outright

---

4. James Kalb, "Skepticism and Dogmatism (Snippet from Book-to-be)," June 6, 2006, http://antitechnocrat.net/node/1472 (accessed August 28, 2019).

the possibility of, an authoritative revelation demanding personal recognition.

Yet the believer in a being who *has* clearly and publicly revealed to man his will for the political order could argue that a studied ignorance regarding the existence of such a publicly accessible divine revelation is intellectually unjustified and politically unjust. For a Roman Catholic, for example, the Church exists as a public institution claiming to be the embodiment and spokesman of a publicly authoritative divine revelation bearing directly on morality and politics. Therefore, the Church is at least a *possible* candidate for a publicly authoritative social institution. Even if one prescinds from the question of the truth of this revelation, the Church's *claim* about itself to be the authoritative spokesman for this truth is still an objective, intelligible fact within societies, and while a political philosopher can deny the truth of this claim, he cannot plead ignorance to the fact of the claim itself, let alone maintain that it is self-evidently false. Thus, in articulating any ideal political order, the political philosopher must deal in some way with the Church's claim to have the authority to define the ultimate meaning of goodness and politics, by either recognizing or denying the Church's public authority to do so. Practical agnosticism to the very possibility of such an authority is, in effect, an implicit moral judgment of the injustice of its ever becoming an actual, living authority, and therefore an implicit theological denial of the authority it may indeed have.

Any moral or political theory involving the question of ultimate political authority that excludes this theological issue from its purview inevitably makes a theological judgment, as D. Stephen Long points out: "Ethics cannot be the province of a philosophical discourse that brackets out theological consideration, unless philosophers assume a being greater than God giving access to goodness."[5] Claiming ignorance or uncertainty of the truth of the Church's claim to public authority, or even just acting as if one were ignorant or uncertain of it by committing oneself to a political theory and

5. Long, *The Goodness of God*, 300.

practice in which the Church's authority could never, without causing grave injustice, be publicly recognized, is effectively to make a
negative judgment about the Church's claim. In practice, it
amounts to a theological judgment against the Church's authority,
and when such a judgment becomes part of a lived social, cultural,
and political tradition, and becomes embodied in its set of practices, one can accurately call such a tradition a religion.

In order to fulfill its basic function of organizing the social activity of human individuals, authority in society must determine,
authorize, and implement practical answers to matters that are
inextricably bound up with religious considerations and commitments: life and death (what is a human being?, whom does the government have an obligation to protect?, who speaks authoritatively
on these issues?); war (what are the criteria for conscientious objection?, for just or unjust war?); sex (is fornication or adultery to be
socially prohibited, celebrated, or ignored?); the family (is marriage
an unchanging social and religious institution, or is its character
open to perpetual redefinition by individuals?); rewards and pun-
ishments (what kinds of behaviors should merit societal approba-
tion and opprobrium?). Social and political authorities must
inevitably consider and make judgments regarding these issues.
Even the decision to depoliticize and privatize these matters, leaving
them to be settled freely by individuals, is socially and politically
significant and habit-forming. Thus, "secular" "non-theocratic"
regimes are de facto religious regimes, in the sense that even if there
were a way fully to depoliticize these sorts of issues, there could
never be "religious neutrality" on the part of the state with regard to
them. If there is a possibility of a God-ordained answer to any of
these questions, and if there is an institution that claims to articulate authoritatively this answer, then societal and political authority
must respond one way or another to this claim. It either believes it
or it does not. Affirmation, denial, or indifference is a non-neutral
commitment involving at least an implicit judgment pertaining to a
politically relevant religious matter, and thus has significant social
and political consequences.

In a dialectical confrontation between non-theocratic liberalism
and Catholicism, then, theological questions such as God's exist-

ence, man's knowledge of God's will, and the political ramifications of this knowledge, are necessarily involved. Any adjudication between a theistic tradition like Thomism and an anthropocentric tradition like secular liberalism must evaluate radically opposed and strong theological standards of political justice and rationality. Moreover, a consideration of the standards of rationality involved in adjudicating theological claims also involves the question of the truth of one's own theological commitments.

Alasdair MacIntyre claims and shows in all his major works that non-Aristotelian rationalities eventually fall "into ineradicable incoherence," that they are inevitably "compelled to acknowledge points at which there is an unavoidable resort to attitudes of unjustified and unjustifiable belief." However, "pragmatic" liberals, that is, those who purport to eschew any philosophical or theological foundation for liberalism, would deny "ineradicable incoherence" in their tradition, and affirm that the primary belief upon which this tradition is founded, that is, the necessary non-existence of publicly authoritative political theology, is perfectly justifiable according to its particular pragmatic standards of rationality. Pragmatic liberalism is not, of course, justifiable according to Thomistic rational standards, but this does not settle the matter, because Thomism itself is unjustifiable according to secular liberalism's standards. Jean Porter makes the point well:

> It is not clear how the rival claims of disparate moral traditions could be adjudicated through an encounter of rival traditions. It is not even clear that moralities can come into conflict, in such a way that we can plausibly regard them as rival traditions. You, collectively, arrange your lives in one way, we arrange our lives in a different way. Is it clear that we even disagree? Even if we do, what would count as resolving our disagreements, since there is no question here of coming to agree on a description of anything? Certainly, we might come to agree on the best way to arrange our lives, but that would represent a change in mores, and not a convergence of thinking about a shared object of enquiry. We do not necessarily need to conclude that moral traditions are a-rational. Nonetheless, it does appear that MacIntyre's account of rationality as tradition-based inquiry is not sufficient, taken by itself, to

resolve the issues raised by contemporary moral pluralism and the interminable character of moral disputes.[6]

Can Alasdair MacIntyre's "tradition-constituted rationality" provide a positive prescription for the right theology to undergird the inevitably theological regimes under which we all must live? It is well known that MacIntyre confines himself to answering strictly philosophical questions, that is, questions the adequate consideration of and definitive answers to which require only the resources of divinely unaided, tradition-constituted-and-dependent human rationality. Thus, I think he is ultimately unable to argue effectively against the theological judgments we have shown to be implicit in the tradition of secular liberalism. Indeed, MacIntyre the *philosopher* is unable to argue effectively against any anti-Thomistic or anti-Catholic prescription for an ideal political order because such a prescription would unavoidably involve theological judgments and commitments, whether these are implicit or explicit. The methodological avoidance of theological judgments and commitments is the primary weakness in MacIntyre's project, for it attenuates the effectiveness of both the vindication of his own theologically-based and theologically-informed Thomistic tradition, and its dialectical challenge to rival traditions.

Any intellectual tradition articulating an ideal political order must necessarily include a judgment as to whether God has communicated His will to man regarding the political order. Neither MacIntyre nor pragmatic liberalism makes any explicit judgment on this question, but the absence of such a judgment on this matter is a judgment. By not prescribing an authoritative role for political theology, both MacIntyrean Thomism and pragmatic, secular liberalism effectively deny that God has spoken authoritatively regarding the proper construction of the political order; in short, they deny the intellectual and political authority of revealed political theology. The primary weakness of MacIntyre's thought is not peculiar to it, for it is attributable to any system of thought bearing on the moral

6. Jean Porter, "Theology, Morality, and Public Life," delivered at The Pew Forum on Religion & Public Life, February 26–27, 2003, accessible at https://www.pewforum.org/2003/02/26/theology-morality-and-public-life/.

and political order that prescinds from theological commitments and judgments. Although Jacques Maritain prescinds from particular theological commitments in his practical political prescription of the "democratic charter," presented in his famous *Man and the State*, he endorses their methodological necessity:

> Integral political science . . . is superior in kind to philosophy; to be truly complete it must have a reference to the domain of theology, and it is precisely as a theologian that St Thomas wrote *De regimine principum.* . . . The knowledge of human actions and of the good conduct of the human State in particular can exist as an integral science, as a complete body of doctrine, only if related to the ultimate end of the human being. . . . The rule of conduct governing individual and social life cannot therefore leave the supernatural order out of account.[7]

What Maritain suggests here is that a *theologically informed* tradition-constituted political philosophy, all other things being equal, would be superior to a theologically uninformed one. Such a joint philosophical and theological enquiry could be vindicated against all rivals, and would serve as the first step to solving the problem of the "non-theocratic" regime that is not what it says it is. Providing a workable practical political model deriving from and justified by this philosophical-theological basis, as well as the political steps to eventually attaining it, would be the next step in the argument.

7. Jacques Maritain, *The Things that Are Not Caesar's: A Translation of 'Primauté du Spirituel'*, ed. Mortimer Adler, trans. J.F. Scanlan (London: Sheed and Ward, 1939), 128.

12

America / Leviathan

Michael Hannon and Robert George[1] are both Catholic thinkers who subscribe to a personalist anthropology and Aristotelian/Thomistic social philosophy, one that interprets the character of the modern autonomous individual as an evil fiction, that recognizes the existence and priority of intrinsic common goods, and that posits the indispensability of social communities ordered by and to such common goods and the virtues requisite for human flourishing. However, there is a substantial disagreement between them. George claims that politics is essentially *instrumental*, that is, not a good in itself, but only good insofar as it enables the flourishing of a multitude of intrinsically good, *sub-political* communities, such as families and churches, made up of persons who discover and possess their good only by participation in such communities. Hannon, on the other hand, claims that politics, or the state and its political activity, is essentially an *intrinsic* good, and as such, even a higher good than the communities it is meant to serve, due to its being more common. Indeed, the political is *the* architectonic natural good (subordinate only to the ultra-architectonic, supernatural common good that subsists in the Church, that is, the City of God), since it alone is responsible for and capable of coordinating the activity of the communities within it, with an eye

1. Michael Hannon, "Man the Political Animal: On the Intrinsic Goodness of Political Community," *Public Discourse*, May 16, 2013, available at https://www.the publicdiscourse.com/2013/05/9897/; Robert George, "The Common Good: Instrumental But Not Just Contractual," *Public Discourse*, May 17, 2013, available at https://www.thepublicdiscourse.com/2013/05/10166/.

to the greatest common good of all, God Himself, and human beatitude in friendship with Him for eternity.

These thinkers are good representatives of the two positions regarding the foundation and end of politics that one finds in conservative Catholic circles. These positions do not appear, prima facie, too dissimilar, for they are, after all, in full agreement on important conservative Christian basics, i.e., that man has an objective, God-given nature; that *good* is an objective, knowable transcendental; that common goods are real spiritual goods of spiritual persons that take precedence over individual, material goods; that men have souls; that the purpose of politics is, ultimately, bound up with the care of souls unto eternal salvation; and that the natural law governs all communities and must be authoritatively recognized. But, though in agreement on these fundamentals, they disagree on the nature and end of political community.

What is the root cause of their disagreement? To discover this, it might help to speculate a bit as to the experiential ground and reasoning process that might have brought them—and us—to their and our positions. What political phenomena, facts, experience, ideas, and considerations might have led George and the *instrumentalists*, on the one hand, to conclude that the political good is merely instrumental, and Hannon and the *intrinsicists*, that this good is truly intrinsic, on the other? I think the first and last place to look for the answer is the American regime itself, and particularly, its founding documents.

Regarding George's position, politics as instrumental good: do not the Declaration of Independence and the Constitution indicate explicitly or implicitly, or perhaps just in presupposition, an understanding of the political common good as instrumental? If government is said to be established to secure the pre-political rights of men, to allow them merely to *pursue* (not enable them to *attain*) happiness, and to secure the general *welfare*, not the common *good*, that is, if the Founding is even remotely Lockean—there is surely a plausible argument to be made that the Founders held the instrumental view of the political common good; at least the overall thrust of the Founding Documents can be interpreted this way. But, prescinding from the question of George's intellectual genealogy for a moment, we can ask why Locke himself might have thought the way he did, that is, rejecting so categorically the traditional Aristotelian account of politics. I think the answer to this is bound up with his experience of the nation-state, only recently on the scene in earnest in Western history when Locke was alive. His experience of the pre- and post-birth of the British nation-state itself—born in the Glorious Revolution of 1688—was an experience that could also explain the Founders' views, as well as George's.

Alasdair MacIntyre has made a persuasive case that the nation-state is not and cannot be the custodian of the common good, for, agreeing with George and the instrumentalists, whatever political good it might embody must be an instrumental one:

> The modern nation-state, in whatever guise, is a dangerous and unmanageable institution, presenting itself on the one hand as a bureaucratic supplier of goods and services, which is always about to, but never actually does, give its clients value for money, and on the other as a repository of sacred values, which from time to time invites one to lay down one's life on its behalf. . . . It is like being asked to die for the telephone company. . . . The shared public goods of the modern nation-state are not the common goods of a genuine nation-wide community and, when the nation-state masquerades as the guardian of such a common good, the outcome is bound to be either ludicrous or disastrous or both.[2]

If this is the case, then the instrumentalist view is right, for MacIntyre is only describing theoretically what has been the case practically in America from the beginning. In 1787, America was a full-fledged nation-state, though in latency in extent and scope; by now, it has been actualized quite fully (it even seems to be in dotage—if dotage denotes a nascent police state). So, both then and now, the American regime is constrained to the kind of goods it can embody and enable by its merely instrumentally good, nation-state essence—an essence that, as William Cavanaugh put it in his land-

<hr />

2. Alasdair MacIntyre, "A Partial Response to My Critics," in *After MacIntyre: Critical Perspectives on the Work of Alasdair MacIntyre*, eds. John Horton and Susan Mendus (Notre Dame: University of Notre Dame Press, 1994), 303.

mark article, is not, and can *never* be, the keeper of the common good.[3]

Now, subscribing to this understanding of the nation-state, identifying it with American politics *ab initio* and *in concreto*, and accepting the idea that the nation-state, by nature, cannot keep anything but instrumental goods, does not mean one has to be a Lockean through and through, in, say, religion, epistemology, and anthropology. And this is why it seems to the instrumentalist perfectly reasonable to accept everything we have said about the American nation-state, if he does indeed accept it, while demurring from Locke and the Enlightenment and affirming the nature and priority of common goods, politics as care of the soul, and the publicly authoritative nature of the natural law and the Roman Catholic Church.

Let us agree that the nation-state, in whatever configuration it happened or happens to be (Federalist or Anti-Federalist, libertarian-market or welfare state, Republican- or Democrat-controlled, lower or higher taxes, Tea Party or Occupy Wall Street ethos, Bush or Obama, Obamney or Hillary or Trump) is what it is—an alliance, not a common good institution, suitable for and capable only of providing goods and services to those *polis* organizations that can (but only with the alliance's instrumental help, as the instrumentalist insists) embody and keep common goods. It is just good philosophy to recognize what is and must be the case, and to act upon it. This, to me, is where George and the instrumentalists are coming from. Whether he would prefer to live under a state that could indeed keep a common good, such as a medieval French city or an ancient Greek *polis*, doesn't matter; the nation-state is here and here to stay, and we must accept its exigencies and limitations so that we can work with it to uphold the mediating institutions that alone can secure those common goods we need in order to flourish and get to heaven.

There isn't much to add to the instrumentalist account to explain the intrinsicist's, other than that what the former considers accept-

---

3. William Cavanaugh, "Killing for the Telephone Company: Why the Nation-State is Not the Keeper of the Common Good," *Modern Theology* 20.2 (April 2004): 243–74; also reprinted in his book *Migrations of the Holy*.

able and normative—the American-alliance-nation-state instrumentally helping sub-political communities to do their intrinsically good things—the latter rejects as unacceptable and impossible. It would be one thing, the intrinsicist says, if the "United Alliance of America" understood itself to be what it is, merely an alliance of *poleis*, securing only the kinds of private, sub-political goods that the individual *poleis* themselves are unable to secure for themselves, such as protection from foreign invaders, coinage of money, interstate commerce regulation, etc.—precisely what the American Constitution presents itself as being, at least prima facie. However, as the intrinsicist seems to think, the American government's true nature as shown in historical action is not a mere alliance, but an alliance-*polis*, that is, a political contradiction, sometimes advertising itself as a *polis*, sometimes as an alliance, but always masquerading as one or the other to attain more and more power for itself at the expense of the good of its citizens, personal and common, individual and collective, soul and body. And this is not an unpredictable outcome, for it is precisely what happens when genuinely political communities are not recognized as what they truly are (namely, more than instrumentally good), and when one expects families and churches to do what only the architectonic political community can do: the coordinating and harmonizing of intrinsic goods in light of the common good, thereby securing it.

In short, this creation of a Frankenstein-Jekyll-and-Hyde politics is what happens when one charges politics with nothing more than providing instrumental goods to sub-political, non-architectonic communities. This is, in effect, to destroy politics, and political nature abhors a vacuum. What you get in its place is not limited government and a flourishing civil society of happy and free persons and intrinsically good communities, but a totalitarian police-state nightmare. In short, for the intrinsicist, the nation-state, in the absence of a *polis* in which the political good is *more than instrumental*, will cease being a mere alliance, if it ever had been one, and turn into a monstrous anti-*polis*, pursuing anti-goods to the detriment and eventual eradication of the common good as well as individual goods. Robert Nisbet has traced the history of this process in his indispensable work, *The Quest for Community*.

For the instrumentalist, on the other hand, there is no need to prophesy doom, for such intrinsically good-making *poleis* are a thing of the past. And even if they were somehow possible in our religiously pluralistic, technocratic, nation-state age, they would not need to exist as long as there were flourishing cultural communities embodying and keeping intrinsic common goods, and as long as the state were confined to the duties deriving from its alliance-essence, assisting these communities in their unique role of securing human flourishing and salvation. Thus, both agree that the nation-state shouldn't try to be a *polis*, but they disagree in this: whether the nation-state can remain and function as a mere alliance in the absence of genuinely political *poleis*. Who is right? How to resolve this debate?

Since its official beginning in 1787, the nation-state of America has indeed presented itself as both a public-interest alliance, aiming only to secure individualist and collectivist goods such as property and security from foreign aggression, and as a common good *polis*, aiming at intrinsic goods such as virtue, peace, and solidarity. The latter aspiration, however, in the present form of an increasingly centralized, managerial, intrusive, incontestable, war-mongering federal government bureaucracy and military-industrial complex, is much more apparent today, and it is working not so much for the common good as for the common evil. This tyrannical tendency of the federal government was much harder to see two hundred years ago because the *polis*-like states at that time still retained a goodly amount of political hegemony and autonomy. After the Civil War, however, and exponentially after IXXI, the Leviathanian nature of the federal government has revealed itself without a mask.

How? Domestically: the Obamacare/HHS fiasco; *Obergefell*; the metastasizing police-surveillance state; the exponentially declining middle class and increasing pauperization of the 99%; the vulgar-ization, brutalization, illiterization, and sexualization of mass cul-ture—caused and supported by monopolistic media conglomerates and the federal government; the criminal rapaciousness, systemic usury, and institutionalized and legally protected mendacity of the 1% (both national and global). The federal government is now opposed to the existence and autonomy of genuine, non-alliance, common good seeking-and-embodying *poleis* within its boundaries. But wasn't it always this way? The individual states never had any *real* rights, *pace* the rhetoric of the Tenth Amendment, which takes away with the left hand what it gives with the right. The Anti-Federalists were right. As Locke would have it, all groups, practices, and institutions that actually aim at the common good, virtue, and human flourishing in the United States are, by definition and law, privatized and depoliticized, relegated to "civil society," or as Rawls called it, the "background culture." Can these flourish better in such a marginalized, depoliticized, and demoralized position, as American political mythology insists? The early history of the United States says no. Can they flourish at all, barring miracles of grace, in such a position? The state of contemporary American culture suggests they cannot.

The U.S. Constitution affords the federal government a political monopoly over every citizen, as the Anti-Federalists warned it would. The newly federated government did not exercise this monopoly at the beginning, as it had *appeared* to delegate much governing authority to the states. In other words, it was de facto precluded from monopolizing political and economic power by those non-Madisonian/non-Lockean, Aristotelian/Pius XI/distributist/agrarian/Tocquevillian/subsidiarist principles and practices that remained in the American political culture—at least for a little while. The states grew less and less sovereign over their own citizens and are now practically non-existent as competing loci of power with the "Federal" (read, Leviathan). Why is it that the states in America gave up their governing autonomy so soon after the Constitution was implemented? And why, after the Civil War, did things get so much worse in terms of centralization of power and loss of states' rights? Was it because authentic classical liberalism was rejected, as George might say? Or was it that classical liberal principles and institutions were fully actualized, as Michael Hanby has compellingly argued?[4]

---

4. Michael Hanby, "The Civic Project of American Christianity," *First Things* (February 2015).

135

In the absence of the balancing dynamic of non-liberal principles, institutions, and practices that embody community-integrat-
ing and substantive human goods, that is, *poleis*, what can a nation-
state do otherwise than create citizens and institutions in its intrin-
sic-good-eschewing image? Was the centralized statism that Lincoln
set in motion in order to "save the Union" intended or unintended
by him? by the Founding Fathers? What does it mean for a state to
be "indivisible" other than that it has become a sacred monolith? If
the main principles of the American Founding, i.e., limited, instru-
mental-good-providing government, religious freedom, and the
preservation of inalienable human rights, are not the root of the
problem, as George, I think, would say, then one has to ask why precisely these principles were not stuck to, why centralization of
power occurred as it did and so quickly, why those genuinely common good communities that were supposed to have worked hand-
in-glove with the alliance-government have suffered so much under
the American regime.

The good can be truly known, embodied, practiced, and possessed only in communities and practices of virtue, as both George
and Hannon, the instrumentalist and intrinsicist, accept. But what
if common good communities of intrinsic worth can only embody
and enable intrinsic goods if they are also, to some extent, *political*
communities, that is, ones with real political and legal teeth, self-
sufficient and architectonic, with actual deliberative, judiciary, and
executive power? What if the ability of smaller intrinsic-good-
embodying-and-enabling communities to survive and flourish
requires the larger society in which they exist to itself be embodied
politically in a more-than-instrumental way? What if the *sine qua
non* of the solution to a government out of control and at odds with
basic human goods is a radical alternative to the alliance-nation-
state of America? If these things are true, then what we desperately
need is a newly revamped and reconfigured and workable Aristotelian *polis*, one subordinate to the divine *polis* of the Roman Catholic
Church. For the political order by nature, even the American one, is
all about intrinsic goods, and ineradicably so. In other words, Aristotle—and Aquinas, and MacIntyre, and Leo XIII—are right.

13

From Socratic Subverter
to Status-Quo Supporter

What MacIntyre Knows

What Alasdair MacIntyre *used* to know, and has been the master teacher of for decades, is that the modern nation-state, particularly in its present Leviathanian-Imperial configuration, cannot, on its own terms and by its own power, do anything truly good for its citizens. MacIntyre has argued consistently and forcefully that political liberalism, whether European or American, due to its essential foundation in the anti-Aristotelian, pro-Lockean privatization of the good, its defective, Enlightenment-inherited notion of practical reason (which inevitably becomes the Nietzschean will to power, albeit a smiling bureaucratic and therapeutic one), its Weberian compartmentalization of agency and authority, and its embodiment, since the late nineteenth century, in nation-states of ever increasing unnatural size and unwieldy complexity, is simply not adequate to the job of true politics, a politics of the common good. Rather, *pace* its stubborn defenders, such as John Rawls on the left and Pierre Manent on the right, the liberally construed nation-state is, according to MacIntyre, simply not a functional political order. Yes, it seems to do "political" things sometimes, but as I argued in the previous chapter, the nation-state is an alliance-pretending-to-be-a-*polis*, an alliance being *sub*-political; and the American nation-state, through having a Lockean/Hobbesian/Rousseauian conception of politics and man (with their opposing elements somehow alchemically synthesized) enshrined in our authoritative documents and political ethos *ab initio*, aims only at preserving life and natural liberty (and property, if you like), but not the *good* life and *moral* liberty. As Kenneth Craycraft has shown, the Founders effectively established the philosophy of liberalism as the "religion" of the nation, leading to the indeterminate and vacuous, Enlightenment/Masonic religion of religious liberty.[1]

But all is well and good, for it is the privilege and prerogative of sub-and-supra-state agencies, practices, groups, and institutions of *civil* society, so the liberal story goes, such as the family, philanthropic associations, and churches, to secure the common good and the flourishing of individuals—not the *state*. Being a morally and religiously neutral agent, by design and common consent, the liberal state *cannot know* what the good is, so it is charged merely to create and maintain safe spaces of civic freedom in which those other quite capable agencies and individuals, the ones that *can* and *do* know the good, can secure it for themselves and the public at large. Of course, *good* is still in some sense determined by the liberal state, as the state, and it alone, is the only agency permitted and authorized to employ coercive power to restrict the practice—and sometimes even the expression, if it is politically incorrect and "harmful" enough—of any conception of the good that inhibits the freedom of others to live out their self-chosen conceptions of the good.

In short, the liberal democratic state is, it itself insists, "non-confessional," and as such is superior to all political orders that came before it. In restricting itself to promoting and defending the *private* interests of its citizens, and only those public interests—the "general welfare"—that are a means to securing private interests, man is liberated from being, as Rousseau famously stated, "everywhere in chains." But, as MacIntyre has argued, by the fact that the liberal state does not dictate to citizens what its interests should be, or try to secure them by its unwieldy and morally ignorant power, it is not a true political order. It is, rather, a "public interest" organization, more like a utility company than a city—though one that sometimes asks us to die for it, and, in William T. Cavanaugh's amplifica-

---

1. Kenneth R. Craycraft, Jr., *The American Myth of Religious Freedom* (Dallas: Spence, 2008).

tion, kill for it. We do sometimes benefit from the state's largesse, but this is accidental to, and many times in spite of, its intentional motives and actions.

In MacIntyre's view, the state, at its best, provides space and resources for the obtaining of certain modest, private goods by and for individuals; and it can secure some protection from criminal depredations, economic fraud, and domestic and foreign violence. Liberal democracy can and has established tolerable public orders. However, due to its bloated size, ubiquitous scope, centripetal centralization, and, most importantly, ideological contradictions, such "benefits" have usually been at the expense of, and even on the backs of, the poor, the marginalized, and the politically powerless. It is also not too friendly to those who accept God's law as standing higher than the state's laws, and who talk and act like it, such as those few non-state-worshipping Christians that still exist in America, e.g., Kim Davis. But whatever good it has done for us, the liberal state always seems to place obstacles to its citizens' moral and spiritual flourishing as the inevitable accompaniment of its blandishments. It tends to morally lobotomize its citizens.

Suffice it to say, MacIntyre has not in the past been a supporter of the American political, cultural, and economic *status quo*. He has repeatedly criticized the contemporary practice of "free market" capitalism for its elitism, irrationality, injustice, and deceitfulness; he has depicted the centralized, bureaucratic nation-state as an "unmanageable and dangerous institution," pretending to be a moral agent but almost always acting like a moral idiot, demanding of its dupes to treat it like a mere utility company, but then, sometimes, asking them to "die for the telephone company"; and he has excoriated the infernal union of consumerist, corporate capitalism and irrational, bureaucratic politics as just another form of the tyrannical liberalism that transcends party lines:

> Liberalism . . . is often successful in preempting the debate by reformulating quarrels and conflicts with liberalism so that they appear to have become debates within liberalism, putting in question this or that particular set of attitudes or policies, but not the fundamental tenets of liberalism with respect to individuals and

the expression of their preferences. So, so-called conservatism and so-called radicalism in these contemporary guises are in general mere stalking-horses for liberalism: the contemporary debates within modern political systems are almost exclusively between conservative liberals, liberal liberals, and radical liberals. There is little place in such political systems for the criticism of the system itself, that is, for putting liberalism in question.[2]

What MacIntyre Doesn't Know

In short, MacIntyre has been, from the publication of his magisterial *After Virtue* in 1981 to his provocative *God, Philosophy, Universities* in 2009, perhaps the most influential and sophisticated Socratic subverter of liberalism and the pretensions of the liberal nation-state in the Western world.

However, in his 2015 plenary lecture, "Justification of Coercion and Constraint,"[3] given at the Notre Dame Ethics and Culture Conference, Alasdair MacIntyre not only posed no challenging questions to the liberal nation-state, but also gave arguments to justify its employment of coercive power, and not just in theory. MacIntyre called for the strong use of nation-state power, right now and right here, in the realms of health, education, military service, and public speech. And judging from the import of his words, MacIntyre was not calling merely for a small-scale, non-Lockean, *polis*-like, natural law founded, subsidiarity-respecting, good-knowing-and-willing, morally capable, alliance-transcending, and otherwise legitimate, trustworthy, modest, and capable political authority to be empowered to secure certain morally robust goods and prevent certain morally repugnant evils through coercion and constraint—something he has called for in the past. The clear import of his words was that the power and authority to regulate health (government-mandated vaccines with no exemptions), dictate education (government prescribed "virtue education"), mandate military service (this indeed seems to be the import of his words), and punish acts of pub-

---

2. MacIntyre, *Whose Justice?*, 394.
3. It may be watched here: https://www.youtube.com/watch?v=9nxoKvb5Uo4.

lic speech (swift and severe penalties for "harmful speech") is to be wielded by none other than the actual nation-state of today, which he once deemed a "dangerous and unmanageable institution."

If an embedded intellectual, talking-head, think-tank elitist, globalist apologist for empire, or spokesman for the industries of education, medicine, or the military, that is, an obvious court sophist and regime propagandist, had said what MacIntyre said, it would be unsurprising; but Alasdair MacIntyre? Is this the same Alasdair MacIntyre who in 2004 wrote this anti-voting manifesto[4] for the same Notre Dame Center for Ethics and Culture (which is, curiously, no longer available on their website)?

> When offered a choice between two politically intolerable alternatives, it is important to choose neither. And when that choice is presented in rival arguments and debates that exclude from public consideration any other set of possibilities, it becomes a duty to withdraw from those arguments and debates, so as to resist the imposition of this false choice by those who have arrogated to themselves the power of framing the alternatives. . . . In this situation a vote cast is not only a vote for a particular candidate, it is also a vote cast for a system that presents us only with unacceptable alternatives. The way to vote against the system is not to vote.

It would be wonderful if health, war, education, and speech could be more effectively, intelligently, beneficially, and justly administered and managed by the liberal nation-state. But certain questions arise when one seriously considers that possibility. On the topic of mandatory vaccinations: why do we find no suspicion whatsoever in MacIntyre's lecture regarding the possibility of government vaccine policy being influenced by a profit and ideology driven scientific establishment working hand in glove with a corrupt Big Pharma? Granting that some vaccines have been very beneficial to humanity, why did MacIntyre not speak about the harmful, sometimes fatal, vaccines conceived and sold to the public in the wedding of these two corrupt institutions? Why did MacIntyre claim, nay,

4. http://brandon.multics.org/library/macintyre/macintyre2004vote.html.

insist, that vaccine technology is based upon the "best science available"? How does he know this? Why would he trust so naively in such notoriously money and prestige driven, government-entangled institutions as contemporary science and pharmaceutical medicine?

Regarding coercion by the state in the realm of education: as MacIntyre has told us many times, the liberal state is based firmly upon the "privatization of the good" (the title of his inaugural lecture as Chair of Philosophy at Notre Dame in 1990), as well as the relativism of moral and religious claims, the quantification and pragmatization of knowledge, and the ideological hegemony of power utilitarianism. Should such a state have its coercive power *increased* so as to dictate not only education policy in general, but also the curricular content, including, as MacIntyre suggested in his lecture, inculcation in those virtues that can best empower students to make moral choices? Which "virtues" would these be exactly? Which choices, and for what ends? Would students be taught to serve the common good and moral, intellectual, and spiritual flourishing, or would they end up serving the gods of mammon and empire, becoming either their mindless devotees or their elite and equally mindless priests? As MacIntyre knows, and as John Taylor Gatto has demonstrated,[5] the mindset of most educrats is the product of a formation and training in the ideology of John Dewey, that is, a concoction of naturalism, collectivism, emotivism, progressivism, materialism, atheism, Darwinism, pragmatism, democratism, and utilitarianism.

Regarding coercion by the state in enforcing military service (MacIntyre didn't explicitly call for a draft, but his words implied that military service and state coercion can go together): is the nation-state, along with its globalist overseers, NATO, the UN, and the Zionist entity in Palestine, as well as the sundry NGOs that wage untold influence over military policy and the financial and armament industries to which such policy is often wedded, and in its

---

5. John Taylor Gatto, *The Underground History of American Education* (New York: Odysseus Group, 2000).

present power configuration of global empire,[6] capable of waging a just war? Have its wars over the past two decades been manifestly *just*? Apparently not, at least if they have been anything like the invasion and occupation of Iraq, which even the most stalwart war hawks now admit was based upon deliberate lies, and thoroughly unjust *ad bellum* and *in bello*. And how about since World War II? In their 2013 book *On Western Terrorism*,[7] Chomsky and Vltchek claim and document that "between 50 and 55 million people have died around the world as a result of Western colonialism and neocolonialism since the end of World War II." And what about the horrific-to-contemplate phenomenon of false-flag, state-sponsored terrorism, which is now, due to the Internet and courageous journalists and writers, no longer a forbidden topic of discourse? In fact, it has now been substantially documented in peer-reviewed journals.[8] Of course, citizens must defend their country against enemies, foreign and domestic—when there is an *actual*, not made up, imminent threat—and sometimes this may require coercion and restraints on certain individual freedoms, but, we're dealing with aggressive wars based on lies.

MacIntyre also called for the state to have the power to limit and punish speech whenever it is "harmful or dishonest." But it must be asked: who decides whether speech is harmful or dishonest, and upon what criteria? I am tempted to say something here about "the

6. David Vine, "The United States Probably Has More Foreign Military Bases Than Any Other People, Nation, or Empire in History," *The Nation* (September 14, 2015), available at https://www.thenation.com/article/the-united-states-probably-has-more-foreign-military-bases-than-any-other-people-nation-or-empire-in-history/.

7. *On Western Terrorism: From Hiroshima to Drone Warfare* (London: Pluto Press, 2013).

8. Lance deHaven-Smith, "When Political Crimes Are Inside Jobs: Detecting State Crimes Against Democracy," *Administrative Theory & Praxis* 28.3 (September 2006): 330–55; "Conjuring the Holographic State: Scripting Security Doctrine for a (New) World of Disorder" (Matthew Witt is lead author), *Administration & Society* 40.6 (October 2008): 547–85; "Preventing State Crimes against Democracy" (with Matthew Witt), *Administration & Society* 41.5 (September 2009): 527–50; "Beyond Conspiracy Theory: Patterns of High Crime in American Government," *American Behavioral Scientist* 53.6 (February 2010): 795–825.

pot calling the kettle black." Couldn't such censoring measures, in the present Orwellian climate of mass propaganda (read Jacques Ellul's *Propaganda* on this) and endless wars and rumors of wars (most if not all based upon lies) result in the empowerment of the federal government to punish more effectively and ruthlessly those who dare to question publicly its propaganda, immoral activities, and self-serving agenda? Of course, manifestly dishonest and harmful speech can and should be justly suppressed, when prudent, by legal force. But, again, Whose "dishonesty"? Which "harm"? Recall that the government of Oceania in Orwell's *1984* was given such *carte blanche* power with similar justifications. Who is to watch the watchers?

*Un*justified Coercion and Constraint

In sum, why was there no hesitation in MacIntyre to give philosophical support to the coercive power of a nation-state that has shown itself more than willing to use its redoubtable powers to promote and protect domestically sodomy, usury, fornication, contraception, and abortion, and abroad to engage in preemptive strikes, regime change, drone assassinations, and aggressive, illegal, immoral wars? This is the same government that has shown itself able and willing to hide its misdeeds with a sophisticated and ubiquitous propaganda ministry that exerts much influence, even control, over mainstream media, entertainment, law, and academia, and to punish with media calumny, legal penalties, and even violence those who blow the whistle on these crimes, expose the lies, and unmask the propaganda. Remember, or learn, that we are dealing with a federal government that, with Obama, has given itself presidential power to detain American citizens indefinitely without evidence or trial—the so-called National Defense Authorization Act.

Are we living under a political order that can be trusted to wield its tremendous coercive power for good, or is the picture more like this: rule by secrecy and deception; rule by bureaucrats, demagogues, unelected agencies and officials, "experts," lobbies, pressure from foreign governments, big banks and big bankers, Wall Street financial elites, the Federal Reserve, special-interest groups, corporate power, globalist elites, NGO's—rule by, first and foremost, secularist and Zionist ideology and power and money and prestige? If things are even remotely close to the picture I have drawn, then prudence dictates that federal and even some state powers should be restricted, decentralized, and enervated, while being distributed to those more local governments and mediating institutions, elected agencies, and individuals—that is, to people of good will, who can and do actually know the good, and can embody and promote a true common good and human flourishing. But even if we live under something less malevolent than my dour description, is it prudent to justify the power and prerogative of the nation-state *at this time*? The time of Obergefell, HHS, and NDAA? The time of a never-ending and escalating "War on Terror," a war that is better named the war *of* terror, for it has only led to *increased* terror, the destruction of millions of innocent Muslims, and the restriction of the liberty of citizens?

All of the coercive and restraining measures MacIntyre called for would be appropriate for a genuine political order, one whose scale allowed for a robust conception of the common good and for the governing agents to know and secure what human flourishing actually entails, but, again, we are dealing now with a "Deep State," a ruling class that is certainly not "neutral towards comprehensive conceptions of the good," but at war, morally and spiritually, with the Good in general and the citizens' good in particular. I used to live in a small town where there are still hints of the "old America," the one de Tocqueville admired, but when you leave small towns and go out to where the federal government and its innumerable agencies have more power and influence, what one finds, as a function of increasing government size and scope, is rule by corruption, deceit, exploitation, and propaganda—in short, soft tyranny. We still have remnants of real political authority, particularly on local levels, and there are good people doing good things on all levels of government, and this is what I still love about the American people, their "don't tread on me!" dignity—but it is the federal government, and now even state governments (which, it would seem, have no real independent power anymore vis-à-vis the Federal, although they might try asserting their power sometime against the feds and see what happens) that is doing the worst treading. So, I can understand desiring to empower local governments and mediating institutions with more coercive authority vis-à-vis the state, to have more authority to change the present health-care racket, more power over protecting their own land and property against state confiscation and robbery, more power over true educational needs instead of educratic insanities, and more power over reasonable limits of free speech (not the silencing of whistleblowers and truth-tellers). But empowering small-scale authorities and agencies to do these things is quite different from empowering bureaucracy, unelected elites, and the federal government to do them.

The contemporary practices, at the federal level at least, of state-mandated education, war, medicine, and the policing of "free speech," are, at worst, abysmally corrupt and destructive of the good, and at best, driven by a combination of financial and ideological forces along with some genuine health, knowledge, and safety concerns, with *some* genuine competency in these areas. Again, I am certainly not against the use of true governmental power in securing the best public education; waging *defensive* and *manifestly just* wars—not wars for empire and *libido dominandi*; providing harmless and disease-preventing vaccines; and ensuring an honest and propaganda-free public square. But the government must actually be a true government, with its agencies acting on a more or less true knowledge of the human good, to do these things. As a Thomist and Catholic, and not a libertarian, I see no problem with true political authority, one with a modest size, a consistent theory and practice of subsidiarity, and a non-liberal, more-or-less Aristotelian/Thomistic, natural law and common good foundation, that is, a state actually capable of knowing and securing the common good, using its power to promote and even enforce the good in the realms of education, the military, medicine, and culture, as well as other realms where the common good is at stake. In this I tend to disagree with the radical Augustinians, such as William Cavanaugh and Stanley Hauerwas—though for all I know, they may be more right than I presently think they are—who are more libertarian, tending towards anarchism in their approach to state power. But, again, I would support more state power only if such a state, in practice and not just in words, were to respect subsidiarity, the antecedent and superior rights and privileges of the family, the superior moral and spiritual, and, dare I say, *political* authority of the Catholic Church on moral and spiritually relevant political issues, as well as all other institutions and practices based upon immemorial and good customs, and the natural and divine positive laws. Does our present nation-state configuration respect these things? Is it even possible for it to do so, based as it is upon a Lockean/Rawlsian privatization of the good and relativism of the true? Is the modern state even capable of recognizing, let along respecting and protecting, any competing authorities or powers? Based not only on its theoretical underpinnings, but also on the history of the state's actual behavior since its birth in the so-called "Wars of Religion" (truly the Wars of the Nation-State, as William Cavanaugh has persuasively argued[9]), it is not so capable.[10]

When the state's coercive power is used on behalf of the true good of its citizens' bodies *and* souls, it is legitimate and worthy of support and consent. But can the coercive power of the liberal, social contract, consent-absolutist, centralized, bureaucratic, managerial, secularist, pluralist, technocratic state, where an increasing pluralism of irreconcilable conceptions of the good is relentlessly promoted and even demanded (multicultural ideology, unrestricted immigration policy), and where equal preference satisfaction (*Casey* and *Obergefell* in theory, abortion and same sex marriage in practice) has become the absolute criterion of "good" government and healthy culture, be used on behalf of the true good of its citizens? No one has argued more persuasively for the need to ask this question, and to ask it seriously, than Alasdair MacIntyre. But, it appears, no more.

---

9. William T. Cavanaugh, "'A Fire Strong Enough to Consume the House': The Wars of Religion and the Rise of the State," *Modern Theology* 11.4 (October 1995): 397–420.

10. As Robert Nisbet argued powerfully in 1953 in *The Quest for Community: A Study in the Ethics of Order and Freedom* (Wilmington: ISI Books, 2010).

Out of the Cave, Into the Light

I mentioned earlier that I would try to explain what might account for MacIntyre's giving philosophical support to the power of the modern liberal state when he has been so adamantly against it, in both theory and practice, for so many years. Honestly, I am not sure, and I hope that I have misunderstood the import of his entire lecture. If I have, I am ready to be corrected. But if I did not misunderstand it, I think there is one plausible explanation: if Alasdair MacIntyre, a respected and influential public Catholic intellectual, were to say plainly that the emperor has no clothes on, by talking about the real dangers of the Deep State, or its imperialistic crimes and domestic tyrannies; if he told the full truth of the decadence and corruption of our political parties—both of them—as well as academia, law, media, police, the military, intelligence, and entertainment, all of which support, and are, to some extent, complicit in these same crimes and tyrannies, he would soon be relegated to the academic, social, and political margins, and he would certainly not be invited to give any more Notre Dame plenary lectures. Perhaps this pressure, along with a naïve (and uncharacteristic for a Socratic philosopher) credulity towards mainstream narratives and claims of the state and its various official mouthpieces, explains why a man who has been for decades the preeminent spokesman in academia of the political defectiveness and duplicity of liberalism and the liberal nation-state, would be willing to give support to the corrupt, mendacious, and money-and-ideology-driven practices of medical profiteering, educational sophistry, unjust belligerency, and truthful speech-policing.

One could see that these practices are as I characterize them if one looked carefully enough at the *actual* practices, and not what their paid lackeys and court sophists say about them, that is, the people who pretend to be statesmen, experts, doctors, educators, lawyers, journalists, and professors, but are actually just paid apologists for a corrupt regime, puppeteers in the cave, with most of them probably completely unaware of what they are doing and who they are really working for. MacIntyre is certainly not one of these, but perhaps he has been overly influenced by them in recent years, as all of us undoubtedly have been. Their malign influence is inescapable now, though we can do things to protect ourselves against it.

To see the actual practices for what they are requires turning one's gaze away from the seductive shadows, and this means, first and foremost, from the mainstream media—in both its left and its right masks. I mean *media* in its fundamental sense—that which *mediates*, but does not actually offer, reality to us. Then we need to look toward the puppets and puppeteers that construct the shadows, the mediated lies, "facts," narratives, reports, etc. Next, we need to expose the counterfeit firelight, which darkens the mind with Manichean scapegoating, inner-circle intrigues, and dogmatic answers with no questions. Finally, we repair to the real light of truth, humility, and courage streaming into the cave. It is Christ, the *Logos*, and the Church, the real world, and good-willed people that iconically mediate His presence. With the Internet we still have ready access to truth-mediating media, and if we can get a decent liberal arts education and a sense of historical context to fill in the Orwellian memory hole, become and remain good-willed, practice natural virtue and become disposed to supernatural virtues, and, above all, practice as much as possible the presence of God in our hearts, in silence, and within the world around us, we can learn, know, and love the Truth and save our souls. We *must* not simply accept mainstream media and government narratives and claims anymore, no matter how much psychological and emotional pressure there is to do so. God will judge us for preferring shadows to reality.

I hope I have at least made a plausible case that Christians and freedom-loving men of good will should think twice about following MacIntyre's blanket endorsement of state power, prerogative, and scope in these four vital areas of human welfare, as well as any area that can seriously affect our souls. Let us remember the big picture. The earthly City of Man has always been and will always be opposed to the City of God, that is, the *true* religion, the Church that embodies it, and all those men and women who love her and what she stands for, whether official members of Her or not. The present-day culture of the West is not liberal, tolerant, rationalist, religiously neutral, enlightened, morally progressive, secular, and non-violent. Notwithstanding the heroic efforts of good people who have created alternative sub-cultures ordered to truth, beauty, goodness, freedom, and virtue—in a word, to God—mainstream culture, including mainstream political and imperial culture, which is now under the empire of mammon and ideology, is becoming increasingly totalitarian, intolerant, materialist, atheist, fideist, spiritualist (dark spiritualism), religiously fanatical (the religion of anti-*logos*), morally decadent, inquisitional, and violent—all its endless and ubiquitous propaganda to the contrary notwithstanding. If you want a good depiction of what American mass culture is becoming, read Thucydides' description of the plague at Athens during the Peloponnesian War:

> The sacred places also in which they had quartered themselves were full of corpses of persons that had died there, just as they were; for as the disaster passed all bounds, men, not knowing what was to become of them, became utterly careless of everything, whether sacred or profane.... Nor was this the only form of lawless extravagance which owed its origin to the plague. Men now coolly ventured on what they had formerly done in a corner, and not just as they pleased, seeing the rapid transitions produced by persons in prosperity suddenly dying and those who before had nothing succeeding to their property. So they resolved to spend quickly and enjoy themselves, regarding their lives and riches as alike things of a day. Perseverance in what men called honor was popular with none, it was so uncertain whether they would be spared to attain the object; but it was settled that present enjoyment, and all that contributed to it, was both honorable and useful. Fear of gods or law of man there was none to restrain them. As for the first, they judged it to be just the same whether they worshipped them or not, as they saw all alike perishing; and for the last, no one expected to live to be brought to trial for his offenses, but each felt that a far severer sentence had been already passed upon them all and hung ever over their heads, and before this fell it was only reasonable to enjoy life a little.[11]

For, at the heart of all cultures, *pace* the Enlightenment and its post-Enlightenment child of nihilistic technocracy—a chip off the

---

11. *The Peloponnesian War*, at 2.52.3.

old block—is always the Sacred, and at the heart of our post-IXXI imperial culture of death and deceit is a terrifying sacred power in mortal conflict with the *Logos*, with Christ. What we need, then, is, not an easy compromise with and valorization of state power, nor a total rejection of it, but its—and *our*—healing, repentance, and transformation. This requires a wholehearted fight against the increasing nihilism and power-worship that has poisoned American political culture, with its ever centralizing, punishing, restricting, censoring, surveilling, taxing, policing, invading, terrorizing, bombing, droning, and lying state practices, and the propaganda that hides them, which cunningly portrays the state as beholden to the people's will and their rights, and promoting only our "freedom" and "security," even while it acts only for its own interests and the interests of immoral and power-insane elites. And now, as MacIntyre's portrayal of liberalism would lead one to suspect, we are dealing with an emboldened ruling class, both left and right (a quite effective controlled opposition), that has become in their own eyes, and, tragically, in the eyes of many American Christians, an unimpeachable, unquestionable authority brooking no opposition. Just consider the reprehensible way many Christian "conservatives" treated the heroic act of Kim Davis against the state.[12]

How this resistance to the state might be translated into Christian teaching and everyday life, as well what a blueprint for building a political culture of love, truth, goodness, solidarity, humility, non-violence, compassion, and beauty might look like, are matters that need urgently to be addressed by Church leaders, lay and clergy, and Christian intellectuals, especially at places like Notre Dame.

---

12. The following chapter takes up this issue in detail.

14

When Christians
Persecute Their Own

E very Catholic, Christian, and man of good will should have
recognized as soon as the decision was made that the so-
called "law of the land" of *Obergefell* is pure lawlessness and
will-to-power, and this, not because the Supreme Court does not
have the constitutional right to interpret law, but because its interpretation, insofar as it makes legal the violation of the natural and
divine law on marriage, is wrong. And it should also be obvious that
the Supreme Court itself, insofar as it accepts no higher law than
itself—however much it may make deceptive references to the
authorities of the Constitution, precedent, scientific consensus,
rights to privacy, *ad nauseum*—is itself a highly questionable political and legal authority. So, what to make of otherwise conservative
and traditional Christians, highly educated ones at that, implicitly
defending *Obergefell* and the authority of the Supreme Court,
Christians who were not too long ago criticizing both unequivocally? With regard to none other than *Obergefell*, we heard these
Christian intellectuals solemnly utter declamations about "the law
of the land" and "the rule of law."

In the meantime, an ordinary, not highly educated woman,
belonging to an obscure Christian sect, one who, we now know, was
steeped in sins related to marriage herself, but who was trying to
obey in a public way what small grasp of Jesus Christ's teachings on
sexuality she had—in this case, a quite accurate grasp of His condemnation of sodomy and sodomite marriage—was discredited,
humiliated, undermined, and indeed persecuted by these same conservative Christian intellectuals. Their criticisms of her and her

refusal to sign same-sex marriage licenses were not remotely as malicious and vitriolic as were those from the secularist left, and they were careful to make distinctions, qualify their condemnation of her defiant act, and otherwise pad and couch what amounted to a betrayal of a fellow Christian in her time of trial. They showed no solidarity with Kim Davis whatsoever.

That Christians, and especially Catholics, have been engaged in attacking, ridiculing, undermining, and, it must be said, scapegoating Kim Davis—who, whatever real faults one may find in her tactics (maybe resigning was the better option) and character (she's been divorced and remarried several times), was actively resisting the tyranny of liberalism of the Kennedy/Obama Regime in its programmatic attack on Christianity and the natural law—is, it must be said, scandalous and disgraceful. I would have thought for sure that conservative Christians, especially Catholics, would have responded to the Kim Davis event, not with statements like "She took an oath and needs to do her job or resign," but with arguments more along these lines:

1. The present Kentucky law states unequivocally that marriage is between a man and a woman. Thus Kim Davis is upholding that law, and that was indeed the law at the time she was sworn in and made her oath.

2. *Pace Obergefell* and its tendentious interpreters, there is no "law of the land" mandating that marriage is not uniquely and exclusively between a man and a woman, and that all civil authorities must secure and facilitate and preside over same-sex marriage. Please show me the *law*. And even if there were such a law, no one is obligated to obey or enforce or facilitate an unjust law, which is precisely what any law is that promotes same-sex marriage or sodomy.

3. *Obergefell* is a blatant attack on the natural law and Christianity and so can be disobeyed by citizens, and treated, not as legitimate law, but as a tyrannical act of force, the imposition of elite ideology on majority rule, states' rights, the Constitution, the natural law, and Christianity.

4. Since the arbitrary will of a small ideological minority has been and is now being imposed on due-process majority rule, on sacred customs, on state laws in good standing, on the freedom of religion

(properly understood), on the freedom of institutions to act in accordance with the dictates of their beliefs (without any compelling reason to the contrary), public resistance to this tyranny is surely a live and legitimate option, with when, where, and to what extent dictated by prudence.

5. No American can be forced to enforce, cooperate with, or facilitate the application of an unjust law, regardless of the present status of her moral character and the precision of her grasp of Christian ecclesiology and dogma. Kim Davis has every right, and perhaps the duty, to disobey the order that she put her name to licenses for sodomite marriage. She could have resigned, yes, and perhaps that would have been the better move. But she had every right not to resign.

Notwithstanding all the sophisticated, absurd mental gymnastics displayed by public, "conservative" Christian intellectuals, such as Rod Dreher, to disparage and even mock Kim Davis in the name of defending the "rule of law,"[1] she was imprisoned because she would not comply with the legal and political support of same-sex marriage, something evil in itself, but which also entails endorsing the practice of sodomy, a sin that cries out to heaven for vengeance. Anyone who denies that Kim Davis was persecuted because she displayed a principled opposition to the homosexual agenda is living in an unreality of legal positivist ideology, state idolatry, subterfuge, scapegoating, and sophistry. And this describes most especially the Catholic and Christian "conservatives" who threw a fellow Christian under the bus, who, indeed, persecuted one of their own, however "soft" in mode. I would never have predicted that this would be the way otherwise upstanding public Christian intellectuals would respond to the beginnings of the coercive persecution of Christians in America. But then again, cowardice, backstabbing, moral incoherence, and hypocrisy are the norm in American culture, so why should one expect anything different from embedded intellectuals

1. See here for an example: http://www.theamericanconservative.com/dreher/kim-davis-political-prisoner-martyr/. In 2017, this same "conservative" journal fired the great Philip Giraldi for writing an article on another journal critical of the State of Israel.

with a vested interest in appearing respectable and sophisticated, and maintaining their intellectual prestige and authority? Those who choose the respect of men over the respect of God already have their reward.

What accounts for the emergence of such a strange group-mind (to use the term of John McMurtry[2]) among Christian conservatives? In addition to, perhaps, a pre-rapture separation of the wheat from the tares, the sheep from the goats, the Peters from the Judases, what we are also seeing is an exemplary instance of the radical incoherency of moral and political discourse and practice in America, something Alasdair MacIntyre has been talking about for decades. We do not have in America, and never had in anything but fits and starts and on the local level, rational and widespread political deliberation eventuating in the rule of laws delivered through such deliberation; rather, we now have, and have had for some time, the rule of arbitrary fallen men, the wills of "experts" imposed on the rest of us with no deliberation, protest, or resistance permitted, unless it be merely private or otherwise sterile and harmless (the Occupy Wall Street protest was not sterile and harmless; hence, its having been violently quashed). And it cannot be otherwise when theological and moral and metaphysical considerations are shunned in public discussion, when legal positivism is mandated ideology, when subsidiarity is systematically violated by a centralized, Leviathanian state ruling as an unimpeachable bureaucratic technocracy in which domestically, as James Kalb has shown, the indiscriminate satisfaction of individual preferences is the exclusive and incontestable criterion for the use of coercive state power, and in which non-domestically, the security and growth of a world empire of "creative destruction" is the primary and unquestioned desideratum. What fills the vacuum when *logos* is banned from the public square and banned as the foundation of law is naked, fallen, human will, the human will of ruling-class elites masking as "reason," "the will of the

2. See "The Moral Decoding of 9-11: Beyond the U.S. Criminal State" (2013), *Journal of 9/11 Studies*, volume 35, 1–67, <Moral Decoding-9-11-2013McMurtryVol 35Feb.pdf> reproduced at http://www.globalresearch.ca/the-moral-decoding-of-9-11-beyond-the-us-criminal-state-the-grand-plan-for-a-new-world-order/5323300.

people" or the "rule of law." What we have is the disordered, revolutionary, and *logos*-averse human will of ruling-class elites ruling for their own self-serving desires, and/or the desires of the true Rulers in the Deep State, the precise definition that Aristotle gives of tyranny in his *Politics*.

Of course, we know that the sexual revolutionaries on the left are lying when they talk about the need to obey "the rule of law" and "the Constitution." Along with the conservatives, they wax pious about "obeying the rule of law," when only yesterday they were decrying the tyranny of the law "imposed on us by elite white Christian males," as they work to overthrow all traditional order to hasten the imposition of their utopian, lawless schemes. They were and are anti-*logos* revolutionaries who are mendaciously using the conservative rhetoric of "oaths" and "law of the land" and the like simply because that ploy can further their attack, perversion, undermining, and destruction of the true rule of law, which is the law of truth and goodness, the *logos*, the moral law and those human laws that correspond with it, ultimately all reflecting and supporting the loving rule of God. If human law explicitly reflects in any way the natural law, as it does right now still in Kentucky, for example, they are all for disobeying it and telling others to do so. However, if a moral evil is imposed on the majority tyrannically, as in *Obergefell*, then suddenly they're pious and solemn and constitutional.

But that conservative Christians on the right are employing their own version of this shell game, indicating the same deference to the Hobbesian conception of the legally positivist secularist state as those they purportedly oppose, is telling. Do they really hope to be able to carve out a safe space, a "Benedict Option" to practice Christianity inside of the very Leviathan they are supporting and enabling? They can disassociate themselves from the Kim Davises of the world all they want, but if the Masters suspect they are doing more than Christian play-acting, that is, if they become a real threat to the regime's authority, they are going to be liquidated, one way or another. Already, outspoken pro-lifers, as well as anyone who publicly casts doubt or questions official government narratives, such as IXXI, no matter how preposterous these narratives may be, are being named and surveilled as "domestic terrorists" by Homeland

Security because of the tyrannical Patriot Act. But then again, it is easy for intellectuals to define any action or speech that causes the ruling powers to oppress an individual or group as being "against the rule of law" or "un-American" or "imprudent," and so never to have to suffer for Jesus Christ in the public square.

The persecution is coming, and it is has been shown to us now in the form of a spiritually and morally wounded, hypocritical in some ways, and theologically unsophisticated woman, one who, surely, has shown herself capable of flouting the Bible and the moral law in her past divorces and remarriages. But what she has done by continuing to resist the state's injustice is heroic, perhaps even motivated supernaturally as a penance for her past transgressions. In any event, God likes to humble the proud with such as these, as Flannery O'Connor portrayed for us. Anyone who scapegoated or ridiculed this woman in public is going to have to answer for it before Our Lord.

Is there a solution to all this, other than simply accepting with courage the persecution that seems inevitable? I don't know, but what I do know is that when Catholics who have access to magisterial teaching on the proper ordering of Church and state and claim to believe it, defer to and promote principles and practices that contradict this teaching, America is doomed. As Orestes Brownson maintained in his 1865 masterpiece, *The American Republic*, the American project cannot succeed without Catholicism. But I would go a step further than Brownson and say that the American project cannot succeed unless Catholicism, or at least a robust, Augustinian, natural law based theism, replaces liberalism as the ultimate source of moral and political authority in the state. In this, I am echoing what Aidan Nichols has written with regard to the moral bankruptcy of English political culture without some sort of integrally implemented confessional state model.[3]

As Brad Gregory has so magnificently recounted in his *The Unintended Reformation*, the Protestant revolutionaries denied fundamental truths declared by the infallible teaching authority of the Magisterium of the Catholic Church, as well as the capacity of her

3. See Aidan Nichols, *Christendom Awake*.

custodians and all faithful Christians to be certain of her possession of the truth. They supplanted this ecclesial and magisterial authority and certainty with *sola scriptura*, an inexorably subjective, "from the inside," and thus incoherent conduit to definitive and saving knowledge about Christ. The Enlightenment liberals, stuck in ecclesial subjectivism, epistemological reductionism, and ontological nominalism, then attempted to build something "objective" on this subjectivist sand, and supplanted the Bible with "reason." The postmodernists then supplanted reason with "irony" and "narrative"— in short, the authoritative "truth" that there is no access to universal truth about reality, let alone the will of God, or at least no way to know that one has access to it. And at the end of this line of revolutionaries, we find ideologues like the late Catholic Anthony Kennedy, as well as those Catholics who, though explicitly renouncing ecclesial subjectivism, nominalism, and liberalism, speak and act in practice as though the Catholic Church were just a private sect; as though the truths of the natural and divine law should never have any privileged authority in law; and as though the American experiment would be a success if only Catholics, Christians, and other men of good will were virtuous, active, and sufficiently educated—that is, with no need for any restructuring of the regime in light of Catholic social teaching, the *philosophia perennis*, and the natural law.

But as the Nietzschean Stanley Fish has demonstrated,[4] the just separation of Church and state is, in a word, impossible, if it is to be accomplished within and according to liberalism and the liberal nation-state—and this includes also the classical liberalism of the American Founders, however much better this form of liberalism was than what we have now. If this is true, it would explain why there was no good and rationally coherent solution to the Kim Davis issue. Within the intellectual, moral, legal, and political constraints of the contemporary American regime, a regime that is utterly incoherent on the relations of Church and state, the just separation of Church and state is, as it were, mission impossible. Either

4. "Mission Impossible: Settling the Just Bounds between Church and State," *Columbia Law Review* 97.8 (December 1997): 2255–333.

Davis goes to jail, or she is permitted to abstain from signing the licenses, or some compromise is made. But whichever outcome is determined by the coercive power of the regime, it is not, and cannot be, a rational determination; for, insofar as the American regime, on both the federal level and the local, constitutionally and legally prescinds in its legal and political deliberations from any consideration of the moral and political and theological claims of the Catholic Church, as well as of the authority of the natural law of which she, the Church, is the unique authoritative custodian, and impedes other citizens from considering these authorities in those arguments and debates in the public square, in Congress, in the Senate, in the Supreme Court, and in any other forum where argument and debate can ensue in law, it renders itself incapable of resolving fundamental political issues, let alone ones that bear upon the supernatural realm, the Church's rights and privileges, and the authority of God.

And this is so because, ultimately, only Jesus Christ has the authority to settle the just bounds between Church and state—for He is the author of both. By the fact of His Incarnation, he brought together Church and state, heaven and earth, divinity and humanity, and after bringing them together, He commanded their proper separation: "Render to Caesar what is Caesar's, and to God what is God's." Therefore, in order to know what we owe to Caesar and what we owe to God today, we must listen to His authentic and infallible mouthpiece, which isn't the Supreme Court or "conservative" court sophists. Unless we have access to the voice of Christ, Fish is right—there is no way of solving the problem. Yet there must be a solution, because Christ commanded us to solve the problem. In short, Christ must have given us a sure and "from the outside" way of determining His will regarding the proper ordering of Church and state. Anything other than a living, visible, unified, universal, hierarchical, concrete, corporal institution whose unity, holiness, universality, and apostolicity could be recognized by all "from the outside" could not afford humans the clear determination of Christ's will in matters political, as well as any other matter. Anything less would perpetuate both the denial of access, and the subjective uncertainty of that access, to the definitive truth regarding

Christ's will for the proper ordering of society and the political order, a denial and uncertainty that would make the just separation of the prerogatives of Church and state impossible, and would thus make a just resolution to particular conflicts between Church and state impossible, such as the Kim Davis conflict. What we would have without it is either outright war, or the Procrustean attempt to make the message of the Gospel fit into the arbitrary will of whoever happens to be ruling in the state—in short, chaos or a hopelessly compromised Christianity. And this is indeed what we have, the latter being exemplified in the sophistry of the Christian intellectuals I have exposed.

15

Speaking the Unspeakable:
Political Correctness on the Right

There is and should certainly be much leeway for discussion of Christian social teaching, and contemporary political and economic issues in light of it. There are those who, understandably and legitimately, lean in different directions, more to the left on some issues, and more to the right on others, more libertarian when it comes to economic matters, more conservative on cultural and moral issues, but all intentionally within the ambit of orthodox Christianity and the *philosophia perennis*, within a cosmos of thought that is in line with the entirety of the Gospel and right reason.

However, a serious problem within Christian discourse among those who consider themselves orthodox Christian conservatives is the existence of a certain secular orthodoxy or ideology masquerading as authentically Christian. Now, some level of ideological taint is inevitable in otherwise sound theological and philosophical analyses and discussions, and no one is immune to this. The only way to counteract ideological infestation, which is a liability of all open and free truth-seeking, is to cultivate open, honest, free, respectful, and rigorous discussion. As I see it, the most important principle of such discussion, for those of us subscribing to authoritatively Christian first principles, is that none but these first principles, including those of right reason or the natural law, be *a priori* secure from critical questioning, and even these can be interrogated to ensure correspondence to reality and precision of articulation. I am not advocating complete skepticism on matters outside these secure realms, as if we are not certain of the truth of anything but the Sym-

163

bols of Faith. But even the most fundamental or self-evident truths need to be probed and developed and questioned to ascertain if we are interpreting them correctly and with sufficient depth and complexity, whether we see their proper relation to other truths, and whether we have distortions in our thinking about these and other truths that flow from them, particularly in their application to the world of time and space and human action.

Christians are defined by their unwillingness ever, under penalty of sin, to reject the truths of Faith. Much else, however, is fair game for discussion. This, to me, is the gift and genius of the Western, Christian intellectual tradition. It is tolerant and generous, in the best sense of the terms, but also uncompromising and truth-seeking. It combines unswerving loyalty and belief with the obligation of critical analysis and flexibility. Socrates has not been banished from the Church, for his gadflying helps us to know and to live the absolute truths of our faith in humility. Thus, political correctness is the death of truth-seeking discussion, and so we must reject it, in both its left-wing and right-wing varieties. However, many evangelical and Catholic Christians see and decry only the left-wing version of political correctness, but not the one that especially tempts *them*. This political correctness of which I speak is not deemed debatable by its staunchest and most outspoken proponents, and not only this; it is assumed *a priori* to be in line with Christian orthodoxy. In fact, any view that contradicts its principles or their application to political or economic reality is determined to be heresy, or proof of unbelief and even of immorality. For example, if one articulates a skeptical position with regard to the justice *ad bellum* and the official narrative *in bello* of the "War on Terror," or if one doubts the goodness, truth, and Gospel-appropriateness of Christian Zionism, basing one's doubt upon, among other things, the treatment of Palestinians in Gaza by the Israeli regime, one may find oneself accused of hating one's country or being anti-Semitic. If one expresses skepticism about the truthfulness of government pronouncements and narratives about dramatic, violent events, and the more or less good intentions of our rulers with regard to domestic security policy and the ever-expanding wars, rumors of wars, and occupations, one may be accused of a kind of modernist skepticism about truth in general, or, horror of horrors, of being a "conspiracy theorist." When a Christian questions this political orthodoxy or even any part of it (let alone suggesting that it is altogether unsound), or attempts to interpret contemporary political or economic events in a way different from this rigid orthodoxy, the politically correct ideologues make blatantly *ad hominum* attacks, engage in shaming tactics, and make threats to one's livelihood. It's a kind of neo-Inquisition.

What are the doctrines of this political correctness on the right? From my experience, the following are claims and "facts" one is *not* permitted to question in public lest one be excommunicated from the conservative temple:

• America exercises its military power only or mostly for the sake of good ends using morally justified means, and any unfortunate results like the death of innocents are unintended and eminently excusable in light of the enormous good that is usually the result.

• American empire is, all other things being equal, good for America and for the world. America is and has always been a force for good in the world, and the more force it has, the better off everyone is.

• America, along with Israel, our greatest ally, is a chosen nation with a special charge from God to liberate, democratize, and Americanize the world. One can criticize how this chosenness is sometimes expressed and executed, but if you don't really believe in the American government and military's intrinsic goodness and chosenness, you're one of the bad guys.

• Zionism and Christianity are perfectly reconcilable, and Christians must support Zionism and the State of Israel, even when there is an appearance of injustice on the part of the Israeli government and military.

• Any criticism of Zionism or the State of Israel, except perhaps superficial criticism regarding occasional and unintended misuse of force, is proof of anti-Semitism.

• In conflicts and wars, the state of Israel is always right and the Palestinians are always wrong. Israel fights defensively and the Palestinians fight offensively. Israelis are the victims, and the Palestinians are the aggressors. Israel never intentionally targets civilians. Israel never uses disproportionate force, except on accident. Palestinians who fight for their people and land are terrorists, not an occupied people with a right to self-defense.

• Capitalism is good. Period. Talk about the problems of usury, fiat currency, and banker machinations is the stuff of conspiracy theorists, Islamists, or weird Catholic monarchists and distributists.

• Christianity in general and Catholic social teaching in particular is entirely reconcilable with the principles of the American Founding, American Constitution, and Declaration of Independence. America represents *Good* Liberalism, rooted in the Good American Revolution and the Good Enlightenment of Locke, and blessed by the Church, while Europe represents the *Bad* Liberalism, with roots in the Bad French Revolution and the Bad Enlightenment of Hobbes and Rousseau.

And here are some politically correct applications of the above:

• All the wars engaged in by the United States were done in the name of freedom and democracy in opposition to the enemies of freedom and democracy, and in order to liberate other countries from these enemies, and so have all been, more or less, just wars.

• We shouldn't make too much of the bad ways Native Americans and African Americans were treated in America, for such treatment was a betrayal of true American principles, not a result of following such principles as "Manifest Destiny" and "The City on a Hill."

• The United States fought World War I to make the world safe for democracy, and World War II to liberate the Jews and save the world from Nazism. The standard narratives about the reasons for these wars, and what happened during them, should not be questioned. There were no secret motives or behind-the-scene players, and the results were overwhelmingly good for America and the world. The Germans in Dresden and the Japanese in Hiroshima and Nagasaki were not treated unjustly—or even if they were, it was a strategically necessary use of force.

• The founding of the State of Israel was eminently just in principle and in the way it occurred, and certainly willed by God. Thus,
the state of Israel had the right to displace tens of thousands of
Palestinians in 1948 and in the ensuing decades of conflicts, a right
established in the Old Testament, blessed by Christianity, morally
required due to the Holocaust, and confirmed by the United
Nations.

• America has engaged in Middle East conflicts for purely defensive or humanitarian reasons against an enemy who poses an
imminent threat to us and the world, so they are just exercises of
force.

• The War on Terror is just, *ad bellum* and *in bello*, and morally
necessary to defend America and the West, and any critique of its
narrative, and U.S. behavior in accordance with this narrative, is
equivalent to hating America and helping her enemies. Perhaps
Iraq was a mistake, but one can't expect perfection in war.

• The official American government, IXXI Commission, mass
media explanation of the September 11, 2001, attacks is authoritative, unquestionable, and eminently reasonable. Any questioning
of it whatsoever is a sign of mental insanity, moral turpitude, trea-
son—and probably all three.

• False-flag terrorism, if it exists, was something only Hitler or
Stalin did, and is now engaged in only by "rogue" states or radical
Muslim regimes, like Iran or Pakistan. America and Israel have
never engaged in it.

What prevents Christians from uniting together to create a political order and culture that is God-pleasing and enabling of true
human flourishing is that these doctrines—ones that support the
ideologies and self-serving behavior of the ruling class, and the narcissistic tribal worship, idolatrous self-exceptionalism, and scapegoating passions of the populace—are protected from any critical
analysis and refutation by none other than the millions of politi-
cally-correct Christians who serve this orthodoxy by not only supporting it but also by policing it. This produces in Christians who
seek the truth a real fear of being harmed in their livelihood and
even in their persons, at the hands of "orthodox" Christians, simply

for articulating positions that challenge, directly or indirectly, this Orwellian political orthodoxy. Christian intellectuals need to become more aware and vigilant regarding the influence of this political correctness on the right, and when they see it, to bring it to public awareness so that it can be challenged in a reasonable way. Only the truth deserves unimpeachable authority.

16

The Conspiracy
Against Conspiracy

A conspiracy theory can be used as a psychological and intellectual crutch, an impregnable bulwark against critical thinking, and an excuse for intellectual laziness. However, to have an *a priori*, intransigent skepticism towards any marginalized theory simply because it's marginalized, or because it accuses a particular person or group not obviously suspicious, or simply because it attributes to a minority of specific agents or groups a disproportionate historical and political influence, is itself to hold a kind of conspiracy theory against conspiracy theories. Indeed, the term "conspiracy theorist" is a misnomer, for it denotes, and should connote, *pace* our Orwellian discourse, those who do *not* accept wild and implausible conspiracy theories, such as the one that assigns the ultimate blame for certain buildings being destroyed from the inside, and in spite of defense technologies second to none in the world, to a known CIA-asset sitting in a cave, choreographing jumbo-jet planes with a laptop.

Before one can attack a so-called conspiracy theory, one needs first to discern if it has some measure of rational plausibility. If it does, one has the duty to take the time and energy to analyze it to see if it is actually false before judging it to be so. One should neither believe nor disbelieve any theory, no matter how far-fetched it appears on the surface, without putting it through at least a small measure of Socratic questioning; if it dies at the first barrage of elementary questions, only then can it be summarily dismissed. Simply because a theory might make one feel uncomfortable—perhaps because it threatens the airtight, comfortable, neatly furnished, intellectual penthouse one has created for oneself, doesn't mean it is worthy of dismissal.

Couldn't the facile dismissal of a certain theory about historical causality—let's say, the theory of the profound global influence of Freemasonry—be itself the symptom not of intellectual integrity but of the very success of the dismissed theory? Might not its elusiveness and impenetrability to intellectual analysis and judgment have been planned? When a demon is to be exorcised, it does everything it can to prevent the awareness of its presence, for it knows that once it is discovered, it has already lost the battle. I once listened to a radio talk show in which it was mentioned that many of those who were early and vocal proponents of the Iraq war were Israeli Zionists. Immediately, the statement was dismissed as tantamount to conspiracy-mongering and racism. I am not arguing one way or the other here about the truth of this statement in regard to this war; I am merely pointing out that the analysis of whether this purported fact was true or not was strategically precluded by the mere mention of "conspiracy theory." If it were true that Israeli influence was disproportionate in the decision to attack Iraq, and more recently to attack Iran and Syria, and if this influence had a vested interest in being hidden, I can think of no better means of doing so than of somehow convincing the media to shut down all public discussion at the mention of even a hint of such influence. Once again, without judging the truth or falsity of the aforementioned statement, is it not plausible to consider the existence of some level of concerted effort to prevent the discussion of the veracity of this fact? Is this a "ludicrous" consideration?

It is interesting to note that many who condemn conspiracy theories in one area of historical causality accept them readily in others. For example, many of the same people who see nothing but Annibale Bugnini's face and a coterie of evil men of "The Rhine" when they think about the Second Vatican Council, condemn as antipatriotic or even treasonous those who detect a certain level of organized deception in the "War on Terror." Again, some of those who would easily admit a strategic and planned effort by a minority of atheistic intellectuals to undermine public morality in the revolution of the 1960s in America are the same people who spew supercilious sarcasm and aspersions of disloyalty when it is pointed out that many of the American Founders and Revolutionaries were Freemasons who had the explicit, publicly noted intention of preventing Catholicism from ever having any effective political, moral, and spiritual influence in the Land of the Free.

If Freemasonry is so easily dismissed, then why was it the subject of more papal encyclicals than any other topic in the history of the Catholic Church? On March 13, 1825, Leo XII published his encyclical *Quo Graviora* condemning Freemasonry, as well as all other secret societies. He wrote:

> They have dared publish works on religion and affairs of state, they have exposed their contempt for authority, their hatred of sovereignty, their attacks against the divinity of Jesus Christ and the very existence of God: they openly vaunt their materialism as well as their codes and statutes which explain *their plans and efforts* in order to overthrow the legitimate heads of state and completely destroy the Church.... What is definitely ascertained is that those different sects, despite the diversity of their names, are all united and linked by the *similarity of their infamous plans.*[1]

Are we to be nervous about conspiracy-mongering when we read these words, or should we be more worried about *not* believing in conspiracies enough when they are at least rationally plausible? Could it be that the most ingenious of their "infamous plans" is to conceal their existence by convincing good Catholics that the belief in such traps is almost always symptomatic of psychological disorder or intellectual laziness and narrowness?

There are two errors to guard against. One is to accept only those theories and grand narratives of the world and history, including conspiracy theories, that make us secure in our easychairs, that exculpate us from any blame for the evils in the world. In an essay contest that posed the question, "What is wrong with the World," Chesterton answered, "I." He told the absolute truth. But the other error, just as dangerous, is to fall into the traps of those diabolically influenced and energized men who would need nothing more for

---

1. Emphasis added.

171

their success than for angelically influenced and energized men to turn a blind eye to their machinations under the invincible cover of being "reasonable."

With respect to official narratives, such as those regarding IXXI, the War on Terror, the Aurora, Sandy Hook, and Charlie Hebdo shootings, and the Boston bombing, one must ask himself: what is it about a government's official narrative that warrants immediate acceptance? For someone to begin to question whether he knows what he thinks he knows with regard to any media-mediated event of which he lacks direct experience, all it takes is merely the realization that such events have indeed been significantly and to a large extent *mediated* to him, and that there is no *a priori* reason to believe that the mediators, especially the corporate-controlled, mainstream mediators, are mediating truth. Indeed, there is every reason to doubt the mainstream mediators' capacity or willingness to convey truth. To demonstrate adequately why *a priori* doubt is more reasonable than *a priori* credulity with respect to official narratives regarding such events as 9/11, the War on Terror, and the shootings reported at Aurora, Charlie Hebdo, Sandy Hook, and Las Vegas, would take an entire book. Suffice it to say that independent investigation of these events turns up glaring inconsistencies and what seems like a disinformation program.

Sometimes the emperor (a symbol here for historical reality) wears majestic clothes of many layers, with convolutions and fringes and perforations not to be easily discerned and appreciated in one easy glance. It would be disrespectful to the emperor not to be willing to take a deeper and more detailed look to gain a true appreciation and perspective. But sometime the emperor is truly naked, and respect for him requires one to admit what is obvious to the unprejudiced, unfearful, truth-seeking eye.

Why is the topic of conspiracy important to Catholics? In a word, idolatry. Now, the fundamental prescriptions of the natural law, rigorously researched and corroborated historical and scientific facts, clear scriptural teachings and magisterial doctrines—these may reach the level of the indubitable. But official, governmental, mainstream-media parroted narratives do not! Any of these may, under rigorous examination and interrogation, be shown to be the most probable theory, but why do so many Catholics treat them, even in the absence of such examination and interrogation, with the same level of submission of intellect and will as they do Catholic doctrine? When we unite unwavering commitment to an ultimate object of allegiance *that is not God or directly related to God* with a belief in the absolute truth and indubitable character of our opinions about this object, and when the commitment and belief are held not only without recourse to adequate rational evidence but even directly against such evidence, we commit an act of idolatry.

As far as I know, there is only one institution whose "conspiracy theory"—a *con-spiratio* among the Father, the Son, and the Holy Spirit—is absolutely true and deserving of complete loyalty and adherence; only one authority structure that both declares and lives up to the declaration that it is especially favored by God, and possesses an explicitly God-given mission to declare truth for all humanity; only one indispensable source and incarnation of divine goodness present in the world. Only the Catholic Church has a truly divine pedigree, foundation, and spirit, which, despite human sin and error, cannot be eradicated or supplanted by another. The Church alone is favored and chosen by God, for it is the new Israel—*she* is the only shining city on a hill—for she is His own bride and body, and He *infallibly brings saving goodness and truth to the world through her alone*. The Church will never lose these divine attributes, and she will continue to display them visibly for all to see until the end of time, however clouded by human error and sin, in her hierarchical and incarnate body and head. *This* is undeniable and indubitable. *This* is not mere opinion. *This* is attested to by all the rational evidence. *Hers* is the cult in which it is not idolatry to worship. *Hers* is the conspiracy theory deserving of all men's belief.

V

Apocalypse

17

The Tradition
of Nothing Worship

Only a flicker
Over the strained time-ridden faces
Distracted from distraction by distraction
Filled with fancies and empty of meaning
Tumid apathy with no concentration
Men and bits of paper, whirled by the cold wind
That blows before and after time,
Wind in and out of unwholesome lungs
Time before and time after.

T.S. Eliot, *Burnt Norton*

The Worship of Nothing

The essence of the Luciferian program is to seduce human beings into believing that their salvation lies in experiencing and acting upon the "freedom of absolute autonomy" that Lucifer inaugurated when he rebelled against God. That hesitation we often feel in our wills, even when confronted with an obvious good, is the sinful inheritance of Adam, but in the religion of Lucifer, it is to be deliberately cultivated as the supreme virtue. The ever-elusive experience of autonomous choice becomes the new sacrament of initiation, the baptism by which we are prepared to participate in the worship of . . . nothing. As the Eastern Orthodox theologian David Bentley Hart maintains, the worship of nothing is the established religion of the modern West:

As modern men and women—to the degree that we are modern— we believe in nothing. This is not to say, I hasten to add, that we do not believe in anything; I mean, rather, that we hold an unshakable, if often unconscious, faith in the nothing, or in nothingness as such. It is this in which we place our trust, upon which we venture our souls, and onto which we project the values by which we measure the meaningfulness of our lives. Or, to phrase the matter more simply and starkly, our religion is one of very comfortable nihilism.[1]

If we want some tangible evidence that the established religion of modern Western culture is the Luciferian worship of nothing, we have only to look for its visible fruits. The most visible fruit of the worship of the living God would be joy, and in a Catholic culture predicated upon this worship, one would see evidence of this joy, particularly among the young. But what do we see when we look at the countenances of many today? Absolute boredom. Michael Hanby writes:

> A world that is "beyond good and evil," in which nothing is either genuinely good or genuinely bad, and no truth, goodness, or beauty are revealed, is a world in which nothing is either intrinsically desirable or detestable. Such a world affords no possibility of seeing and using things as holy, which means to some degree letting them be, because in such a world there can be no holy things. Boredom is therefore the defining condition of a people uniquely in danger of losing their capacity to love, that is, a people uniquely in danger of failing to grasp "the mystery of [its] own being" and losing its very humanity.[2]

Abstracted from Abstraction by Abstraction

Since nothing, literally, does not exist, how is it possible for humans to worship it? How can men encounter, let alone worship, no-thing? How did Lucifer choose nothingness over the overwhelming irre-

---

1. David Bentley Hart, "Christ and Nothing," *First Things* (October 2013).
2. Michael Hanby, "The Culture of Death, the Ontology of Boredom, and the Resistance of Joy," *Communio* 31.2 (Summer 2004): 187.

sistibility of the presence of God? Charles DeKoninck gives us a clue:

> One can say, "It is possible to be and to not be at the same time and in the same respect"; "The part is greater than the whole," though one cannot think such things. But yet, they are grammatically correct phrases. Transcendent power of language: one can say both the thinkable and the unthinkable. Power to use the purely irrational. I can say, "I do not exist." And with that I can found "I exist" on pure non-being. I say it! Who will stop me? Let them stop me. I will say it again. Myself, and myselves. Before long, a society of myselves. The liberty of speech is discovered: speech set loose from intellect. . . . Free, finally. In the beginning, the word of man.[3]

Perhaps Lucifer employed his unimaginably powerful intellect to create and then immerse himself in an abstract and unreal universe of words—"liberty" and "equality" come to mind—thereby severing himself from the concrete and real Being of God. I think man's worship of nothingness is made possible with a similar misuse of language, through a relentless program of abstraction. Since his creation, man has attempted to flee the ubiquitous reality of God through creative abstraction from the natural things of His creation and the supernatural plan of His redemption. Fallen man has always been offended at the "scandal of particularity," always seeking to live in a universe of his own devising, always abstracting from the concrete, contingent, particular, fleshy, historical realities in which he, as a creature of matter and spirit, finds himself, and through which God has chosen to communicate Himself to him.

All was well in the Garden until Adam and Eve began abstracting: "It can't be this particular fruit on this particular tree that could be so significant to God and to our happiness!" For the ancient Greek philosophers, God's existence was knowable; for the Jews, He was a living presence. But that he would limit Himself to a backwater village in the Middle East, or become anything less than a divine conqueror, was foolishness to the former and a stumbling block to the

---

3. Charles De Koninck, "On the Primacy of the Common Good: Against the Personalists and the Principle of the New Order," in *The Aquinas Review* 4 (1997): 86–87.

latter. Martin Luther accepted the truth that the universal became particular in the Incarnation, but denied that this Incarnation should be seen as continuing mystically in a particular, historical, visible institution demanding man's obedience. Enlightenment man accepted the existence of God and absolute truth, but demanded that these be universally accessible solely through man's reason. "Enlightenment" would be the result of abstracting from one's particular and contingent cultural and religious "superstitions" to attain the universal truth transcending them. But such a position was tantamount to abstracting the Incarnation out of reality, to rejecting the entire supernatural order made manifest in and through Our Lord, and denying the necessity of His grace and teachings for an accurate understanding and practice of even natural truth and virtue. Postmodern man appeared to have overcome this error, rightly rejecting Enlightenment man's facile claim to have discovered self-evident absolute truths in abstraction from particularist commitments. He discovered that the historical, the cultural, the societal, that is, the particular, cannot be so easily cut out of the picture. "Self-evident"—to whom? A fair question, that. Yet by denying the possibility of attaining universal truth through and in its particular embodiments, the atheist-oriented postmodernists rejected the reality of transcendence for the abstraction of pure immanence. In short, every error of man throughout history has been the result of missing the balance between immanence and transcendence, the human and the divine, the particular and the universal, by abstracting out some particular realm of natural or supernatural reality.

Extra Traditionem Nulla Salus

It is in the simple enjoyment of humble, everyday things—"boats and boots," to use the words of C. S. Lewis—that we stay in contact with creation and the Creator, where abstractions break down and we encounter the living God. As G. K. Chesterton noted, "The simple sense of wonder at the shapes of things, and at their exuberant independence of our intellectual standards and our trivial definitions, is the basis of spirituality."[4] It is only inside the universal and bloodless abstractions of our own making that we can escape real things. There we may, as Adam and Eve, hide from God and become, like Lucifer, indifferent to Him.

One way of ensuring contact with reality is immersion in the living, breathing Roman Catholic tradition, which we might compare to Chesterton's praise for "a thick steak, a glass of red wine, and a good cigar"—no abstractions there. Recapitulating what we have said so far: the intimate encounter with God immunizes us to nothing worship, the robust encounter with real being is the prerequisite for divine encounter, and authentic tradition enables the intelligible encounter with reality. The devil knows all this, being an expert logician, and so he desires above all the annihilation of authentic tradition. His main target is Catholic Tradition, for it provides the surest means to an intimate encounter with both natural and supernatural reality.

The diabolically fomented World Wars of our past century sapped much of the life out of the religious and cultural tradition of the West, with the anti-traditional abstractions of communism, fascism, and Nazism serving as demonic parodies of the Catholic Church. But Lucifer's *coup de grâce* would be saved for the next century. To his dismay, his all-out destructive assault on tradition in the first half of the twentieth century had provoked a robust counterattack by men of good will in the second half. Lucifer learned his lesson: men cannot exist without some sort of tradition. Thus, instead of attempting again the direct destruction of the Western Christian tradition (rendered rather vestigial, decrepit, and paltry, it must be admitted, from his first assault), this time he pursued a subtler but more effective method. Realizing that any authentic tradition, even a barely-breathing one, is a receiver and transmitter of the divine, his stroke of genius was to inspire the construction and establishment of an abstract anti-tradition that would receive and transmit nothing. Although similar in its unreality to the abstractions of communism, fascism, and Nazism, it would bear such a striking

---

4. G. K. Chesterton, *A Defence of Nonsense, and Other Essays* (New York: Dodd, Mead & Co., 1911), 11.

resemblance to the Christian tradition that it would escape detection. Implemented surreptitiously and cloaking itself in the form of its host, it would serve as the tradition to end all tradition. Not only would there be no counterattack this time, men of good will would have no idea what hit them—or even that they had been hit.

Secular liberal democracy is the cave, liberalism the shadows on its walls, and "conservative," "liberal," and "radical," shadows of various shapes and sizes. For those in the cave, reality is contacted by comparing and choosing among the shadows; certain shadows appear "true," while other shadows seem "false." But since shadows are all they know, it cannot be said that they really know any of these shadows at all. They do not know the shadows *as* shadows. They may use the word "shadow" in their many echoey cave discussions, but they do not know of what the shadows are. Indeed, if they ever recognized the shadows as shadows, they would escape the cave.

People in the modern West may use the term "liberalism," and identify "other" points of view in contrast to it, but because they are inside liberalism and do not know it, they do not recognize the liberalism of liberalism. They do not see it as an alien, artificial ideology projected upon the walls of their minds by the elitist puppeteers of academia, religion, bureaucracy, and media, but simply as "just the way things are." They are like fish that never recognize their immersion in water because they know of nothing else. Liberalism claims to provide a religiously neutral social framework within which individuals can autonomously determine their own vision of the world in perfect freedom. But we must reject liberalism's official public claim that it lacks any particular conception of the good and any restrictions on others' conceptions of the good. Since liberal culture is founded upon a particular conception of the good and a particular doctrine of truth—namely, the good of the privatization of all claims to truth, and the truth of the irreducible plurality of conceptions of the good—and since the publicly authoritative rhetoric of liberal culture denies having any substantive conceptions of its own, what liberalism amounts to is an established and intolerant belief system—a religion—that indoctrinates citizens into disbelieving in its very existence. Just as the puppeteers must ensure that the shadows are never recognized as shadows, else the cave be identified as a cave and the prisoners break their chains, liberalism must never be exposed as liberalism, that is, as a historically contingent, non-necessary, man-made ideology. It must at all costs be identified with "the facts," "the way things are," as the inexorable social reality. In short, as the great Nietzschean ironist Stanley Fish, a cave-puppeteer with a genius for exposing his fellow puppeteers to the light, has confessed: "liberalism doesn't exist."

The problem, however, is that it does, and its existence is no longer limited to an abstract idea or a revolutionary experiment—it is now a well-established social reality. The liberal incubus has found a willing consort in the decrepit culture of the secularized West, and unfortunately, we citizens of the modern liberal democracies of the West are its traditionalists. Cavanaugh's name for liberalism is the "worship of the empty shrine," and, according to Cavanaugh, its main temple is the United States of America:

> The public shrine has been emptied of any one particular God or creed, so that the government can never claim divine sanction and each person may be free to worship as she sees fit.... There is no single visible idol, no golden calf, to make the idolatry obvious ... officially the shrine remains empty.... The empty shrine, however, threatens to make a deity not out of God but out of our freedom to worship God. Our freedom comes to occupy the empty shrine. Worship becomes worship of our collective self, and civil religion tends to marginalize the worship of the true God. Our freedom, finally, becomes the one thing we will die and kill for.[5]

And the priests of the empty shrine have become quite zealous of late to evangelize, both through preaching in a variety of media (McDonalds, MTV, pornography, condoms...) and, especially since 2003, through inquisition—democracy and freedom at the end of a gun, a white phosphorous bomb, or an electric shock to the genitals. The god of the American state is a jealous god, commanding its devotees to kill for it. As Cavanaugh writes: "You may confess on your lips any god you like, provided you are willing to kill for Amer-

---

5. William Cavanaugh, "The Empire of the Empty Shrine: American Imperialism and the Church," *A Journal for the Theology of Culture* 2.2 (Summer 2006): 15.

ica"—and to be killed for it. As MacIntyre wryly puts it: "It is like being asked to die for the telephone company."[6]

With a track record of human sacrifice, how has the empty shrine of liberal nothing worship (to conflate names for a moment) managed to escape our detection? The short answer is that it has removed our eyes. Authentic traditions, both natural and supernatural, embody and transmit the ultimate realities of man's existence, the transcendent origin, end, and meaning of things that cannot be grasped by the isolated individual, and cannot be fully rationalized or defined. Ultimate reality must be experienced through and in its incarnation in tradition. It is in this sense that tradition is the eye that allows men see the spiritual, eternal, and transcendent meanings hidden in the physical, temporal, and mundane facts of everyday existence. Participants in the anti-tradition of liberalism, however, are prevented from ever seeing themselves as participants in a tradition, even though they are its slaves. They are blinded to their God-given identity as members of a common good higher than themselves, even as they serve as mere cogs in the liberal machine.

How does liberalism do this? Like any demon, its power over us lies in its ability to imitate the divine. America's worship of freedom at the empty shrine bears a striking resemblance to the Church's worship of the Holy Trinity in the Eucharist. First of all, like the Catholic Church, the empty shrine defines itself as both universal and particular: as a universal idea, that of equal freedom for all, and as a particular country with a particular history, the United State of America. Like the Holy Trinity, absolute freedom is transcendent, ubiquitous, and infinite. Discourse about freedom, like talk about the Trinity, is necessarily abstract, since to speak in a concrete manner about that which transcends any particular object would be to profane it by limiting it, a kind of idolatry. Since America is not only an abstract idea but also a real place, its worship is both immanent and transcendent, like the mystery of the Holy Eucharist. The immanent body, blood, and soul of the Eucharist are a thirty-three-year-old Jewish carpenter from Nazareth, but these are inseparable from His higher identity as the transcendent and eternal Second

6. "Partial Response," 303.

Person of the Blessed Trinity. The immanent land, citizens, and government of freedom-worship are a 250-year-old regime located in North America, but these are inseparable from its higher identity as the very locus of transcendent and eternal freedom. Thus, American worship of freedom competes with the Holy Eucharist. But to most Americans, the empty shrine seems the more holy of the two:

> According to [Michael] Novak, the shrine has been "swept clean" in democratic capitalism not out of indifference to transcendence, but out of reverence for it, and out of "respect for the diversity of human consciences, perceptions, and intentions." Transcendence is preserved by the freedom of each individual to pursue the ends of his or her choice.[7]

The freedom cult includes all others, even the cult of the Eucharist, and so it is more universal, more "catholic," and therefore more divine than the Eucharist. By not prescribing any particular object of public devotion, America's empty shrine appears to allow all devotions to exist and thrive more successfully than if there were an exclusivist, established cult, such as Catholicism.

However, all of this is a grand illusion. As David Schindler points out: "The state cannot finally avoid affirming, in the matter of religion, a priority of either 'freedom from' or 'freedom for'—both of these imply a theology."[8] By prescinding from the particularity of religious truth in the organization of the American body politic, the American Founders enshrined a theology, a religion. The implied theology of its First Commandment, the First Amendment, is that the order of nature is separable and separate from the order of grace, temporal matters from spiritual ones, reason from faith, freedom from truth, the state from the Church. Though some of the Founders favored Christianity as an ideal civic religion, the American Founding was essentially exclusivist, anti-pluralistic, dogmatic, and Masonic. It was an implicitly anti-Catholic theological *establishment*, not just a "prudential accommodation" of religious plural-

---

7. Cavanaugh, "Empire of the Empty Shrine," 7.
8. Schindler, *Heart of the World*, 83.

ism, as is commonly thought. In other words, liberalism doesn't exist—there is no such thing as an empty shrine.

We have now identified our demon. The Tradition of Nothing Worship is not the worship of religious truth, but of religious freedom; not faith in the Incarnation, but belief in belief; not the desire for God, but the desire for desire. It has no definable substance, no particular content, no concrete object for worship, for it is only an abstraction. But then, it is the worship of nothing. We know that worship of the Catholic religion produces saints, but what does the worship of nothing produce? James Kalb gives us the terrifying answer:

> Since [for liberalism] it is choice itself that makes something good, one does not choose things for their goodness but simply because one chooses them. Choices thus become arbitrary, and human actions essentially non-rational. On such a view, the rational component of morality is reduced to the therapeutic task of clarifying choices and the technical task of securing their satisfaction efficiently and equally. . . . It is the outlook of a psychopath.[9]

From the First Amendment's "Congress shall make no law respecting an establishment of religion" to Eisenhower's "Our form of government has no sense unless it is founded in a deeply felt religious faith, and I don't care what it is"[10] to George W. Bush's "The ideal of America is the hope of all mankind. That hope still lights the way. And the light shines in the darkness. And the darkness will not overcome it"[11]—it's all the same Masonic gospel. G. K. Chesterton was right: America is a nation with the soul of a church. And with its cohort, Zionist Israel, it has established countless mission churches in Europe and throughout the world. It is now attempting to gouge out the eyes of the Muslims in the Middle East, whose collective sight is already quite dim. The "darkness of Islamism," to use the words of Pius XI, is about to get much darker, and as we attempt to blind our "enemies," we become all the more blind.

---

9. James Kalb, "Liberalism, Tradition, and Faith," *Telos* 128 (2006): 114.

10. Quoted in Patrick Henry, "'And I Don't Care What It Is': The Tradition-History of a Civil Religion Proof-Text," *Journal of the American Academy of Religion* 49.1 (March 1981): 41.

11. President Bush's remarks on September 11, 2002.

18

The Satanic Sacred

Freedom Isn't Free

J ust four days after the Charlie Hebdo event, the world wit-
nessed a march in Paris, in fact, the largest in French history,
including two million people (with three million more French-
men marching in solidarity with the Parisians) and forty world
leaders. The march was held to commemorate and mourn the six-
teen people who were murdered at the Charlie Hebdo offices and at
a Kosher deli, but it also had the purpose of emboldening and
encouraging freedom-loving people, who must now risk their lives
merely to exercise their right to free speech. *Nous sommes tous
Charlie Hebdo maintenant.* The official government narrative of the
event was that a few radical Muslim terrorists—and precisely those
designated by the authorities immediately after the attack—murdered eleven employees of a newspaper simply because of the content of that newspaper, as well as five more Jewish people simply
because they were Jewish. The official government-authorized
meaning of the event was that violence employed against the free
use of speech would not be tolerated in France. And any public
utterance that did not fall perfectly in line with this authorized narrative and meaning met with the hostile force of the French state.
Criticism of the blasphemous cartoons attacking the religious
beliefs of millions of Christians and Muslims, and any hesitation in
accepting with trust and gratitude the new French status quo of surveillance, suspicion, and censorship, was considered intolerant, big-
oted, and even criminal, for such could indicate only animosity
toward free speech and thus solidarity with murderous terrorists.
    In short, very soon after the largest free-speech march in Euro-

pean history—perhaps the *only* free-speech march in European history—there was a massive government crackdown on free speech, and precisely where that march took place. Included in the hundreds of "dangerous enemies of free speech" who were arrested by the Paris police in the wake of Hebdo was an eight-year-old French Muslim boy, detained and questioned by the police due to the dangerous content of his post-toddler speech. And only a month after this, a French citizen was sent to prison for two years merely for questioning the accuracy of certain episodes of another officially authorized narrative.[1] The most obvious consequence of the Charlie Hebdo event was not the expansion and increased tolerance of free speech, but a radical suspicion and circumscription of it, an unprecedented escalation of government surveillance and legal suppression. Daniel Spaulding from *The Soul of the East* reported:

> Over the past several decades, France has prosecuted numerous individuals for engaging in state-designated "hate speech." The French novelist and gadfly Michel Houellebecq, depicted in a satirical cartoon on the cover of Charlie Hebdo the same day of the terrorist attack, was at one time tried, and later acquitted, for making remarks derogatory toward Islam. And a mere few days after the Charlie Hebdo shooting, the comedian Dieudonné M'bala M'bala was arrested on the dubious charge of "glorifying terrorism" after decrying his previous persecutions at the hands of the French authorities for alleged "anti-Semitic" comments. If convicted he could spend several years in prison.[2]

In his book, *There's No Such Thing as Free Speech, and It's a Good Thing, Too*, Stanley Fish writes:

> "Free speech" is just the name we give to verbal behavior that serves the substantive agendas we wish to advance; and we give our preferred verbal behaviors *that* name when we can, when we have the power to do so, because in the rhetoric of American life,

---

1. http://france3-regions.francetvinfo.fr/basse-normandie/2015/02/11/coutances -vincent-reynouard-condamne-deux-ans-de-prison-ferme-pour-negationnisme-6 53515.html.

2. Daniel Spaulding, "Free Speech Farce," *The Soul of the East* (January 30, 2015), http://souloftheeast.org/2015/01/30/free-speech-farce/.

the label "free speech" is the one you want your favorites to wear. Free speech, in short, is not an independent value but a political prize, and if that prize has been captured by a politics opposed to yours, it can no longer be invoked in the ways that further your purposes, for it is now an obstacle to those purposes.[3]

The Charlie Hebdo event and the behavior that followed it provide solid evidence for the truth of Fish's words. There was an unmistakable Orwellian cast to the event, suggesting the existence of an esoteric agenda underneath the exoteric one. If Fish is correct, and free speech is just the name given to verbal behavior that serves the agenda of capturing some political prize, *who* in Paris were seeking such a prize, and *what* was it? The who is easy: the French-Anglo-American-Israeli-European ruling classes, comprised of personnel in government, intelligence, technology, military, finance, academia, media, and entertainment, the organizers of the *Je Suis Charlie Hebdo* campaign and march, the budding Paris surveillance industry, the bureaucratic drafters and enforcers of France's version of the Patriot Act, the South Park-esque cartoonists of the Charlie Hebdo newspaper and their fans, and finally, every person wearing a *Je Suis Charlie* T-shirt (in spirit, if not on body). But what was the political prize? As we shall see presently, the *what* question is much more complex than the *who*.

When an explanation for a massively violent event and its concomitant crisis emerges as the official, unquestionable, and authoritative narrative; when it includes, and without empirical evidence or investigative inquiry, the assignation of innocence and exceptionalism to the victims, and utter depravity and terrifying power to the designated criminals; when dissent from this narrative is socially forbidden, even to the extent of legal harassment and prosecution; when it spawns behavior in contradiction with itself, such as committing acts of terror in the name of eradicating terrorism, or restricting and punishing free speech in the name of expanding and protecting it; when the narrative is immediately supported, echoed, and policed by the vast majority of the ruling classes, including

3. Stanley Fish, *There's No Such Thing as Free Speech and It's a Good Thing Too* (Oxford: Oxford University Press, 1994), 102.

189

both the mainstream and "alternative" (gate-keeping) left and right; when it successfully unites and synthesizes otherwise opposed factions of the populace—liberals with neoconservatives, libertarians with statists, humanists with Nietzscheans, theists with atheists; when rational scrutiny and frank discussion of obvious explanatory holes in the narrative are forbidden; and when the ritualistic, annual remembrance of an event and recitation of its hallowed story—particularly the harrowing portrayal of the demonic villains to which it assigns all blame for both the increasing domestic strife among citizens and the perpetual Manichean war against the newest "enemy"—instills and evokes primordial fear and religious awe in the populace; when the narrative of an event or series of connected events possesses all of these attributes, or even just a few of them, we know we are dealing with no ordinary phenomenon. We have something whose apparent mystery and power strike at the very heart of the collective consciousness, searing it with something akin to the divine. What we are dealing with, in a word, is the *sacred*. And it just so happens that the Charlie Hebdo event and narrative bear all the aforementioned characteristics. But isn't the sacred an extinct relic of our benighted, superstitious, medieval past?

The Sacred (Secular) State

Secular modernity is neither secular nor modern. Of course, we no longer live under the medieval sacral regimes of throne and altar or post-Reformation confessional monarchies. And who can doubt the peculiarly modern rise of science and technology, the radically new kinds of political and economic institutions, the undisputed reign of democratic ideology, and our unprecedented religious pluralism? However, these obvious historical facts and features are not what are primarily signified by the words "secular" and "modern." Their inseparable concomitant is a "just-so" story of the genealogy of modernity, which goes something like this.

Only in secular modernity did man finally achieve his liberation from oppression and ignorance, from superstition, magic, tyranny, and priestcraft, from the dark forces of religious power, fanatical belief, and sectarianism. Man achieved this liberation primarily through the secularization of reason, morality, and society, which was effected through the separation of religion from the political order, Church from state. Ever-increasing religious and ideological pluralism ensued as soon as previously oppressed men of good will were permitted to exercise freely their reason and act on their consciences. It is true that when Christendom was broken up in the wake of the Reformation, religiously intolerant, confessional, monarchical states emerged, but these evolved quite quickly, historically speaking, into the secular, tolerant-minded, pluralistic, democratic states we have today. The rise of secular society after the sixteenth- and seventeenth-century "wars of religion"[4] was rendered possible only by the removal of "religion"[5] from all positions of political significance and power. Good-willed, reasonable people were ready and willing to accept the desacralization of the state, so the story goes, after centuries of witnessing incessant bloodshed over religion. Sequestered, depoliticized, and privatized, religion and the sacred would now no longer cause war, divisiveness, and oppression, and the newly liberated, autonomous, politically secular individual could finally thrive. In the religiously tolerant, secular, pluralistic liberal democracy governed by the rights of men, not the rights of God, the sacred would still have a place, as well as a capacity to exert influence over politics; but now it would have to coexist with the many competing, private "sacreds" residing in the same city, proliferating and dwelling together in peace precisely because none is permitted to obtain societal, cultural, and political power, let alone a monopoly on power. In short, secular modernity was born at the moment when the archaic, violence-inducing sacred lost its public, political hegemony and influence, having been relegated to the sub-political, private sphere of men's fancies and

---

4. To see why this phrase must be put in scare quotes, see the pioneering revisionist work of Cavanaugh, especially "A Fire Strong Enough to Consume the House."

5. As Cavanaugh shows, "religion" in its newly depoliticized and privatized form is a creation of the modern state: see *Migrations of the Holy*.

hearts. What took its place in the public square is what should always have been there in the first place: the inalienable right of the individual to self-determination, to freedom of thought, action, speech, property, and religion.

This is the familiar tale told of modernity. And this much can be said with certainty: in modernity, man attempted, for the first time in human history, to construct a political order *not* based upon the religious or the sacred. While not denying the right of every citizen to believe (if he wants) in a sacred, superhuman, cosmic, divine, transcendent power as the true ground of man's existence, both personal and social, the theoreticians of the modern paradigm—thinkers such as Machiavelli, Hobbes, Locke, Rousseau, Kant, Madison, and Marx—justified, by appeals to reason, common sense and consent, historical inevitability, enlightened sentiment, or even the will of God, the replacement of any power or will higher than man with secular values and rights codified in a social contract, the general will, a constitution, or the party line. And yet, the continual irruption and increasing proliferation of violent, crisis-making events that bear the sacred features described above—unimpeachable narratives, an ethos of fear and awe, the sudden unification of factions, etc.—indicate that the phenomenon of the sacred is as publicly present, influential, and authoritative in secular modernity as it ever was in the ancient "religious" world. We need only think of other recent sacred events, such as Sandy Hook, the Boston bombing, the Aurora shooting, the ISIS beheadings, the Sydney chocolate-shop massacre, and all the other post-9/11 crisis events that constitute ongoing episodes in the "War on Terror," whose pilot episode was that most sacred of all American events, IXXI. Can modern man really live without the sacred? And when he has repudiated the traditional sacred, or perhaps has just forgotten about it, is he bound to concoct sacreds of his own, in his own fallen and depraved image? It is the argument of this chapter, and the overall contention of this book, that a community cannot exist without a sacred component, and that, when modernity rejected the traditional sacred of monotheism, the shrine did not remain empty.

An objection might be raised here. Even if it were a delusional mistake to try entirely to desacralize politics and power, did not secular modernity bring us the freedom of religion, the rule of law, civil equality, and representative government, that is, unquestionably beneficial institutions and practices unheard of in the premodern world? We can say with certainty that modern liberal democracy, insofar as it has provided the political, legal, cultural, social, and psychological space for the free exercise of reason and conscience, and insofar as it has helped men to flourish physically through its scientific, technological, and medical advances, is a considerably good thing. But what is the price we have paid for these secular advances? Was the dethronement of the traditional sacred from its rightful place at the heart of society, culture, and politics worth it? "For what shall it profit a man, if he gain the whole world, and suffer the loss of his soul?" (Mk 8:36).

Sacred Nihilism

One way to characterize the sacred is as that which is considered absolutely *good*—under, around, in obedience to, and in pursuit of which men order their individual and corporate lives. Insofar as secular liberalism denies that such a metaphysical, ethical, and spiritual good, if it exists at all, can or should have any public authority in civil society, it is delusional and hypocritical. Since secular liberal culture is founded upon a particular conception of the good, namely, the *sacral good* of the privatization and desacralization of all claims to truth, and a particular doctrine of truth, the irreducible plurality of conceptions of the good and the sacred; and since the publicly authoritative rhetoric of liberal culture includes a denial of having any substantive sacred conceptions of its own; what liberalism amounts to is an institutionalized religious sacred—but one that indoctrinates citizens into disbelieving in its very existence. The "secular" state is a sacred power exercising hegemony over all competing sacreds, which it has effectively privatized and neutered. Thus, its own sacred dogmas become unimpeachable, unquestionable, incontestable, and, most importantly, invisible. It judges all beliefs and actions in accord with these dogmas, and executes its definitive judgments through its terrible liturgical violence and murderous ritual scapegoating, masked by the language of rights, democracy, freedom, security, diversity, equality, and tolerance. Orwell, eat your heart out.

All political orders require a mechanism for engendering and preserving unity, and the sacred has always been the source and engine of this unity. It is no different in our "modern" day. The Charlie Hebdo murders, though horrific and tragic, were exploited, and perhaps even orchestrated, through a kind of psychological and spiritual sorcery, the effect of which was to create a unified, regulated group-mind in the French people and in the West at large. At the shrine of Charlie Hebdo, "free speech" became God, but a god with no essence, no divine identity, no supernatural content. It is a cunning idol, nevertheless, commanding only toleration, and promising only freedom. Yet it tolerates—and encourages—blasphemy and ridicule of precisely those competing sacreds it seeks to vanquish, the God of Abraham, Isaac, and Jacob, and the personages of Muhammad and Christ—and it persecutes any who dare to critique its sacred nihilism. The desacralization, profanation, and degradation of Christianity and Islam is, since Charlie Hebdo, the official meaning of "free speech."

IXXI and the Satanic Sacred

Although Charlie Hebdo was a sacred spectacle, IXXI was *the* exemplar of secular modernity's sacred. It will suffice to point out its uncanny resemblance to traditional sacred mythology, ritual, and sacrament. Sheldon Wolin writes:

> The mythology created around September 11 was predominantly Christian in its themes. The day was converted into the political equivalent of a holy day of crucifixion, of martyrdom, that fulfilled multiple functions: as the basis of a political theology, as a communion around a mystical body of a bellicose republic, as a warning against political apostasy, as a sanctification of the nation's leader, transforming him from a powerful officeholder of questionable legitimacy into an instrument of redemption, and at the same time exhorting the congregants to a wartime militancy,

demanding of them uncritical loyalty and support, summoning them as participants in a sacrament of unity and in a crusade to "rid the world of evil."[6]

James Alison has given a penetrating Girardian account of the IXXI event worth quoting in full:

> And immediately the old sacred worked its magic: we found ourselves being sucked in to a sacred center, one where a meaningless act had created a vacuum of meaning, and we found ourselves giving meaning to it. All over London I found that friends had stopped work, offices were closing down, everyone was glued to the screen. In short, there had appeared, suddenly, a holy day. Not what we mean by a holiday, a day of rest, but an older form of holiday, a being sucked out of our ordinary lives in order to participate in a sacred and sacrificial centre so kindly set up for us by the meaningless suicides. . . . And immediately the sacrificial center began to generate the sort of reactions that sacrificial centers are supposed to generate: a feeling of unanimity and grief. Phrases began to appear to the effect that "We're all Americans now"—a purely fictitious feeling for most of us. It was staggering to watch the togetherness build up around the sacred center, quickly consecrated as Ground Zero, a togetherness that would harden over the coming hours into flag waving, a huge upsurge in religious services and observance, religious leaders suddenly taken seriously, candles, shrines, prayers, all the accoutrements of the religion of death. And there was the grief. How we enjoy grief. It makes us feel good, and innocent. This is what Aristotle meant by catharsis, and it has deeply sinister echoes of dramatic tragedy's roots in sacrifice. One of the effects of the violent sacred around the sacrificial center is to make those present feel justified, feel morally good. A counterfactual goodness which suddenly takes us out of our little betrayals, acts of cowardice, uneasy consciences. And very quickly of course the unanimity and the grief harden into the militant goodness of those who have a transcendent object to their lives. And then there are those who are with us and those who are against us, the beginnings of the suppression of dissent. Quickly people were saying things like "to think that we used to spend our

6. Sheldon Wolin, *Democracy Incorporated* (Princeton University Press, 2008), 9.

lives engaged in gossip about celebrities' and politicians' sexual peccadillos. Now we have been summoned into thinking about the things that really matter." And beneath the militant goodness, suddenly permission to sack people, to leak out bad news and so on, things which could take advantage of the unanimity to avoid reasoned negotiation. . . . What I want to suggest is that most of us fell for it, at some level. We were tempted to be secretly glad of a chance for a huge outbreak of meaning to transform our hum-drum lives, to feel we belonged to something bigger, more impor-tant, with hints of nobility and solidarity. What I want to suggest is that this, this delight in being given meaning, is satanic.[7]

All human beings "delight in being given meaning," but the meaning given to the masses through the IXXI and Charlie Hebdo events is as meaningless as it is idolatrous and psychopathic. Charlie Hebdo informs us that those who aren't comfortable with public, state-supported mockery of other citizens' religious beliefs are equivalent to murderous terrorist fanatics. Through IXXI and the War on Terror that followed, the United States, as the metonymic Twin Towers and the World Trade Center, was transformed into a suffering and resurrected God, scourged and crucified by the forces of pure evil that "hate our freedoms," but brought back to life by Bush, Rumsfeld, Cheney, et al., as mediators of the immortal righ-teousness of the American people. Our priest-warriors inaugurated an endless "shock and awe" crusade against the demons of this world, one that not only "keeps us free" but also effectively manages to separate the sheep from the goats, the saved from the damned— "Either you are with us, or you are with the terrorists," the divinized oracle uttered. IXXI comes to mean the definitive, once for all, divine confirmation of "our" exceptional righteousness, and, con-comitantly, the irredeemable wickedness of the "other," defined by magisterial fiat as anyone not willing to worship American power. Of course, Americans had some faith in the truth of this meaning before IXXI, but only on IXXI was that faith confirmed and vindi-

7. James Alison, "Contemplation in a World of Violence: Girard, Merton, Tolle," a talk given at the Thomas Merton Society, Downside Abbey, Bath (November 3, 2001), available at http://girardianlectionary.net/res/alison_contemplation_violence.htm.

cated, seemingly by God Himself, using as his divine sign demonic planes crashing into our tallest shrines.

> Death in war—what is commonly called the "ultimate sacrifice" for the nation—is what periodically re-presents the sense of belonging upon which the imagined nation is built. Such death is then elaborately ceremonialized in liturgies involving the flag and other ritual objects. Indeed, it is the ritual itself that retrospectively classifies any particular act of violence as *sacrifice*. Ritual gesture and language are crucial for establishing meaning and public assent to the foundational story being told. The foundational story is one of both creation and salvation. At the ceremonies marking the fiftieth anniversary of D-Day in 1994, for example, President Clinton remarked of the soldiers that died there both that "They gave us our world" and that "They saved the world."[8]

Charlie Hebdo was a psychological-spiritual operation through which the French masses, already alienated from the true sources of meaning, truth, goodness, and beauty found in the beliefs and practices of traditional monotheism, were initiated into the satanic sacred, the worship of the empty shrine of nihilism.

Two Cities

Since IXXI, individual liberty has been vastly curtailed, and global violence has exponentially increased. Wars and rumors of wars abound. Perhaps the next terror event, whether staged or not, will trigger the final annihilation of our freedoms and the complete establishment of a global police state, if we aren't nuked out of existence first. The apocalypse seems to be upon us. So, what should we do?

No doubt we should do all we can to restrict the scope and power of modern states and international institutions of global governance, as well as expose the machinations of the "Deep State" that actually rules us. We must preserve what is left of the freedoms of

---

8. William T. Cavanaugh, "The Liturgies of Church and State," *Liturgy* 20.1 (2005): 25–30.

speech, protest, and worship by non-violent means, and by self-defensive force if necessary. Moreover, if our analysis is correct and modernity is merely the replacement of one bloody sacred for another—we used to have bloody crusades and wars for Christ or Muhammad, now we have them for democracy and freedom—it would seem reasonable for us to turn our efforts towards banishing any semblance of the sacred from the public square so as to separate it from all political, coercive, and violence-making power and thus from its corruption. This would protect both the sacred from profanation and the state from idolatry. In other words, if Western governments are indeed shrines and purveyors of satanic nothing worship, then we need to strip them of all sacred authority and power.

It cannot be denied that a less powerful and more—much more —decentralized government-military-financial-educational-intelligence-media complex is the *sine qua non* of any solution. If, however, we take the reality and power of the sacred as seriously as it deserves, we should be as discontented at seeing the sacred remain merely a private affair as we are at seeing it counterfeited, mocked, and profaned. God exercises, whether we recognize it or not, social, cultural, and political reign over the world—we live now in a theocracy, always have, and always will, until the end of the world. And this rule is not just over individual hearts, but over institutions and states, over men organized collectively for the common good and for His honor, even if they dishonor Him and order the sacred commons to their monstrous, vampirish appetites. *He* is the ultimate common good, the ultimate ground for any human society, and if He is relegated to the private sphere of idiosyncratic and irrational fancy, something not so good will always take His place. Just as there is no such thing as free speech, there is no such thing as an empty shrine.

Thus, we must work not only to dethrone the satanic sacred, the Abomination of Desolation now residing in the Holy of Holies, but also to replace it with the authentic sacred, the worship of the living, holy, all-powerful, all-knowing, all-just, all-merciful God. To dethrone the satanic sacred that has usurped the seats of earthly power in Western society, we first must repent of our own complicity in its rites and ceremonies: accepting the scapegoating status quo because it flatters, protects, and keeps us feeling comfortable, and refusing to speak truth to power out of fear. After a thorough examination of conscience, we must unmask the satanic face hiding right out in the open so as to help those blinded to its existence and horrific nature to escape the unholy fear it engenders, the tortuous psychological and spiritual deceptions it incessantly enacts, and its totalitarian control of public discourse. As Neil Kramer says: "For the ordinary person, the primary power of Empire rests not in its might or cunning, but in its invisibility. People who are not mindful of its presence do not comprehend their conscious and spiritual incarceration."[9]

> The City of God is founded on a love of God that leads its citizens to contempt for themselves, counting all earthly things as worthless.... Augustine argues that the temporal ought to be ordered to the eternal (*Civ. Dei* XIX,17), but that this ordering will never be achieved entirely harmoniously till the second coming of the Lord. For, there is a second city here on earth in addition to the city of God—the *civitas terrena*, the earthly city. This city is founded on a love of self to the contempt of God (*Civ. Dei* XIV,28). And these two cities are in conflict.... The earthly city is always opposed to true religion.... Justice consists in giving each his own, thus no society is just that does not give God the worship due to Him.[10]

The City of Man has always been opposed to true religion, to the truly sacred. This opposition has only increased in our "secular age," and exponentially since IXXI. At the heart of every culture is always the sacred, and at the heart of our post-IXXI, pathocratic, imperial culture of death and deception is a terrible—but entirely vincible—sacred power in mortal conflict with the *Logos*, the merciful, loving, and truly sacred Person who protects, guides, and saves those who are willing to recognize, adore, and trust in Him.

---

9. Neil Kramer, "Invisible Empire" (May 22, 2014), available at http://neilkramer.com/invisible-empire.html.

10. Edmund Waldstein, "Religious Liberty and Tradition" (January 2, 2015), available at http://thejosias.com/2015/01/02/religious-liberty-and-tradition-iii/.

19

Modernity and Apocalypse

Taking the kids from our districts, forcing them to kill one another while we watch—this is the Capitol's way of reminding us how totally we are at their mercy. How little chance we would stand of surviving another rebellion. Whatever words they use, the real message is clear. "Look how we take your children and sacrifice them and there's nothing you can do. If you lift a finger, we will destroy every last one of you."

The Hunger Games[1]

Either you are with us, or you are with the terrorists.

George W. Bush[2]

You can foresee the shape of what the Antichrist is going to be in the future: a super victimary machine that will keep on sacrificing in the name of the victim.

René Girard[3]

Modernity's Soteriology?

O ne might define modernity in the West as essentially that which happened to Christendom after it was dehellenized, nominalized, and secularized. In its Enlightenment mask, it is an ahistorical, non-ideological, world-view-neutral account of "the way things are and have always been," bereft of the superstitious, irrational, freedom-suppressing and ruler-serving, ancient-medieval theoretical and practical apparatus of scholasticism, priestcraft, oppression, and feudalism; in its post-Enlightenment

1. Suzanne Collings, *The Hunger Games* (New York: Scholastic Press, 2008), 18–19.
2. George W. Bush, "Address to a Joint Session of Congress and the American People," September 20, 2001.
3. René Girard, *Evolution and Conversion—Dialogues on the Origins of Culture* (London, New York: Continuum, 2007), 236.

201

persona, it is a parasitical cultural growth aping Christianity and Christian culture while repudiating it in its nihilistic, anti-*logos* core. Modernity is Christ without the cross, in its liberal democratic manifestation, and it is the cross without Christ, in its totalitarian strains. Modernity is an anti-Aristotelian tradition of rationality, depriving persons of the knowledge of their good and the ability to attain it personally and corporately. It embodies the moral and spiritual fruits of the Gospel's affirmation of ordinary life, to use Taylor's expression, the dignity of each person, and the freedom of the children of God—along with the negation of the Christian soil, trunk, and branches that engendered these fruits. Modernity is a liturgical and ecclesial counterfeit of the Church, attempting to unify in its artificial Leviathanian body all people in a national and global church of peacemaking and violence-restraining violence. It is the sundry failed attempts at cultural, economic, political, and spiritual order within a seemingly inescapable nominalistic, theological framework; the result of the extrinsicist separation of nature and grace and the triumph of secular reason; the priority of freedom-from in the anti-trinitarian cultural form of the machine. And it is the dethroning of a theology of primordial peace and the apotheosis of an anti-theology of fearsome violence.

There are, of course, other "just so" stories in this more conservative vein, as well as many persuasive non-theological, secularist-friendly, progressivist narratives. Indeed, the narratives of modernity are seemingly endless and incommensurable, notoriously resistant to definitive adjudication and harmonious negotiation. What is needed is an adequate synthesis in which the partial truths of all the myriad stories and accounts can lie together.

If one teased out the most plausible and compelling threads in each narrative, could one find a meta-thread winding through them all and holding them together? Let me posit that such a thread can be found in the work of René Girard, and that absent this thread, modernity cannot be properly understood. Supernaturally powerful, non-violent, and authentically Catholic engagement with the modern world requires an engagement with Girard's thought. Girard's work is not only indispensable for understanding our present predicament of escalating violence in the "clash of civilizations," but also, and more importantly, our future, one which Girard characterizes as *apocalypse*. These are bold claims, and I hope to make them persuasive in this chapter.

The late René Girard, who was a professor of language, literature, and civilization at Stanford University, is the preeminent expert on the phenomenon of scapegoating, or the "single victim mechanism" as he puts it. Girard's oeuvre is prolific and complex, including not only a rigorous psychological, sociological, anthropological, theological, and literary account of scapegoating, but also a persuasive analysis of the foundation of religion and culture in collective violence and ritualized murder.[4] Girard has applied his formidable skill and erudition in literary criticism in the analysis of the myths employed by religious and cultural authorities to obscure their violence, including an examination of modern and contemporary Western culture's scapegoating violence and ideological obfuscation. What follows is a summary of the fundamental principles of Girard's thought, an analysis of the West's "War on Terror" based upon those principles, a discussion of modernity and apocalyptic violence in the light of Girard's most recent work, and a brief account of the pertinence of Girard's thought for Catholic social thought and practice, particularly in America.

Scapegoating Then

The New Testament describes St Peter denying thrice that he knew Jesus Christ. Obviously, he was under immense pressure. But what kind of pressure could have led a three-year intimate of Jesus of Nazareth *almost* to betray his master? I say *almost* because his full

---

4. It must be said that Girard's understanding of the nature of the political order, as well as the relationship between nature and grace, is in tension with Thomism. Indeed, if he is denying the political order's inherent *telos* to the human good, it would be contradictory not just to Thomism but to the entire *philosophia perennis*. But that's a topic for another essay. Girard's insights into the nature of political *evil* are accurate and profound, and, I would argue, surpass the work of the Thomists in this area. In this respect, he is especially helpful in understanding modern politics.

betrayal of Jesus was preempted by Jesus Himself, whose prophetic words about the crowing cock when recalled by Peter prevented the latter's fear-provoked denial from becoming deliberate persecution. The standard explanation for Peter's behavior is lack of courage: he feared that he would be killed if he admitted to being a friend of Jesus. There is, of course, truth to this, but it is only a partial explanation. René Girard proposes an alternative and rather startling explanation: "Peter's denial should *not* be read as a reflection on the psychology of Peter, on the personal weakness of Peter, it should be read as the revelation of the scapegoat mechanism. We should have no revelation of it since even Peter, the best of the disciples, joins the mob."[5] As we shall see presently, identifying and understanding this "mob" is the key to explaining not only Peter's personal behavior, but our own, and not only this. Cultures themselves, and hence political orders, are created and sustained in the crucible of this peculiar and mysterious mob-pressure. Only a vivid awareness of the truth about scapegoating, its ubiquity and seeming inexorability, and, most importantly, our own complicity in it, can enable personal, corporate, and, it must be said, ecclesial emancipation from its psychological, cultural, and political clutches.

According to Girard, the first culture was founded by Cain, that is, upon fratricide, with the divine proscription of murder the first law. Murder, as the omniscient God the Bible depicts must have known, would be imitated and repeated in this originary culture, and thus serve as the original violence of all other cultures throughout history in the now fallen world. However, the law proscribing murder was not obeyed: Cain's murder of Abel would be perpetually imitated on both a personal and cultural level. The reason humans murder other humans, and why they found and preserve cultures upon violence is, according to Girard, *mimetic desire*. For Girard, desire is not naturally ordered (at least in its specific movements) but socially constructed, and though we do have an innate, natural desire for the good, the actual form this desire takes in individuals, the particular objects that are seen and desired as good for

5. Markus Müller, "Interview with René Girard" (June 1996), available at http://www.anthropoetics.ucla.edu/apo201/interv.htm.

each person, are the result of social modeling and imitation. In short, we desire what we see others desiring. Consider the toddler in the nursery, whose desire for a particular toy is enkindled by nothing other than another toddler's reaching for it.

Since there is a scarcity of desirable objects, mimesis results in competition, until a point is reached when other men's desires become scandalous, literally, "stumbling blocks," to us. At this point, there is a cultural crisis, and imminent violence is inevitable—inevitable, that is, without some kind of release valve or transference mechanism. Cultures, as well as the political orders that embody and protect them, would never have come into existence without such a mechanism. Since cultures and political orders do exist, there must be some force that counteracts or channels the frenetic and violence-prone psychological storm of mimetic desire. This Girard identifies as the "accusing finger," the "single victim mechanism," or—Satan:

> The shift from "all against all" to "all against one" permits the prince of this world to forestall the total destruction of his kingdom as he calms the anger of the crowd, restoring the calm that is indispensable to the survival of every human community. Satan can therefore always put enough order back into the world to prevent the total destruction of what he possesses without depriving himself for too long of his favorite pastime, which is to sow disorder, violence, and misfortune among his subjects.[6]

One has only to consider the story of Creation, in which Eve imitates the desire of the Serpent, a desire both for the forbidden fruit and a desire to blame Him who had forbidden it. The "accusing fingers" are then displayed in spades—Satan at God, Eve at Satan, Adam at Eve.

But men do not just imitate the concupiscible desires of others for scarce goods; they also model for each other the irascible desire to confront and overcome evil. Though the evil of selfish mimetic desire is caused by the desires of men themselves, the notion that a powerful, outside, superhuman force is somehow responsible for

---

6. René Girard, *I See Satan Fall Like Lightning* (Maryknoll, NY: Orbis, 2001), 37.

205

the cultural crisis is an irresistible one, and so the community trans-forms its now uncontrollable desires into one collective desire for vengeance. The "accusing finger" becomes the new mimetic model, and it enables the community at the point of violent anarchy to attain "peace" by ridding itself of the "cause" of its crisis. The scape-goat, who is both the source and solution to the crisis, is thus iden-tified, murdered, and, through the religio-cultural myths created to justify and obscure the single victim mechanism, divinized. The rit-ual reenactment of the "founding murder," whether through actual murder, as in the ancient worshippers of Moloch or the pre-Colum-bian Aztecs, or through surrogates, as in the animal sacrifices pre-scribed by Moses in the Old Testament, is what sustains culture and politics in the fallen world.

Returning, then, to the courtyard of the Jewish High Priest, we can now see that Peter was swept up in the single victim mechanism that had already overtaken the Pharisees. When the accusing finger was pointed at Jesus, Peter was unable to resist what his commu-nity's leaders determined: "It is better that one man die for the peo-ple than that the whole nation perish" (Jn 11:50). However, due to his three-year acquaintance with Jesus, by which he was gifted with a mimetic model whose only desire, according to Girard, was to imitate the self-giving desire of the Father, Peter was able to snap out of his scapegoating trance. This, for Girard, was nothing short of miraculous, for no human power is able to resist the scapegoating dynamic. It is only through imitation of the divine, non-scapegoat-ing Jesus that men and cultures can be saved from murderous vio-lence, for He is the only man whose desires do not cause scandal and cultural disintegration when imitated. Cultures centered on and dedicated to Him would, thus, have no need for the scapegoating mechanism to keep peace. Only His power can enable men and whole societies to resist the accusing finger, and so it is only when a culture embraces and embodies the Gospel that it can preserve itself without resort to sacrificial murder. This is the heart of Girard's apologetic for Christianity, a peculiarly empirical, psychological, cultural, political, and anthropological defense, without explicit recourse, apparently, to the authority of divine revelation. It is, itself, a revelation of sorts, but one that any open-eyed person can see—if, that is, he desires to see the truth of his scapegoating complicity.

Scapegoating Now

The Gospels, according to Girard, are the only religious literature we have that was authored by those in solidarity with the victim, and so they alone reveal the truth about religion and the "divine saviors" of fallen historical communities—the truth that Satan casts out Satan to preserve Satan's rule over mankind. Paul Nuechterlein writes:

> The true God ... is revealed as on the side of the victims, not that of the idolatrous perpetrators. If we maintain the post-modern concern that truth claims, especially about God, lead to violence, then Girard's answer is that the true God revealed in the cross of Jesus Christ is always the victim of human violence, not the perpetrator or instigator of any new violence. ... Anthropology guides us into a true theology by understanding that the true God is non-violent; humankind is solely responsible for its own violence.[7]

It is the conceit of modern secular culture that, unlike the barbaric, religious cultures of the unenlightened past, it has preserved itself and progressed morally without the need for publicly authoritative religion, let alone ritualized murder. Yet, if Girard is correct, no merely human-centered person, culture, and civilization can do without the single victim mechanism; sacrifice is essential to society, and there can be no effective, non-violent cultural engenderer

---

7. Paul Nuechterlein, "The Anthropology of the Cross as Alternative to Post-Modern Literary Criticism" (October 2002), available at http://girardianlectionary.net/girard_postmodern_literary_criticism.htm. I do not agree with the suggestion here that *all* violence is prohibited by the Gospel. Joshua's genocide of the Canaanites, the Inquisition, and the Crusades are not necessarily forms of scapegoating in principle, though acts of unjust violence and scapegoating were committed. I do not follow most of the Girardians in condemning all religion-inspired and justified violence. Jesus Himself did not refuse to use violence; consider his use of whips to drive the moneychangers out of the Temple. The point to emphasize is that violence in the hands of those subscribing to religions that reject the Gospel, implicitly or explicitly, will always be a form of scapegoating.

and preserver other than the one, divine, non-scapegoating victim-savior. Either we scapegoat ourselves in recognition of our culpability in the sacrificial murder of the Innocent One, whose death exposed the single victim mechanism and thus deprived Satan of his power over the world; or we side with the Pharisees and the Romans of yesterday and today, and remain unconverted scapegoaters in denial.

What form might such scapegoating take in our proudly tolerant and humanistic culture—one haunted by the Gospel certainly (as Flannery O'Connor would say), but not converted by it, indeed, a culture that explicitly rejects scapegoating in its maudlin concern for victims? According to Girard, modern culture does possess some buffers or *katechons*[8] for mimetic desire that serve to mitigate cultural violence. Two of these are the free market, by which desires are multiplied and satisfied without the immediate threat of scarcity and conflict, and our modern juridical system, predicated, rhetorically at least, upon a commitment *not* to scapegoat, where one is innocent until *proven* guilty, that is, not *determined* to be guilty through the indisputable accusing finger of the community. Yet juxtaposed with these seemingly pacific procedures of cultural order that indicate an apparent ethos of victim-concern and non-violence is the modern phenomenon of "apocalyptic violence" and "private" scapegoating. Modern nation-states are virtually in perpetual war with each other and with those stubborn states that need to be "democratized"—in the twentieth and twenty-first centuries alone, World War I, World War II, Korea, Vietnam, Latin America, the Cold War, Bosnia, Israel and Palestine, Israel and Lebanon, Afghanistan, Iraq, Libya, Syria, and, as I write this, aggressive plans against Iran. What is particularly apocalyptic about this violence is that all involved persons and state-actors insist upon the moral righteousness of their use of violence and the moral depravity of their oppo-

---

8. The term comes from 2 Thess 2:6–7: "And you know what is restraining him [the Antichrist] now so that he may be revealed in his time. For the mystery of lawlessness is already at work; only he who now restrains it [*ho katechon*] will do so until he is out of the way." A *katechon* is therefore anyone or anything that restrains the satanic from irrupting in its unmitigated malice.

nents; add to this a continuing escalation of the lethalness and destructiveness of the forms of violence employed. Liberal, secular democracy is purported to be peaceloving, yet genocidal violence, of the domestic unborn and the foreign "enemies of freedom," is deemed somehow necessary and inevitable for peace. As Nathan Colberne puts it:

> Humanity maintains its faith in the power of violence to provide peace (demonstrated most vividly in the belief that maintaining a nuclear arsenal will prevent the use of nuclear weapons), but with the exposure of the scapegoat mechanism, we are deprived of the single technique that could justify our faith in the efficacy of violence to maintain peace.[9]

About the cosmic character of contemporary political violence, Mark Juergensmeyer has written:

> Looking closely at the notion of war, one is confronted with the idea of dichotomous opposition on an absolute scale. . . . War suggests an all-or-nothing struggle against an enemy whom one assumes to be determined to destroy. No compromise is deemed possible. The very existence of the opponent is a threat, and until the enemy is either crushed or contained, one's own existence cannot be secure. What is striking about a martial attitude is the certainty of one's position and the willingness to defend it, or impose it on others, to the end. . . . Such certitude on the part of one side may be regarded as noble by those whose sympathies lie with it and dangerous by those who do not. But either way it is not rational.[10]

Here I go beyond Girard to claim that the great historical and contemporary violence engendered by the secularized nation-state indicates that ancient, religious scapegoating and ritualized violence have not only not ceased in the modern era, but have mutated into something incomparably more sinister and destructive. This is due to the political culture of modernity and late modernity being at

---

9. Nathan Colberne, "Engaging Girard: Is a Girardian Political Ethic Necessary?," *Journal of Religion, Conflict, and Peace* 4.1 (June 2010), available at http://www.religionconflictpeace.org/node/73.

10. Mark Juergensmeyer, *Terror in the Mind of God: the Global Rise of Religious Violence* (Berkeley: University of California Press, 2000), 148–49.

once cognizant of and opposed to the Gospel's revelation of the single victim mechanism. The Gospel has exposed, to those who will listen, the inherent hypocrisy, idolatry, and violence of all non-Christian cultures and political orders. But modernity won't or can't listen to its message. Anglo-American and European political history is peculiarly guilty of this hypocrisy, idolatry, and violence, for it conceives of the post-Glorious, French, and American Revolution settlements as *the* beacons of "religious freedom" to the world, as the only truly "Christian nations." Surely, America, as a political order and culture, is religious and peace-loving—but what religion are we talking about, and what price for peace? Religious belief and practice are free in America—but are they so in more than a private capacity? Ultimately, it seems that only those religions are tolerated that accept, or at least do not publicly protest, the public religion of the state, which is the worship of state power itself, a power predicated upon perpetual Manichean enemies and scapegoating.

Modernity: Birth-Pangs of Apocalypse

Girard provides an outstanding summary of his thought on modernity and its relation to apocalypse:

> My work has often been presented as an investigation of archaic religion, through the methodology of comparative anthropology. This approach aimed at elucidating what has been called the process of hominisation, this fascinating shift from animality to humanity that occurred so many thousands of years ago. My hypothesis is mimetic: it is because humans imitate each other more than animals that they had to find a way of overcoming a contagious similitude, prone to causing the complete annihilation of their society. This mechanism—which reintroduces difference at the very moment when everyone becomes similar to one another—is sacrifice. Man is born of sacrifice and is thus a child of religion. What I call, following Freud, the foundational murder— namely, the killing of a sacrificial victim, responsible for both the disorder and the restoration of order—has constantly been reenacted in rites and rituals, which are at the origin of our institutions. Millions of innocent victims have thus been sacrificed since

the dawn of humanity to allow their fellow men to live together or, more precisely, to not destroy themselves. Such is the implacable logic of the sacred, which the myths dissimulate less and less as man becomes more self-aware. The decisive moment of this evolution is Christian revelation, a sort of divine expiation in which God in the person of his Son will ask man for forgiveness for having waited so long to reveal to him the mechanisms of his violence. The rites had slowly educated him; now he was ready to do without them. It is Christianity that demystifies religion, and this demystification, while good in the absolute, proved to be bad in the relative, for we were not prepared to receive it. We are not Christian enough. One can formulate this paradox in another manner and say that Christianity is the only religion that will have foreseen its own failure. This prescience is called the apocalypse.[11]

In spite of modernity's *katechons* having performed their restraining function for hundreds of years, there is still much mimetic violence in today's world—indeed, more than ever before. But to the true believers in these *katechons*, the violence we still see in today's world can only be the result of a deficient application of these *katechons*: a market not free enough, a state not centralized and powerful enough, the stubborn existence of hierarchical and morally absolutist institutions and regimes. Violence enacted by the enemies of modernity and its professedly non-scapegoating practices and institutions, such as the September 11 attacks, is the result of those few, surd elements of what should now be entirely an extinct, archaic-religious, scapegoating culture. These simply have not yet been fully modernized by the peacemaking influence of the secular state, the globalist economy, the ADL, the World Bank, the NSA, NATO, the United Nations, the bombs of democracy, apartheid against archaic and barbaric peoples, or the blandishments of consumer, virtual, entertainment, and erotic culture. As the modern, secular, anti-scapegoating state and the modern, victim-concerned culture it embodies have become more pervasive and influential, these violent dinosaurs have indeed radically decreased

11. René Girard, *Battling to the End: Conversations with Benoît Chantre* (East Lansing: Michigan State University Press, 2010), 9–10.

(modernity insists), and terrorist attacks such as IXXI are merely the last, violent gasps of a terminally ill, ancient-medieval model that only persists due to the West's anemic tolerance of and complacency towards the futile resistance of those few fundamentalists and fanatics who are not yet resigned to modernity's inevitable triumph. And thus, the occupation and destruction of sovereign countries, drone killings, a domestic police state, NSA spying, and threats of a nuclear attack on sovereign and non-aggressive states, such as Iran, are only the reasonable measures the secular, peacemaking West has undertaken to ensure that this triumph becomes a reality sooner rather than later, for the good of all peoples. The so-called peace-making state, the free market, international law and transnational organizations, a commercialist, utilitarian culture of mass-produced consumer products, technology, science, the privatization of religious belief and practice, the declaration of and enforcement of human rights and the dignity of every human, the universal concern for victims that is institutionalized in law and government—all of these *katechons*, according to modernity, prove modernity's moral superiority, even its more perfectly *Christian* character; for, these institutions and practices require no scapegoats: no human sacrifices, on the one hand, no suppression of religious freedom, on the other—and they have brought about an unprecedented material prosperity and elevated moral consciousness to boot!

So much, then, for the conventional account. Some of these mechanisms have indeed produced undeniably good temporal effects, for, as Jacques Maritain once argued, whatever good there is in modernity's practices and institutions is due to the Incarnation's sacralization of the image of God in every human, and the dynamic this sacralization has activated in the West, including the eradication of all dehumanizing hierarchies, repressions, and proscriptions. However, through a Girardian lens, things look less rosy: the prolongation and escalation of violence, with millions upon millions of human sacrificial victims—the unborn, the elderly, the handicapped, the poor and middle class in the first world, the vast majority in the third world; religiously, culturally, and intellectually starved souls; the normalization of political propaganda; pathological sex and violence in media and entertainment; massive indebtedness; masses of brave new world soma addicts (in forms Huxley couldn't have dreamt of); the so-called collateral damage of millions of innocents in perpetual wars; the perpetual fear and terror of the national security and surveillance state; wars and rumors of wars; the real threat of nuclear Armageddon.

In other words, scapegoating has not just continued since the advent of modernity, but in the contemporary Western world has both escalated beyond control and cloaked itself in an all but unrecognizable form—it is now engaged in out of a concern for and in the name of *victims*. The politically correct on the left persecute those they deem the persecutors in the name of the persecuted. The "War on Terror" terrorists of the right terrorize those they deem the terrorists in the name of the victims of terror—those made victims by terrorists that they themselves have, to a large extent, created, such as ISIS.[12] What is particularly apocalyptic about this new, secular, post-Christian scapegoating violence is that we are *in denial*, we know not what we do; each person and state-actor insists upon the cosmic righteousness of his use of violence and the demonic depravity of his "enemies"—all in the name of concern for victims.

Modernity, for Girard, is now witnessing the birth-pangs of the apocalypse, conceived, as it were, two thousand years ago through the Gospel's revelation of the scapegoat mechanism as the original sin of all cultures, a revelation accepted by the Church and embodied in medieval Catholic culture, but still tainted with the religious violence it was supposed to eradicate. This revelation was either thoroughly rejected, as in secularist Europe, or relegated to one private opinion among others, as in America. In both, it was replaced by an officially established "gospel" of secularized victim-concern, with the divine victim, the only effective means to avoid the apocalypse of scapegoating violence, himself scapegoated through indifference and incomprehension. What ensued was the unleashing of, in Paul's words, "the man of lawlessness," now in his full fury—the uncontrollable, escalating mimetic desire of undifferentiated and

---

12. Garikai Chengu, "America Created Al-Qaeda and the ISIS Terror Group" (September 19, 2014), available at http://www.globalresearch.ca/america-created-al-qaeda-and-the-isis-terror-group/5402881.

equal, autonomous, relativistic persons in a secularized, mechanistic, individualized, immanentized culture bereft of any authoritative, corporate, transcendent meaning and purpose—and now without the safety valve of the archaic mechanism of religiously authorized human sacrifice. Girard writes:

> The trend toward the apocalypse is humanity's greatest feat. The more probable this achievement becomes, the less we talk about it.... I have always been utterly convinced that violence belongs to a form of corrupted sacred, intensified by Christ's action when he placed himself at the heart of the sacrificial system. Satan is the other name of the escalation to extremes. The Passion has radically altered the archaic world. Satanic violence has long reacted against this holiness, which is an essential transformation of ancient religion.[13]

The "War on Terror": Satan Casts Out Satan

Perhaps the most globally-witnessed examples of satanic, scapegoating, apocalyptic violence were the attacks of September 11, 2001. The way we have interpreted and explained this event—and this includes Girard himself—is as a terrorist attack resulting from the resentment, perhaps justified, and religious fanaticism of some extreme elements within the modernity-hating political culture of radicalized Islam, an attack on, from their perspective, "The Great Secular Satan," and rendered justifiable by a certain tendentious and primitive interpretation of Islam. Due to Islam's fatal flaw, namely, its misinterpretation of Jesus Christ, the divine Victim, as only a prophet of the later and definitive Koranic truth about God given to and through Muhammad, Islam has never transcended its Judeo-pagan, violent, archaic, theological core, according to which violence is inherent in God Himself and thus commanded by Him. In other words, IXXI was the violent, resentful, mimetic response of those few, archaic "others" living outside the peacemaking *katechons*

---

13. Girard, *Battling to the End*, 216–17.

of modernity, those who have obstinately rejected modernity's loving concern for victims and its sacred proscription against doing violence in the name of religion.

Is this an accurate depiction of the cause of IXXI and the War on Terror, or is it just another religious myth obscuring our own complicity in scapegoating? Is not the War on Terror just the kind of single victim mechanism needed to keep the masses unified and pacified in their belief in their own righteousness?[14] This is not to say that terrorists influenced by a violent and nihilistic interpretation of Islam have not also engaged in scapegoating, but there is reason to believe that this kind of Islamic scapegoating has been used, managed, and exploited by Western military, financial, and governmental elites to further their own more destructive scapegoating. In other words, is it not possible that the relatively small number of mostly ineffective terrorists, notwithstanding their real hatred of the United States, have been created and manipulated behind the scenes to become useful "enemies" to those of the elite who financially and culturally benefit from warmaking? This appears to be what is happening with ISIS.

At the risk of being called a "conspiracy theorist" (a term invented decades ago by the CIA and employed systematically, as professor Lance deHaven-Smith has shown, to discredit doubters of the official story of the JFK assassination),[15] I wonder if the birth of the latest "cosmic conflict" doesn't bear the marks of a scapegoating mechanism. There is much empirical evidence that the War on

---

14. Section V of *Rebuilding America's Defenses*, published in 2000 by the "Project for a New American Century," entitled "Creating Tomorrow's Dominant Force," includes the sentence: "Further, the process of transformation, even if it brings revolutionary change, is likely to be a long one, absent some catastrophic and catalyzing event—like a new Pearl Harbor."

15. Lance deHaven-Smith, *Conspiracy Theory in America* (University of Texas Press, 2013); cf. Ginna Husting and Martin Orr, "Dangerous Machinery: 'Conspiracy Theorist' as a Transpersonal Strategy of Exclusion," *Symbolic Interaction* 30.2 (2007): 127–50: "If I call you a conspiracy theorist, it matters little whether you have actually claimed that a conspiracy exists or whether you have simply raised an issue that I would rather avoid.... By labeling you, I strategically exclude you from the sphere where public speech, debate, and conflict occur." See also chapter 16 above.

Terror is far more complex than the official plot of "those who hate our freedom want to destroy us." On the contrary, it would seem that the hatred and will-to-destruction can also be found within, confusing the convenient wartime distinction of "us" and "them." Looking below the surface reveals a project of *deliberate, knowing, conscious* scapegoating, which is unheard of in history and in Girardian terms. I would propose systemic psychopathy as the cause of this unprecedented phenomenon, following the work of the Polish psychiatrist, Andrew Lobaczewski, whose work on "political ponerology," making use of psychology, sociology, philosophy, and history to account for such phenomena as aggressive war, ethnic cleansing, genocide, and police states, was the fruit of his intimate experience of political evil in Nazi and Soviet occupied Poland.[16] Here's a narrative to consider: With the cooperation of a governmentally, militarily, and industrially controlled media, the new scapegoaters—particularly the neoconservative cabal in the Bush administration—pointed their accusing fingers at certain oil-rich and otherwise strategically located countries, and, most importantly, the "enemies" to the continuing expansion of the State of Israel. With the populace not clued in to the arbitrariness of the pointed finger, and now swept up in mortal fear, like Peter in the courtyard, and in the throes of mimetic, irascible desire, certain countries could now be forcefully "democratized"—that is, exploited and occupied, right out in the open and with the support of an emotionally duped populace. This violence (e.g., over 1,000,000 Iraqis dead, mostly innocent civilians) would thus be ritually legitimated, for they are our enemies, after all, the enemies of freedom and democracy. And even the overwhelming documented evidence that Saddam Hussein posed no real threat to the United States, had no WMD, and bore no responsibility for IXXI has not undone the spell. Now we're involved in supporting, of all things, ISIS in Iraq and Syria, with NATO as our proxy, and soon, if some of the most strident war hawks have their way, off to Iran, with the same lack of credible evidence of any threat to us or any other

16. Andrew Lobaczewski, *Political Ponerology* (Otto, NC: Red Pill Press, 2007).

country. Only God-blessed America can save the world from these demonic monsters—as the record spins over and over again.

In short, there is good reason to see the War on Terror—again, without dismissing any real threats of terrorism to our country or the government's right and obligation to use force against them—as a state-sponsored, reactionary instance of deliberate, systemic scapegoating. Without our designated "enemies," we'd lose our very identity. James Tracy writes:

> The repression and revised imposition of September 11th and the attendant "war on terror" on the public mind have important implications not only for the integrity of public discourse, but also for the collective sanity of western culture and civilization. As crafted by dominant news media, 9/11 has become the cracked lens through which we view and conceive of our own history, identity, and purpose.[17]

Former President George W. Bush in an address to a joint session of Congress on September 20, 2001, declared: "Either you are with us, or you are with the terrorists." This appears to me to be a secularized and politicized version of Christ's authoritative spiritual portrayal of the choice between divine allegiance to Him and allegiance to Satan in his lying, murderous ways: "He who is not with me is against me" (Mt 12:30). If we follow Girard, we should see that, insofar as we are not fully living the Gospel, we are *all* terrorists now, for we inhabit a post-Christian Western culture and political order in massive denial about its own use of murder to preserve itself from its own self-created apocalyptic violence, as it careens towards ever-expanding cosmic conflicts between "us" and "them." It is the same old, self-made, staged battle of "all against one" that enables the many to feel—but not *be*—saved from "evil" and "sin" (religious fundamentalism) at the expense of those permitted to be sacrificed, i.e., those determined to be "our" official enemies. For example, Iran has been targeted by the U.S. and Israel for many years now, and, officially, it has neither attacked any country since

17. James Tracy, "9/11 Truth, Inner Consciousness, and the 'Public Mind'" (March 18, 2012), available at http://memorygap.org/2012/03/18/deep-events-alternative-news-media-and-the-return-of-the-repressed/.

its inception as a republic, nor even threatened to.[18] It has been proved beyond any doubt that it does not have a nuclear weapons program.

By supporting the unjust violence justified deceptively as the War on Terror, not only have Christians been complicit in a perversion and exploitation of the Gospel, they have also convinced themselves of God's approval of it. But as Girard has shown, the victims, however sinful, are never truly as guilty as they need to be for the mechanism to work. The guilt is imputed, not deserved, for scapegoating chooses its victims arbitrarily. The War on Terror is, at root, just another example of Satan casting out Satan. Being an authentic Christian means being on the side of all the victims in all instances of violence, including political violence masking itself as liberation and democratization. Muslims and anyone else who carry out terrorist attacks are not, of course, to be excused as mere victims, for anyone can employ violent scapegoating, and must be held accountable. But those who give blind allegiance to their own nation render themselves blind to the colonization of their own minds and souls by nationalist and now globalist scapegoating. And Christians who refuse to utter any word of condemnation of their own regimes for manifestly immoral acts are guilty of rejection of the Gospel. The aggressive "preventive warfare" employed by America in occupying Iraq was, there can be no doubt now, a grave evil. The Rome Statute of the International Criminal Court, referring to the Nuremberg Tribunal's words, states: "To initiate a war of aggression, therefore, is not only an international crime; it is the supreme international crime differing only from other war crimes in that it contains within itself the accumulated evil of the whole." Yet Christians have supported this supreme crime, and some are now calling for the same evil to be inflicted upon Iran, a country that has attacked no one since its founding as a republic in 1979, and before then since the nineteenth century. We have the right and duty to protect ourselves from violence, as the just war tradition teaches. But the policy of preemptive strike has nothing to do with this tra-

18. Stephen Lendeman, "Inventing an Iranian Threat" (August 26, 2012), available at http://www.globalresearch.ca/index.php?context=va&aid=32508.

dition. It is Hobbesian, through and through. Supporting such violence as "necessary" and even personally salvific is pledging one's allegiance not to America, but to Satan.

If modernity's soteriology is the apocalypse, then a massively violent, global-scale event like IXXI and the War on Terror it spawned should certainly be identified as a failed instance of ritualistic scapegoating that has served only to escalate global violence. According to Girard's analysis of IXXI taken from a recent interview, the Muslim hijackers, who we naturally locate outside of Western modernity, were actually well within it, due to the phenomenon of mimetic doubling and mirroring. Jean Pierre Dupuy puts it this way:

> The image that appears to emerge—in place of the "clash of civilizations" slogan invoked by those who do not understand the state of the world—is that of a civil war within a single global civilization, which has come into being kicking and screaming. It is within this framework that we must analyze the stunning mirror games in which Al Qaeda and the West have become entangled. In the face of an event as horrible as the tragedy of September 11, we have generally sought the reasons for the nonsensical and incredible in the radical otherness of those responsible, thereby reassuring ourselves.... What could be more different from our liberal, secular, and democratic societies than a gang of Muslim fundamentalists prepared to offer their lives in order to maximize the extent of the damage they cause? Few analysts have understood that the key is to be found not in a logic of difference, but, on the contrary, in a logic of identity, similarity, imitation, and fascination.[19]

Is the upshot of this analysis of IXXI, then, that, in a certain sense, we were attacked by ourselves, with the archaic, scapegoating, Islamic "other" nothing but a mirror of us? The Archbishop of Granada Javier Martínez has described it this way:

> The secular society lives in daily violence, violence with reality. This violence shows that nihilism cannot and does not correspond to our being. But it shows also, in a very concrete way, how the

---

19. Jean-Pierre Dupuy, Robert Doran, and Caroline Vial, "Anatomy of 9/11: Evil, Rationalism, and the Sacred," *SubStance* 37.1, issue 115: Cultural Theory after 9/11: Terror, Religion, Media (2008): 40.

secular society annihilates itself by engendering the very monsters that terrify it most and that it itself hates most: the twin monsters of fundamentalism and terrorism. After 11th September 2001 and 11th March 2004, it is more and more obvious that Islamic terrorism, like Islamic fundamentalism, for all its Muslim coloring and a certain vague connection with traditional Muslim ideas and practices, is not understandable or thinkable without the West; it is mostly a creature of Western secular ideologies. It is pragmatic nihilism using Islam instrumentally, very much like the emergent modern nation-states used in their own political interest a Church institution like the Inquisition.[20]

But why would modernity create, so to speak, its own monsters and its own sacrificial victims? According to Girard, it would be to engender cultural and political unity and, to a real extent, confer salvation, just like any ancient scapegoating mechanism. It must be said that IXXI, though horrific and tragic, was exploited spiritually by its victims and those who identify with them. Did not we purge our guilt and fear through the seemingly salvific and redeeming catharsis of the accusing finger and the ritual mass identification with the innocent victim—the sacrificed American regime? Was not Ground Zero transformed into a sacred, sacrificial site at which Americans could bury their sins and feel the redemption of ritual identification with the innocent victims, while justifying any subsequent violence in its name, such as preemptive strikes against and occupations of countries having nothing to do with the attacks? If Girard is right, all cultures, even postmodern, secular, technologically advanced ones, especially in the throes of an insoluble mimetic crisis, must construct *katechons*, and when the ones it previously erected are found wanting, violent and public sacrificial ritual is the inevitable fallback. When one considers the post-Christian context in which this event occurred—a country trying its best to be completely secular but still haunted by the memory of the divine scapegoat—its success in securing an effective purgative catharsis and forging cultural and political unity would depend upon the event's likeness to the Sacrifice of Calvary.

20. Martínez, "Beyond Secular Reason."

220

Modernity and Apocalypse

In light of Girard, in light of modernity's programmatic repression and privatization of the transcendent, leading to (I would argue) a cultural neurosis of simultaneous repulsion from and fascination with the sacred, and in light of the War on Terror's unmasked identity as a worldwide, murderous, scapegoating terror campaign of mimetic violence, the true meaning of the September 11, 2001 attacks is something like this: the inauguration of the reign of the archaic sacred in the midst of modernity; a ritual human sacrifice ushering in the apocalypse for which an unrepentant modernity lusts in its necrophilic heart of hearts, much like the pigs running off the cliff at Gerasene in Mark's Gospel, after being invaded by the demonic Legion fleeing from Christ. When one considers the apoplexy that ensues when IXXI's nature, purpose, and significance are questioned by those who do not automatically defer to its authoritatively promulgated meaning, that is, to the myth that was created by the regime's sacrificial priests to obfuscate its true character and orchestrators, it is clear we are dealing with the archaic sacred in the heart of modernity. Girard:

> On September 11, people were shaken, but they quickly calmed down. There was a flash of awareness, which lasted a few fractions of a second. People could feel that something was happening. Then a blanket of silence covered up the crack in our certainty of safety. Western rationalism operates like a myth: we always work harder to avoid seeing the catastrophe. We neither can nor want to see violence as it is. *The only way we will be able to meet the terrorist challenge is by radically changing the way we think.* Yet, the clearer it is what is happening, the stronger our refusal to acknowledge it. This historical configuration is so new that we do not know how to deal with it.[21]

Children, Beware of Idols

At the outset of this chapter, I stated that supernaturally powerful, non-violent, and authentically Catholic engagement with the mod-

---

21. René Girard, "On War and Apocalypse," *First Things* (August 2009), available at http://www.firstthings.com/article/2009/08/apocalypse-now.

ern world requires an engagement with Girard's thought. It has been the purpose of this chapter to engage Girard's thought as it pertains to Catholic thought and action in contemporary Western culture. A full Girardian program for interpreting and applying the principles of Catholic social teaching is an urgent need, and I hope to have contributed at least a persuasive argument for its urgency.

For the present, I think we can glean one fundamental insight and one indispensable directive for Catholics, both lay and clerical, from the Girardian analysis I have undertaken here. The insight is that the liberal, secular, humanist model of political order—one in which any conception of the sacred, as well as all religious belief and practice, is normatively privatized, necessarily pluralistic, and publicly non-authoritative, and where neither the public authority of the cult of the Gospel, nor the mechanism of ritual scapegoating is not and can never be tolerated, let alone hegemonic—is not just patently false, but a massive deception. IXXI and the War on Terror demonstrate that scapegoating has never been renounced by the West, but only masked by the discourse of Enlightenment "reason," and that, *pace* pluralist dogma and the separation of Church and state, the sacred is as authoritative and intolerant as ever it was in pre-modern society, and the Empire is itself a public religious cult that brooks no competitors. Thomas Breidenbach, who has written an erudite, groundbreaking account of IXXI as an imperial sacrificial cult, writes:

> What 9/11 ultimately reveals is a ritual landscape and technology the secular mind is largely if not wholly unequipped to apprehend, largely because of its own sentimental attachment thereto. It follows that the rationalist has been carefully conditioned not to believe in (and therefore not to perceive) the very technology being used to complexly condition him and his community. However ironically, rationalism dismisses as superstition the precise method, craft, or secretive *science* being used to channel the collective desires, fears, and animosities of the West into an effective external aggression that many rationalists themselves may nominally oppose, an aggression which their opposition (as a demonstration of the imperial collective's overall freedom) serves in a crucial sense to bolster. Meanwhile, most of the self-professed reli-

gious faithful are similarly unwilling to confront the intra-communal or ritual dimension of 9/11, since to do so would reveal their participation in a satanic (human sacrificial) culture.[22]

It is not just the rationalists, naturalists, atheists, and skeptics who do not, cannot, or will not see the reality of violent scapegoating in their midst and their complicity in it, but also the "self-professed religious faithful." And our ignorance is, perhaps, a more culpable one, since we are not atheists and skeptics regarding the reality of the sacred and of the divine, of the spiritual and the supernatural, of the existence of the demonic. The obstacle to the penetration of the Gospel in our culture is not so much the culture's rationalism, naturalism, and atheism, or even its "dictatorship of relativism," as Pope Benedict XVI was wont to say, but its simultaneous denial of and resignation to human sacrifice. This is the insight that both Church leaders and educated lay people do not seem to grasp. Further, Catholics are themselves prone to this idolatrous dynamic insofar as they participate in, or at least do not fully renounce, the imperial culture that embodies it—in all its "Catholic-friendly" disguises. The more orthodox and pious among us tend towards the "conservative" forms of imperial culture, propping up an economy of exploitation of the poor and the middle class, consumerism, usury, fiat money, and bankster hegemony under the guise of the "freedom of the market" and the evils of "socialism" and the "welfare state," citing tendentiously interpreted social encyclicals in defense of precisely those capitalist ideologies and practices the Church condemns. Politically, the neoconservative fascism ("You are either with us or with the terrorists") of the Orwellian national security-surveillance-propaganda state—bound up with government-sponsored false-flag terrorism, the racial/tribal scapegoating idolatries of Zionism and American exceptionalism, and Manichean Islamaphobic propaganda—are defended as an object of patriotism

22. Thomas Breidenbach, *IX XI: A Study of the Ritual Dimension of Contemporary Western Imperial Statecraft* (unpublished, 2014). See his published companion book of IXXI poetry *The Wicked Child / IX XI* (New York: The Groundwater Press, 2014).

and a suppression of the enemies of Christianity and freedom, both domestic and foreign. Those with a more "liberal" bent support the other dehumanizing aspects of the imperial culture, the egalitarianism and deracination that, under the guise of cultural diversity and tolerance, deprives peoples of those ethnic and cultural heritages and traditions indispensable for their moral and spiritual flourishing, as well as the moral relativism and nihilism that destroy the natural foundation of human culture in sexual complementarity and fruitful marriage. Both factions of the imperial culture give worship to the nation-state as the sole repository of political and legal authority, accepting its absolute determinations of what is sacred in public life—government narratives of terrorist attacks, on the one hand, government identifications of "hate crimes," on the other— and, in accord with the dictates of pluralism, accepting its relegation of all ecclesial, magisterial, and religious authority to the realm of the sub-political, background-cultural, and idiosyncratically private. Insofar as the human element of the Catholic Church has been co-opted into thinking and behaving according to these categories, it has made the Gospel an instrument of imperial culture: that is, it has engaged in idolatry.

As the de facto established religion of IXXI and the War on Terror reveals, however, America is not religiously pluralistic—it is, and has always been, *confessional*. The problem for Catholics in public life, then, is not publicly authorized *atheism*, but *satanism*, as Girard presents it:

> We have experienced various forms of totalitarianism that openly denied Christian principles. There has been the totalitarianism of the Left, which tried to outflank Christianity; and there has been totalitarianism of the Right, like Nazism, which found Christianity too soft on victims. This kind of totalitarianism is not only alive but it also has a great future. There will probably be some thinkers in the future who will reformulate this principle in a politically correct fashion, in more virulent forms, which will be more anti-Christian, albeit in an ultra-Christian caricature. When I say more Christian and more anti-Christian, I imply the figure of the Anti-Christ. The Anti-Christ is nothing but that: it is the ideology that

224

attempts to outchristianize Christianity, that imitates Christianity in a spirit of rivalry.[23]

What we are dealing with is a sacralized, satanic, imperial culture rooted in an established religion of ritual scapegoating and human sacrifice—but appearing to the vast majority as something worthy of assent, for it masks itself superbly by counterfeiting the desires, aspirations, and commitments of everyone along the political, ecclesial, and ideological spectrum. This, then, is the primary Girardian *insight* for Catholics: the recognition of the satanic sacred for what it is. This is extremely difficult, for it is a sacred that hides itself, as Neil Kramer describes:

> For the ordinary person, the primary power of Empire rests not in its might or cunning, but in its invisibility. People who are not mindful of its presence do not comprehend their conscious and spiritual incarceration. For those who decide to inquire into Empire, initial investigations usually begin with scrutiny of interconnected fraternal and secret organizations and their relative aristocratic families. Then there are the think tanks, corporations, and institutions that have been sequestered by Empire. This leads on to analyzing the logical deleterious effects on society, law, science, industry, culture, education, language, and media.[24]

The primary Girardian *directive* for Catholics is nothing else than the wholehearted rejection of the imperial culture at the heart of today's City of Man, one that has eclipsed the City of God through its counterfeit, satanic imitation of it.

---

23. Girard, *Evolution and Conversion*, 236.
24. Kramer, "Invisible Empire."

20
Why Mysticism is Not an Option

Only someone who has broken out of the restricted horizon of ideology can see clearly what has been left behind. And only those who have fully contemplated the abyss can be sure of having attained the spiritual truth capable of overcoming it.[1]

David Walsh

Józef Życiński, in his magisterial *God and Post-Modern Thought*, writes:

To live the faith of Abraham is to be ready at a day's notice to pack the tents symbolizing everything that is dear to one and to go to a new, unknown place, which God will indicate, completely independently of rational calculations or our emotional predilections. To live the faith of Abraham in the cultural context of postmodernity is to be able calmly to pack up the tents of congenial concepts and arguments, not in order to set out on a desert path, but to set them up again in a different context and in a different form, in a place indicated by God. In an Abrahamic testimony of faith, one may not lose heart on account of the wildness of new places or on account of a feeling of loneliness in a foreign landscape. We must constantly seek the face of the Lord (Psalm 27:8), listening carefully to His voice, which could be either a discreet whisper or a delicate breeze (1 Kings 19:12). We need to love God more than the logic of convincing deductions and the collection of respected authorities, to which we like to refer in times of difficulty. We need to accept the provisionality of contingent means, in order that the Divine Absolute might all the more clearly reveal in them his

---

1. Walsh, *After Ideology*, xii.

power. Only then does the contemporary "wandering Aramaean" reveal the style in which, amidst the darkness of our doubt, flashes the light of the great adventure of our faith.[2]

I think Życiński's words are compelling, particularly these: "We need to accept the provisionality of contingent means, in order that the Divine Absolute might all the more clearly reveal in them his power." They also echo and confirm the prophetic thought of Romano Guardini. If Guardini and Życiński are right about what it means to live in the fullness of the Abrahamic faith today, schismatic and Jansenistic forms of Catholic traditionalism in general, and the Benedict Option in particular, are simply not adequate for living the life of faith in today's world and enabling others to do the same, for they are not the proper response to how things actually are and will be quite soon. To help us see how things really are, or at least, to present a view of our situation for which the Benedict Option may not even be an option, let alone the long-term solution to our problems, I would like to present the thought of one philosopher and one theologian who look at two aspects of our world: Taylor, the existential, and Guardini, the spiritual. Taylor teaches us that modernity is inescapable, and Guardini that intimate union with God Himself—with nothing other than the humanity of Christ between Him and our sin-purged egos—is no longer an option, but an absolute obligation and necessity. What I hope my presentation of these authors will do is not so much answer all our questions, but show us that we need to keep asking them, in deeper and deeper ways; for honest and courageous inquiry is precisely what in the end will defeat the evils we are facing.

In his book, *The End of the Modern World*, written in 1956, the great Italian-born and German-educated Catholic theologian Romano Guardini writes:

---

2. Józef Życiński, *God and Post-Modern Thought: Philosophical Issues in the Contemporary Critique of Modernity*, trans. Kenneth W. Kemp and Zuzanna Maślanka Kieroń (Washington, DC: The Council for Research in Values and Philosophy, 2010), 130.

The new age will declare that the secularized facets of Christianity are sentimentalities. This declaration will clear the air. The world to come will be filled with animosity and danger, but it will be a world open and clean.... As unbelievers deny Revelation more decisively, as they put their denial into more consistent practice, it will become the more evident what it really means to be a Christian. At the same time, the unbeliever will emerge from the fogs of secularism. He will cease to reap benefit from the values and forces developed by the very Revelation he denies. He must learn to exist honestly without Christ and without the God revealed through Him; he will have to learn to experience what this honesty means. Nietzsche has already warned us that the non-Christian of the modern world had no realization of what it truly meant to be without Christ. The last decades have suggested what life without Christ really is. The last decades were only the beginning.[3]

Nothing but the "free union of the human person with the Absolute through unconditional freedom will enable the faithful to stand firm—God-centered—even though *placeless* and *unprotected*." He goes on:

> Loneliness in faith will be terrible. Love will disappear from the face of the public world, but the more precious will be that love that flows from one lonely person to another, involving a courage of the heart born from the immediacy of the love of God as it was made known in Christ.... Perhaps love will achieve an intimacy and harmony never known to this day.

Guardini sees no real possibility for "safe" havens of Christian culture, and even if we could create them, they have the real potential of stunting our spiritual growth. God is calling theists to a higher level than mere orthodoxy and orthopraxy, indeed, a heroic and mystical level, of faith, obedience, and trust—unshakable, naked, intimate, experienced union with God, communicating this supernatural reality wherever we go and to everyone we meet. Like Christ, we will have nowhere to lay our heads (cf. Lk 9:58).

---

3. Guardini, *End of the Modern World*, 101.

Benedict Option—or Mandatory Mysticism?

Although the Benedict Option is a crucial strategy for theists to protect their families and to preserve Christian consciousness and community, it may not be sustainable in the long term. If Taylor is right, the immanent frame is our home. But if Guardini is right, our situation is a gift, indeed, a priceless treasure, for God will give each of us who ask for it the grace to endure the darkness, barbarism, and loss of many of our customary sensible and cultural signs of God's love and presence.[4] We will emerge with our idols and crutches and safety nets broken and useless. Thus we will be able to know God as He is and be conduits for His Love.

We can surely try to opt out of the decaying culture and to shore up theistic culture in small enclaves of likeminded devotees of Tradition and the Transcendent, but whatever we do, we must do the one thing most necessary, as Mary did at the feet of Jesus, while Martha was busy with other things she thought more important. We must all become mystics now, in intimate and real contact with Jesus Christ, so that we can be His hands, heart, voice, and presence in our ever-darkening world. As the great German theologian Karl Rahner once prophesied: "The Christian of the future will be a mystic, or he will not be at all." Rahner again:

> Do not despair when experiencing despair: let the despair take all away from you, since what is taken from you is only the finite, the unimportant, even if it may have been ever so wonderful and great, even if it may be yourself with your ideals, with your smart and detailed plans for your life, with your image of a god that looks more like you than the incomprehensible One. Allow all the exits to be blocked, for they are only exits into the finite and paths into dead ends. Do not be frightened by the solitude and forsakenness in your internal prison, which appears to be as dead as a grave. For if you stand firm, refusing to flee from despair, and in the despair over the loss of your former idol that you called God you do not doubt the true God; if you stand firm, which is a true

---

4. This is not to deny that Catholicism cannot exist without some sensible signs and a certain cultural penumbra; these it generates by its own inner power—the more so, the more healthy it is.

miracle of grace, then you will realize suddenly that your grave-like prison cell is locked up only against what is meaningless and finite, that its deathly emptiness is only the vastness of God's presence, that silence is filled with a word without words by the one who stands above all names and who is all in all. The silence is *his* silence. He is saying that he is here. . . . He is here.[5]

I end this book with a quotation from a paper of one of my humanities students at Wyoming Catholic College. She wrote this after studying postmodern philosophy and literature, both the godless authors—Conrad, Camus, Derrida, and Foucault—and the godful—Dostoyevsky, Eliot, O'Connor, and Girard. She says it all:

> Living in the modern era is a gift. Despite the broken traditions, abolished communities, and heap of worn-out philosophies, this era is still a gift. In one way, man can no longer distract himself with human constructs. They have all failed, and anyone who lives in denial of this failure will be forced to face tragedy at some point like the grandmother[6] (even if that point only comes at his or her own death). In another way, man is called to even more intimate encounter with God as a result of this Wasteland. Quite literally, we have been placed in a society that purges us of pride and confidence in human accomplishment. The disparity of the Wasteland calls for deeper love and communion, but God provides a more intimate way of encountering Himself to overshadow this disparity. And this is a gift.

---

5. Karl Rahner, "Lent—My Night Knows No Darkness," in *The Mystical Way in Everyday Life*, ed. Annmarie S. Kidder (Maryknoll, NY: Orbis, 2010), 44–45.

6. A character in Flannery O'Connor's "A Good Man is Hard to Find."

About the Author

THADDEUS KOZINSKI taught philosophy and humanities for ten years at Wyoming Catholic College, where he also served as Academic Dean. He is the author of *The Political Problem of Religious Pluralism: And Why Philosophers Can't Solve It* (Lexington Books, 2010), and a forthcoming book on Aristotelian logic. His essays have been published in *Modern Age, First Things, Telos, Public Discourse, ABC Religion and Ethics, Catholic World Report,* and *The Imaginative Conservative.*

Printed in Great Britain
by Amazon